A SAVAGE FACTORY

An Eyewitness Account of the Auto Industry's Self-Destruction

Robert J. Dewar

AuthorHouse™
1663 Liberty Drive, Suite 200
Bloomington, IN 47403
www.authorhouse.com
Phone: 1-800-839-8640

First published by AuthorHouse 9/10/2009

ISBN: 978-1-4389-5293-2 (sc)
ISBN: 978-1-4389-5294-9 (hc)

Library of Congress Control Number: 2009900764

Printed in the United States of America
Bloomington, Indiana

This book is printed on acid-free paper.

AUTHOR' S NOTE

I want to explain to readers that the foul language and racial remarks were put in the book simply because I want A Savage Factory to be a true and accurate account of the degrading and demeaning way that Ford Motor Company talks to, and about, employees and customers. This is the actual language used at the Sharonville Transmission Plant during my tenure as a first line supervisor, and paints an accurate picture of normal verbal communication between managers, foremen, hourly workers, and the UAW. I apologize for any offense taken by my written account of actual conditions in the plant.

I also want to acknowledge people who gave me assistance with writing this book. First, my daughter and her husband, Sharon Dewar and Alex Yates took the picture at the Sharonville Transmission Plant and designed the jacket cover for the book. They also edited the book and gave invaluable assistance in getting the book to market. My wife, Barbara Dewar provided technical computer assistance, as I am weak in this area.

Books on publishing, marketing, and promotion by Steve Weber, Dan Poynter, and John Kremer guided me in this, my first book. Michael Larsen, a very successful author's agent from San Francisco give me extremely valuable advice on how best to market A Savage Factory, as well as what pitfalls to avoid. Finally, Homer Hickam, a best selling author and his wife gave me encouragement and advice. I am grateful to all of these people, without whom A Savage Factory would never have gotten to market.

CONTENTS

PROLOGUE

I always believed, as I had been taught, that Americans are "free." But schools do not teach us about economic bondage. Being free is more than a political concept. Independence from oppression is not cheap and they don't teach that in school, either.

My quest for economic freedom took me from a tarpaper shack in the bituminous coal fields of Western Pennsylvania to the largest transmission factory in the world. The story I share with you is true. Only the names of the people have been changed.

CHAPTER 1:
THE SHARONVILLE JUNGLE

As I pulled off Sharon Road and passed through a mound of earth and barbed wire fencing that looked more like a prison than a factory, I felt a surge of excitement. I had just quit a management position at Procter & Gamble to take a job as a first line foreman at Ford Motor Company's Sharonville Transmission Plant. It was a step down in status, a big step up in salary, and it was going to be my last job in corporate America. When I saved enough money, I would kiss corporate life goodbye and strike out on my own.

I slipped into a parking space in the lot designated as Management Parking Only, pocketed my keys, and got out. I was still about 100 yards from the guard shack, and the immensity of the Sharonville Transmission Plant struck me. There it was, at the end of a lot built to accommodate nearly 6,000 cars. The gray cinder block walls of a two million square foot industrial plant that occupied hundreds of acres of land. An endless expanse of concrete with dirty, 20-foot-high windows, and a loading dock capable of feeding an entire fleet of eighteen wheelers. Steam or smoke, I could not tell which, punctuated a blustery sky above the plant's flat roof and partially obscured the overbearing letters on the immense white sign that spelled a single word: FORD.

I wasn't the only new kid on the block that day at Sharonville. Two other aspiring managers, dressed appropriately for an interview, sat beside me in the Salaried Personnel Office. We were just striking up a conversation when a man roughly the size and shape of a Sherman tank burst through the door.

He did not look like a manager, yet the clerk stiffened in her seat as he came in. He gave us a disgusted side glance, spat a stream of tobacco juice at a corner waste can and missed, then said, "Which one of you guys worked at P&G?"

I volunteered that I had just quit my job at Procter & Gamble. He sneered at me, looked at the clerk, and said, "I'll take this here one on out to Zone 3."

The clerk nodded and said, "Okay, Ed. I will forward his paperwork to Roger." The tank spun around, without saying anything to me, and I made the assumption that I was supposed to follow him.

Ed rumbled from the office without a backward glance, and I scrambled after him as we made our way through a maze of corridors in the salaried personnel complex, and then turned toward a set of double doors that opened into the factory. I followed Ed into a different world, the likes of which I had never seen.

What had been the distant muttering of a tenor volcano when heard from the heavily insulated front offices was now an infernal roar. Machines, some nearly the size of a house, were lined up end to end as far as the eye could see. They whirled, clanked, churned, and groaned. Some spit fire and sparks; others shot hot metal shavings into the air. Still others spat streams of what appeared to be dirty, diluted milk that flowed into metal enclosures, and then disappeared back into the machines.

Clouds of blue-gray mist, laced with millions of minute metal particles hung in the air and brought to mind a movie about poison gas attacks in World War I. Fork trucks darted between machines and down endless aisles without regard for the workers who jumped out of the way as they approached with horns blaring.

The factory floor was made of rectangular wood blocks, about the size of street bricks, saturated with filthy black oil that gave the plant an odor of sour rot as if the entire Industrial Revolution had died and was decaying right here in Sharonville.

As we threaded our way through the warren of aisles, Ed, or at least I assumed his name was Ed because that is what the clerk called him, never spoke to me, extended his hand, asked my name, or acknowledged my presence. The feeling that I had somehow stumbled into Hell was confirmed by the faces of the damned that tended the monstrous machines.

They were hard, resentful faces; unhappy, miserable faces; dulled, stunned faces. Above all, hostile faces. Out of the corner of my eye I saw a man glaring at me, and I could read his cursing lips. It was impossible to hear what he was saying above the deafening roar of the machines, but I wondered why he hated me. He did not even know me. I speculated that my clothing, which was typical attire at P&G, but stood out as an anomaly amongst the filthy, oily confines of Sharonville, might have been offensive to him. Someone dressed like me had no business in the hellish realm of the hourly.

Ed turned and shouted, but the noise was so intense I could not hear him. He moved his head so it was six inches from my face, and the smell of tobacco juice and body odor overcame the aroma of rotting oil.

He pulled a pair of safety glasses from his back pocket and snarled, "Put these on. You don't never come out on the floor without no safety glasses. How the hell you supposed to write a man up for not wearing no safety glasses when you ain't got no safety glasses on your own self? The UAW would laugh you right out of the hearing room."

After a long trek through the roar of the machines and the clouds of haze, we arrived at a filthy cement block structure built like a battlefield bunker. I soon learned that this was the General Foremen's office. As soon as we went inside the decibels were subdued, and it was obvious that the structure was soundproofed so that people inside could communicate without shouting in each other's ear.

Inside there were four dirty, dented gray metal desks. Ed herded me to the desk occupied by a man who looked like a fully clothed skeleton. His face was a mass of wrinkles, and his right eye was obviously false. A yellowish liquid like Elmer's Glue, or the snot under a three-year-old's nose, seeped from the fake eye, which was turned to the right even though his good eye was looking to the left.

The skeleton was aware that Ed and I were standing in front of his desk, yet he ignored us. Ed acted like being ignored was normal etiquette at Ford Motor Company, and risked a long shot at the corner waste can. The tobacco juice fell short and ran down the side of the trash can over ageless stains of previous near misses.

After an uncomfortable minute or two, the skeleton looked up and examined me with his good eye like a customer in a butcher shop evaluating a steak. He shook his head slowly with an expression of utmost despair and moaned, "You aren't telling me that this is the boy wonder Roger hired from P&G, are you?"

Ed spat another stream in the general direction of the waste can and said, "I just do what I'm told. I was told to go to salaried personnel and get the guy from P&G and that is what I done."

The skeleton got up and moved around to the front of his desk.

He said, "I'm Larry, senior general foreman of Zone 3. This here is Ed. Ed is general foreman. Ed is your boss. You report to Ed. Ed reports to me. I report to Roger. Let me tell you up front. I don't give a hairy rat's ass how many college degrees you got or where you worked before. You don't work there no more. You work at Ford. At Ford Motor Company there is only one thing that counts – your numbers. You don't make your numbers, you better have some good reasons, and you better have a stack of 4600s.

"Don't be coming in here saying 'here is what professor so and so said,' because I don't give a fuck about professor so and so. He don't work at Ford.

"Don't be coming in here and saying 'here is how we did it at P&G.' I don't give a fuck how they do things at P&G. I work at Ford Motor Company. Just so we understand each other.

"If you don't make your numbers, Ed will be on your ass like stink on shit. If he still can't get you to make your numbers, he will have your ass in front of my desk. You don't want to be in front of my desk. I won't fuck with you. If you can't cut it, I'll haul your ass up to Roger. Roger will give you one more chance. That's all you get at Ford. After that you will be back out on Sharon Road looking through the fence, wondering what in the hell happened."

Larry paused. His withered, skeletal face softened for an instant turning almost human as he looked at me and shrugged, "I don't make the rules. I just do my job. Ford is a hard place to work. But you make a lot of money. You do your job, you'll be okay. You don't do your job, you'll be gone."

Then he turned to Ed, "Take him out to 258 and get him broke in."

Ed had been wiping his safety glasses to remove the oily fog left by the haze from the floor. He looked a little surprised and said, "You sure you want him in 258? You want a brand new foreman in 258?"

Larry spun around and said, "Did I stutter? What did I say? I said take him out to 258 and get him broke in. Roger hired him for 258. He is supposed to be a P&G hotshot. Roger figures he can handle 258. It ain't my decision and it ain't your decision. Take him out to 258."

Ed shrugged his shoulders indifferently, put his safety glasses on, and headed out the door. I followed, past the long lines of clanking machines, hostile faces, and toxic clouds of machine vapors. We reached a rusty, oil smeared green metal desk with a bent leg that seemed to be half digested by a row of large machines that shot red hot sparks every few minutes.

Ed put his face close to mine so we could communicate and shouted, "This here is Department 258, Torque Converters. 258 is a bitch and a half. You don't make your numbers in 258, you shut down assembly. You shut down assembly and we ain't making no transmissions. When we don't make transmissions, final assembly plants in Michigan, Kentucky, Georgia, Alabama, and Canada shut down. If that happens, your ass is grass and Roger got a lawnmower."

Ed turned to me, almost sympathetic, and said, "If it was up to me, I would never put a brand new foreman in 258. I don't care how many college degrees he got or where he worked before. It don't make no sense. These sons a bitches will chew up a foreman and spit him out if he don't know what he's doing. But it ain't up to me. Roger hired you for 258, and Roger is the big boss."

I glanced around, but could not tell where one department ended and the next began. There were yellow lines on the floor, but I did not know their significance. I wondered how the three inch yellow lines adhered to the oil soaked wood blocks. Everything was tied together in a continuous, unending web of steel, conveyor belts, and rows of machines seemingly connected like the intestines and organs in a person's body.

I looked at Ed and said, "I can handle 258. When does my training start?"

"Right now. Your best bet, until you get your feet on the ground, is to stay here by the desk. From this desk you can watch just about every sorry piece of meat in 258. Let 'em know you are watching them. Let 'em know you ain't gonna take no shit. They think you ain't looking, they'll fuck your brains out."

Ed started my training tour of Torque Converters, Department 258. He pointed across the aisle where two men were taking various parts from large steel baskets and hanging them in slots on a moving monorail. The monorail snaked through a steaming washer, came out of the other end dripping wet, and then climbed to the ceiling, snaked around in an "s" pattern, and wound past four men who took the parts off the monorail and assembled them.

Ed motioned toward the two men hanging parts and said, "Right there is operation 10, the first thing that happens to converters. If operation 10 ain't running full, you won't make your numbers. Watch them two stock handlers. Make sure they hang a part on every hook. Make sure the hilo keeps ZE34 racks fed in. They think you ain't watching them, they'll start missing hooks. Then the assemblers won't have no parts to build. Those two stock handlers can fuck you harder than anybody else in 258, other than your set up men.

"Now over here what you got is four assemblers. They are called minor assemblers. Any assembler that does not assemble the final transmission is a minor assembler. Major assemblers work on assembling the final transmissions. Different job classification, same pay.

"What you got on that monorail is the impeller housing, a cover plate, and a turbine. Minor assemblers have the stators, the 812 washers, the fiber washers, and the yellow washers at their work stations. They assemble the converters. When the monorail gets past the last assembler it should be empty. If it's not empty, that means them assemblers aren't building their parts, or it means the welder is down. If they ain't buildin' their parts, you put a 4600 on their ass. If the welder is down, you find out why.

"Minor assembly is operation 20. The assembled converter goes up that conveyor to operation 30, the welders. You got one automatic welder that welds the converters from each minor assembler. You got four assemblers and four automatic welders. You got two automatic welder operators. Each one tends two welders. There is one set up man for all four welders.

"Like I said, they are automatic welders. The only time they should be down is for cleaning tips or adjusting the angle of the guns. You watch them welders. If you don't see fire and sparks from each one, you better find out why, and you better find out quick. Each welder gets you one fourth of your numbers. A quick way to not make your numbers is to have a welder down.

"After the converter leaves the welder, it goes down this conveyor to the turnover. At the turnover you got a plate feed and clamps. One of them steel plates, that looks like a pancake with a ring in the middle, slides down. Then the clamps grab the converter, turn it upside down, and set it on the steel plate. It got to be turned over because it gets welded upside down, then has to be flipped over so it can be tested, oil filled, and balanced.

"They can't fuck you too much on the turnover. About the most they can do is take a stick or something and jam up the plate feed. You see anybody messing with the plate feed, you put a 4600 on his ass. The turnover is operation 40.

"After operation 40, the converter goes down the conveyor to the Inteco, operation 50. You can get your brains fucked out on the Inteco. It is a real delicate piece of equipment. Electronic, pneumatic, shit like that. They think you ain't looking, a man can pound his fist on the electronic panel and the damn thing will be down for two hours. You see a man that even *looks* like he is going to fuck up an Inteco, you rack his ass.

"What the Inteco does is it leak tests the torque converter. It sticks a tube down the hub and sucks out all the air. Then it pumps in nitrogen. Then a sniffer sniffs around the weld to see if any nitrogen is leaking out. If it is, the Inteco kicks the converter down that side conveyor to the weld repair booth. There is a man in the booth, and he manually welds the leaks on the converters kicked out by the Inteco."

I looked closely at the Inteco. It was about the size of a backyard storage barn, and clanked and hissed each time a torque converter went into it. The repair booth was approximately the same size as the Inteco. There was a slit in the side of the booth, and a pair of eyes watched me through the slit, like a peeping Tom. I was also very aware that 25 pairs of other eyes were watching every step I took.

Ed spit a stream, aiming for the base of the conveyor, and asked if I had any questions.

I said, "Not at the moment, but I'm certain I'll have a million questions as I get into the job of managing 258."

He nodded and continued with my training.

"After the converter gets leak tested, it goes to operation 60, oil fill. As it goes over the conveyor a metal stop pops up and stops it under the nozzle. The nozzle comes down automatically into the impeller hub, and fills the converter with transmission oil. Then the nozzle retracts, the stop pops back down, and the converter continues on the conveyor. There ain't a whole lot they can do to fuck you on the oil fill."

As Ed talked, I could see that there were two distinct production lines in 258, a north line and a south line. They were exact duplicates of each other. The two north welders fed the north line and the two south welders fed the south line. Ed walked about 20 feet past the north Inteco and stopped in front of a monstrous machine the size of a hunting cabin. It was encased by a wire cage and had a panel of gages, lights, meters, needles, and control knobs that brought to mind the Starship Enterprise.

"This here is operation 70, the automatic balancers. You got a north automatic balancer and a south automatic balancer. The balancers are the biggest bitches you got in 258. The only ones that knows anything about them is your set up men. If a balancer goes down, you ain't going to get your numbers, it's that simple."

I stood in awe of the automatic balancers. The converter was grabbed by a set of enormous claws, lifted up, pulled into the machine like a python swallowing a rat. Then it was spun around at high speed. The panel of lights blinked and winked and arrows on gages jumped back and forth. Then the spinning abruptly stopped.

Next a welding arm came out of the machine like a prehistoric monster lunging at prey. There was a shower of red hot sparks as it hit the converter and welded a small metal weight at a precise spot. Needles, gages and blinking lights caught my eye. Then a steel arm shoved the torque converter out of the balancer like a bouncer ejecting a drunk from a bar, and the next converter was abducted into the machine.

Ed seemed satisfied that I was sufficiently impressed by the size and complexity of the two automatic balancers. He put his face close to mine as though he wanted to tell me something important, but did not want to shout loud enough for anyone else to hear. These instructions were for my ears only.

"You see them two guys playing checkers between the balancers?"

I indicated that I did.

"Them two guys is your automatic balancer set up men. They ain't supposed to be sitting there playing checkers and looking at fuck books. But let me tell you something, just between you and me. If they are playing checkers, it means them balancers are running like scared niggars at a Ku Klux Klan meeting. If they *ain't* playing checkers, that is when you gotta worry. Your balancer set up men can fuck you harder than everybody else in 258 put together. You know why?"

I shook my head no.

"Because every converter you make got to run through one or the other of them balancers, and them sumbitches know how these balancers work. They can put them balancers down and Einstein, Jesus Christ and his twelve apostles wouldn't be able to figure out what they done. They can also keep them balancers running for you. What I'm trying to tell you is, it doesn't pay to fuck with your balancer set up men if you want to make your numbers. Know whatta mean? But you didn't hear it from me. If you say I said it, I'll call you a damn liar."

I had enough manufacturing experience to know what Ed was trying to tell me. He was saying that in the strange world of Ford Motor Company, all the animals in the barnyard are not equal. It depends on whether a man could hurt me more on my numbers than I could hurt him with paperwork.

Ed yelled to the two men playing checkers, "This here is your new foreman. His name is Bob."

The two set up men got up and climbed the step over ladder because they could not hear what Ed had shouted. When they were next to us Ed repeated, "This here is your new foreman. His name is Bob."

They gave me the once over and nodded with expressionless faces. I extended my hand to the closest, and he looked at me like I was insane. Ed had a horrified look on his face. My hand hung limply in midair and then I dropped it back to my side. The two set up men turned and resumed their game of checkers. They had been summoned. They came. They did what they were told. That was all that was expected of them.

When they were out of earshot Ed gasped, "Holy Christ, man, you don't offer to shake hands with an hourly man. Didn't you learn nothing at P&G? What the hell do they do over there? Go around shaking hands with the hourly? It don't matter if they are set up men or not, they're still hourly."

Ed shook his head as though I was a hopeless imbecile.

This stunned me, because at P&G a manager knew each of his employees personally, and developed good, solid interpersonal relationships. Organizations function on the strength of mutual respect and the depth of interpersonal relationships. This was such a basic, elementary management concept.

I pondered how Ford was even able to function if management and labor operated like warring street gangs. But I decided it was pointless to discuss this issue with Ed, so I nodded my head to indicate that I had blundered, and we moved on in my training.

At the back side of both the north and south balancer was a small piece of equipment that resembled a tire changing machine in a service station, and one man stood at each machine.

Ed said, "These are the standby balancers. Sometimes the automatic balancer kicks out a converter that is not properly balanced, and the standby balancer operators balance it by hand. The standby balancers are operation 80."

I looked at what I assumed was the end of the department. Finished torque converters rolled down long conveyor belts and hit a metal stop. There were two men on the north line and two men on the south line unloading the converters into the large steel baskets that I had seen all over the plant. Ed had called them ZE34 racks.

When a ZE34 rack was full of torque converters, one of the men pulled a lever, which released the basket, and it rolled down large roller conveyors to another steel stop. Then people took the converters out and hung them on a giant overhead conveyor that had hooks about four feet tall and looked like the letter "J".

Ed said, "This is the ass end of 258. Operation 90 is the last operation. Them four PR Burrs unloads the converters into the racks. After that they ain't our problem no more. You see them yellow lines on the floor? Them yellow lines mark the end of 258 and the beginning of final assembly.

"You got yellow lines all around each department. Anything happens on the other side of them yellow lines, ain't your problem. Your problem is to get me 2400 converters each shift. You get me 2400 converters, or less than 2400, plus enough 4600s to make up for what you didn't get, then you done your job."

I scanned the faces of the men at the back end of 258 and saw the same hostility, the same dulled, disinterested expressions that I had seen all over the plant. They were all watching me. These men whose bodies were nothing more than an extension of the machine they ran. They had been dehumanized to the point where they identified themselves by the machine they ran, and their lives were regulated by the bells, whistles, and time clocks of Ford Motor Company.

I wondered if these men had human characteristics when they resumed their private lives at the end of their shifts, or whether industrial dehumanization carried over into their personal lives. If, indeed, they had personal lives, since the Sharonville Transmission Plant never shut down.

I cocked my mouth to Ed's ear and said, "I have a million questions. When does my formal training program start? Now that I have done a walk through of my department, the formal part of my training will be a lot more meaningful."

Ed twisted his face, shooting me a look like I was hopelessly stupid and said, "What the hell are you talking about, formal part of your training? I just gave you your training. I told you about every machine. I told you what to watch out for. I told you all the ways they can fuck you. You been trained. There is a clipboard up on the desk. A good foreman will always carry a clipboard. The hourly will not know what is on the clipboard, but they know you can write shit down if you got a clipboard. They figure well, hell, that foreman looks like a prick. He got a clipboard. We better not fuck with him. Know whatta mean? Now 258 ain't the only department I got responsibility for. Take over 258 and ride it like a cheap whore on Saturday night."

With that Ed spit out a stream of tepid brown juice, wiped his mouth on his sleeve, and said, "Another thing. Take off that fucking suit jacket. This ain't no fashion show. You're a foreman, not a model for Brooks Brothers suits."

Then he disappeared into the deafening noise and the blue grey mist and I was left to run 258.

I looked at my watch. My training had consumed 39 minutes. I recalled my three month training program at Procter & Gamble, which included lectures, hands-on training, and seminars. But as Larry had pointed out, I did not work at Procter & Gamble anymore. I worked at Ford Motor Company.

I walked back up to the front of 258, feeling every eye in the department following me. I took off my suit jacket, hung it on a rusty corner of the desk, undid my necktie, and picked up the clipboard. I hoped that my expensive suit jacket did not get hit by the periodic shower of fiery sparks that exploded from welder number one.

I studied the papers on the clipboard, which looked like gibberish. It was then that I became aware of a major decrease in the noise level. All four welders had stopped hissing, whirling, and shooting out sparks. There were no converters moving down the conveyor belts. All the machines had stopped and 258 was at a dead standstill.

I looked at the two men that were supposed to be hanging parts across the aisle. They were just standing there, watching me. One of them was lighting a cigarette. I felt the presence of someone directly behind me, and casually turned around.

There was a big black guy standing four feet behind me. I guesstimated him to be six-two, six-three, and weigh about 225. He was about my age, had a sweaty red bandana tied around his head, and a scar on his left cheek that looked like it had been made by a slicing knife. Beads of sweat rolled down his face and landed on his dirty coveralls. He stared at me like an inmate on death row. I stared back.

Then he said, "You're the new foreman?"

I said, "That's right. My name is Bob. What is your name?"

"8942 is my last four."

"Last four? What do you mean last four? I asked you what your name is."

"It don't matter what my name is. At Ford everybody is just a number. My last four is 8942."

"I still don't know what you mean by last four."

"Man, you another one of them green weenies, ain't you? Ford done went out and hired another green weenie. You would think they would have learned by now. At Ford people go by the last four numbers on their Social Security card. Here men ain't men. Men is numbers. Nothing more than numbers. My last four is 8942. That is all you need to know about me. You don't need to play like you give a shit about me. All I am is somebody whose ass you gonna nail. You don't know jack shit, do you? Coming in here dressed like you was important. Nobody is important at Ford. You are just a number, just like me."

"I am learning. This is my first day."

8942 snickered and said, "Most of you guys ain't here long enough to learn where the shithouse is."

"Most of us guys? What do you mean most of us guys?"

"Fancy ass college boys in fancy ass clothes that come in here and think they know something because they read books and shit and got some kind of paper that says they are real smart. Well I am here to tell you that your Howdy Doody ass don't know jack shit, no matter how many books you done read.

"Everybody knows your kind. You think you are better than us. You figure you're so smart that you're gonna tell us how it is. But that ain't how it shakes out. You want to know how it shakes out? Here is how it goes down.

"You don't get your numbers because you don't know jack shit. They take you in the office and ream your ass up one side and down the other. They say you ain't getting your numbers because them guys in 258 is fucking you out of your numbers. 'Write them up.'

"So you start writing people up. Then you get even worse numbers. They take you back in the office and rip you a new asshole. They say, 'you ain't writing up enough people and that is why you ain't making your numbers.' You start getting sick. You go to a doctor. He puts you on pills.

"But them pills don't help none, because no matter how good the pills are, you still got to come back in here seven days a week. You still got to face the front office. They still be screaming for more 4600s, because you ain't making no where near what they say you have to make on your numbers. Then one day you just can't face it no more. You come in and quit, and everybody laughs as you walk out the door. Then they go out and hire another green weenie. They got to, because nobody with a brain will take the job.

"They come around to the hourly and say, 'Look, man, we want to promote you into management. We want to make you a foreman.'

"But the hourly says, 'Fuck you. I got a union to protect me. If I put on that necktie, I ain't got shit and you can fuck me around any way you want. So you take that management job and shove it up your ass.'"

8942 threw his head back and started laughing. Then he said, "We got bets on you, man."

"Bets? What kind of bets?"

"On how long you gonna be here before you get sick; before you can't stand coming into this place no more. Some guys figure you are good for three, four months. I say no way. I got my money on three weeks. In three weeks yo ass is history and I pull in a lot of jack. When you hit the road in three weeks or less, I done made over five hundred dollars."

"So you think that I will be at Ford for only three weeks?"

"Three weeks tops. I seen enough green weenies to know. The fancier their clothes is, the quicker they gone. You come in here with the fanciest clothes I seen in a long time. But you could be gone even quicker if you fuck with me. You could have one of them industrial accidents that you read about in the Wall Street Journal. You dig, man?"

With one last baleful glare and a disgusted shake of his head, 8942 spun around and disappeared behind welder number four. Then, like a symphony orchestra, Department 258 started back up again. It was then that I heard a telephone ringing. At least it sounded like a telephone. There was so much noise I could not be sure. I looked around the desk. Sure enough there was a phone on the upper left corner.

I picked it up and said, "Hello."

Someone was talking to me, but it was all garbled, like he was talking through a plastic barrier. I felt something wet and gooey on my ear, and I looked at the ear piece. It was covered with a thick, black grease of some kind. I looked across the aisle. The two guys at operation 10 were splitting a gut laughing and pointing to black grease dripping on my white shirt.

I wiped it off and said, "Hello. This is Department 258."

The voice on the other end said, "We're losing Fairfax. Get your GAWDAMN south line unloaded."

"Excuse me,"

The voice said, "If you lose Fairfax you ain't going to have no excuse. We are within eighty pieces of losing Fairfax. Eighty fucking pieces."

The phone went dead, and I headed for the back end of 258. I looked at the south line. Converters were backed up all the way to the two automatic welders, which were shut down because the line was full. As I hurried down the line I noticed something that I had missed before. All the torque converters on the south line had a wide orange stripe on them, while those on the north line did not.

The bottleneck was at the end of the south line. The two guys who were supposed to be unloading were not unloading. One of them was sitting on a five gallon bucket smoking a cigarette. The other was leaning against the ZE34 rack admiring the foldout of a Playboy magazine. Everyone was watching me to see how I would handle this first crisis of my Ford career.

A short fat guy drove up on an orange golf cart, slammed on the brakes, and slid across the oil slick floor. He did not have a happy face.

He shouted, "Who in the hell is supposed to be running this place?"

I said, "I am the new foreman in 258."

"No shit? Well, Mr. new foreman you had better get the Fairfax line unloaded before they run out of converters. Right now they are hanging the last ZE34 that they have."

I walked over to the idle unloaders and said, "I want these converters unloaded. Put down the can of coke, the magazine, and get this line unloaded."

The guy with the coke looked at me, then looked at his coworker and said, "Who is the clown in the fancy duds?"

His coworker shrugged and said, "Beats me. I ain't never seen him before."

I said, "I am the new foreman in 258. I want those converters unloaded right now. Your job is to unload converters. Get them into a ZE34 rack."

He said, "Oh Yeah? Well, if you are the new foreman, then where in the hell is our relief men? If you are the new foremen, tell me how come I been unloading for damn near three hours, and I ain't had no relief. I gotta take a piss, man. You know how much them converters weigh? No, wait, how would you know how much a converter weighs, let alone what it is like to unload steady, with no relief, for three hours. A man that wears fancy suits ain't never done no work in his life. I gotta take a piss. Get me a relief man. While you are at it, call my committeeman. Get the Wop down here."

I said, "You got it wrong, fella. I don't do what you say. You do what I say. Now get those converters unloaded."

He looked at his coworker and said, "Did you just hear this new foreman refuse to call me a committeeman?"

His coworker said, "Damn right I heard it."

The two men unloading the north line chimed in and said, "We heard it, too. We heard pretty boy refuse to call a committeeman."

The short, fat guy shook his head and said, "You just lost Fairfax."

Then he jumped back on his golf cart and spun down the aisle, shaking his head in disbelief.

Ed suddenly appeared out of the smoky haze, walking fast, dousing the floor with tobacco juice.

He shouted, "Jesus Christ. We're losing Fairfax. You been in 258 for about an hour and you already lost Fairfax."

I said, "Well, Ed, to be honest, I don't even know what Fairfax is. You never said anything about Fairfax. I got this phone call. Then these guys said they have not gotten relief. Then some fat guy drove up and said I was losing Fairfax, and I don't even know what that means."

The blood drained out of Ed's face, he got a horrified look and said, "You don't even know what Fairfax is? How many of them college degrees you got? How in the hell much did Roger pay you to come to Ford? You been here less than two hours and you caused an assembly plant to shut down. You come with me."

I followed Ed like a scolded schoolboy headed for the woodshed. As we walked I could see most of the men in 258 laughing as though they were watching a Three Stooges comedy. We ended up in front of the human skeleton. Larry was not wearing a happy face.

He snapped his pencil in half, pitched it with amazing force into the tobacco stained trash can, and said, "I just got a call from Fairfax. Right now 1800 men are clocking out because they have no torque converters. Do you know what kind of hell comes down the line when we lose an assembly plant? What in the FUCK happened? No. Never mind. I do not want to know. It is not my problem. Therefore I do not give a rat's ass.

"Roger hires a high dollar man from P&G and that man loses Fairfax, then I do not have a problem. Roger has a problem. Take him to Roger and have him explain how he managed to lose Fairfax on his first day on the job, before lunch break. Get him out of my sight."

I meekly said, "The thing is, I don't even know what Fairfax is."

Larry's mouth dropped wide open, and for a minute I thought he might be having a heart attack. He said, very slowly, as if to fully digest each word

"You.....do.....not.....even.....know.....what.....Fairfax.....is. You do not even know what Fairfax is. HAS THIS FOREMAN BEEN TRAINED?"

Ed shook his head vigorously and said, "Hell yes he has been trained. I spent a good hour with him in 258. He got as much training as any foreman ever gets. I showed him every operation. I told him what to look out for. I told him how those people could fuck him at every operation. He should have been watching his PR Burrs on the south line. He ain't got no excuse for losing Fairfax."

Larry shook his head hopelessly and said, "Take him to Roger."

CHAPTER 2:
ROGER AND THE WOP

I followed Ed about 300 feet to another dingy, dirty cement block building that gave the appearance of having sprung out of the wood block floor like some mutant fungus. We went inside. Surprisingly, it was a clean, well organized professional office, complete with a secretary busy at her typewriter.

Ed said, "Roger in?"

The secretary nodded, and Ed knocked on Roger's door.

A quiet, firm voice said, "It's open."

I followed Ed inside. He closed the door and we were standing in front of Roger's desk. He did not look up or acknowledge our presence, which evidently was a standard signal at Ford that said, 'I'm more important than you, so just stand there until I feel like talking to you.'

Ed shifted nervously from foot to foot like one might stand at the last day in front of Saint Peter awaiting his terrible judgment. After an uncomfortable interval, Roger laid his pen down and looked up at us.

Ed said, "Roger, this here is that new foreman you hired from Procter & Gamble. We put him out in 258, like you said to do. He went and fucked it up and lost Fairfax."

Roger scrutinized me like a customer would examine a car on a dealer's lot. Then he looked at Ed and said, "I know we lost Fairfax, Ed.

It's my job to know everything that goes on in Zone 3. You better get back out on that floor before they bang us even further."

Ed quickly exited, relieved that he was off the hook and I would face the full wrath of Roger.

Roger was the most professional looking manager I had seen during my half day at Ford Motor Company. He was short of stature, and almost boyish looking. I guessed him to be 45 years old or so, and about five feet five or six. I doubted that he weighed more than 150 pounds. Though he was short, he had a commanding presence. He spoke softly, but each word was pregnant with authority.

His suit jacket was hanging neatly on a wooden coat rack. He wore a crisp white shirt and a necktie perfectly centered by a gold plated tie clasp in the shape of the Ford logo. His hair was professionally styled. Under the coat rack was a pair of overshoes, which I assumed Roger wore during the few times that he went out on the oil-soaked floor, to protect his expensive shoes. There was no doubt in my mind that in Zone 3, Roger was The Man.

Roger asked if I went by Bob or Rob.

I said, "Bob," and he nodded, gazing more through me than at me with cold, piercing, emotionless black eyes.

He said, "I'm Roger. I run Zone 3. Nothing goes down in Zone 3 without me knowing about it. Nothing happens in Zone 3 unless I make it happen."

He picked up my folder and said, "You have an interesting resume. In fact, one of the most interesting resumes that I have seen. That's why I made you an offer I knew you couldn't refuse, even though we've never met. I tell Salaried Personnel who to hire and how much to pay them. I try to pick winners for Zone 3. Looks like you pulled yourself up by your own bootstraps."

He paused, studying me as if trying to penetrate inside my head. "Did you really work in a pick and shovel coal mine before you were fifteen years old, and live in a tarpaper shack on the side of a hill?"

I said, "Yes, I did."

Roger smiled slightly and said, "I see that you were the only one in your family to graduate from high school. Yet you were able to work your way through college and then win a full scholarship to the University of Southern California. Then you nailed down a management job at Procter & Gamble."

I nodded, and Roger continued, "You graduated from Penn State with a 3.4 and had a 3.7 when you got your MBA. Then you went through the full P&G management training program and ran their Duncan Hines operation. Tell me, Bob, what made you leave a comfortable management job at P&G for a foreman's position at Ford Motor Company?"

I looked Roger in the face, and decided to be completely up front with him. If it did not set well with him, so be it. I would not be the same kind of two-faced deceptive phony that surrounded me in the management suites of Procter & Gamble.

I looked directly into his piercing eyes and said, "I am not going to lie to you. I came to Ford for the money. You offered me a salary that would choke a horse. I see my future as not working for Ford, Procter & Gamble, or any other corporation. I want to work for myself. I am not an organization man. I come from a long line of independent men that must be their own boss. My long term goal is to have my own business. I have to call my own shots in life. But that takes money, and lots of it. I came to Ford because I can make more money here than anywhere else. The simple truth is, as soon as I have enough money saved to pay off my mortgage and float my own business, you will be getting my resignation."

Roger leaned back in his chair and studied me. My response took him completely by surprise. I did not know if that was good or bad. After a few seconds he responded.

"You sound like a man who knows where he is going and how he intends to get there. It takes a man with some big balls to tell me on your first day of work that you will only be here long enough to save the money that you want. I like that. I like it a lot. I never had a foreman be that honest with me, or one who had concrete future plans."

He had a half-cocked smile and stared at me, "All the college graduates that we hire have their heads stuck so far up their asses that they can see their belly buttons from the inside. They are nothing more than overgrown kids that have been coddled by Mom and Dad since they popped out of the womb."

Roger's tone shifted to that of tangible disgust as he seemed to drift off, looking into the recesses of his memory. "They never had to take responsibility for anything. They don't know how to do anything. They never had to work a real job. Then they come in here and we put them out on that floor. Some last a week or two. Some have actually made it for several months, but sooner or later they get their balls cut off by the hourly and handed to them in a plastic bag. Some don't ever come back. One guy never even came back for his pay check. It's still laying in Salaried Personnel in an envelope with his name on it. He ran back home to Mommy and Daddy and they said 'You don't have to work a nasty job. Come back home and live with us.' These types of people are as useless as tits on a boar hog."

I was surprised and pleased by Roger's response. He reminded me of one of my Chief Petty Officers in the Navy. He was a hard ass. But if he respected you, he was a man that could be dealt with. Unless I was missing something, Roger respected who I was and what I was trying to do in life. He smiled and continued.

"Let me tell you something, Bob. Coming to Ford for the money is nothing to be ashamed of, and nothing that anybody is going to hold against you. How many men do you think work here because they like to build transmissions? Not a single one. Everybody at Ford Motor Company is here for the money. You can make more money at Sharonville than anywhere else in Southern Ohio, Northern Kentucky, or Eastern Indiana. No other company pays overtime to management. At other companies management is expected to spend whatever time it takes to get the job done for their base salary. But Ford pays overtime to management for every minute they work after eight hours and 45 minutes. You get time and a half. On Sundays you get double time. On holidays you get double time plus holiday pay, which is triple time. We never shut down, 24 hours a day, seven days a week. Easter Sunday, Thanksgiving, July fourth, you will be out in 258 pumping out converters and pulling down enough jack to write your own ticket in life." He smiled with pride and then asked, "Have you ever heard of the Cleveland Clinic?"

A little surprised by the question I said, "Sure. It's a famous hospital. Supposedly has the best doctors in the world, and well-known people go there to be treated."

Roger said, "That's right. Well, my wife's uncle is a heart surgeon at the Cleveland Clinic. He has operated on movie stars, corporation presidents, and a king. Last year I made more money than he did."

He paused, looking at me, letting the thought sink in. "But that's enough about money. Let's talk about transmissions. Do you know why Sharonville works seven days a week? Do you know why I hired you?"

"I suppose Sharonville never shuts down because Ford is selling so many cars that we have to run around the clock to keep up with car assembly. I imagine you hired me because I have two college degrees, solid management training, and several years experience."

Roger said, "Wrong and wrong. Sharonville never shuts down because automatic transmissions are the controlling factor in how many cars and light trucks we can build. All the other Ford facilities have ample, if not excess, capacity. But that is not true for automatic transmissions. On paper Sharonville and Fairfax have enough capacity to just keep up with assembly plants, and nothing more. Ford plans to build another transmission plant, but so far they are only plans. In fact, we could sell more cars and light trucks if we could build more automatic transmissions. If Sharonville misses a beat, assembly plants start to shut down. When assembly plants shut down, the Men From Up North are not happy campers."

Roger stared at me dead straight in the eyes to ensure I was absorbing every word and emphasized, "You will learn that you do *not* want to piss off the Men From Up North. Some call them the Detroit Mafia. Of course, what they are talking about is corporate headquarters at Dearborn. In a very real sense, Sharonville determines how much money Ford Motor Company makes because it determines how many cars and light trucks we can build. Do you know what the controlling department is at the Sharonville Transmission Plant that determines how many transmissions we can make?"

I was almost afraid to hear the answer, so I just shook my head.

Roger said, "Torque converters control how many transmissions we can make. The torque converter is the heart and guts of the automatic transmission. It is what makes the transmission automatic, as opposed to manual. Department 258 makes the converters not just for Sharonville, but also for Fairfax. When 258 goes down, it shuts down two transmission plants, which in turn shuts down final assembly plants in four states and Canada. Are you getting a clear picture of how important 258 is to Ford Motor Company?"

I said, "Yes, I am. But explain to me about Fairfax. Ed and Larry went off the deep end because they said I shut it down. But they never explained to me exactly what Fairfax is."

Roger seemed a little annoyed. He said, "Fairfax is our sister automatic transmission plant. It is located in the village of Fairfax, twenty miles east of Cincinnati. Fairfax is the oldest automatic transmission plant in the United States. It was the first automatic transmission plant ever built. That was 1951, and sales of cars with automatic transmissions skyrocketed. Fairfax couldn't keep up. So Ford built a second plant at Sharonville. They gave the Sharonville plant enough capacity to make torque converters for both Fairfax and Sharonville. Then they took out converter manufacture at Fairfax to expand final assembly of transmissions. Now Fairfax merely assembles transmissions. We supply both us and them with converters. Did Ed explain to you how to tell the difference between a Fairfax and a Sharonville torque converter?"

"No. He did not."

"I am going to have to talk to him about how he trains new foremen. A Fairfax converter has a spline with a quarter inch inset, and a Sharonville converter does not. If you look down the impeller hub you can see the spline. If it has an inset, it is a Fairfax converter. Also, we swipe a strip of orange paint across the top of the impeller housing to identify Fairfax converters."

Roger leaned forward in his chair, folded his hands on his desk, and got a hard look on his face.

He said, "Do you know what's the main impediment to producing automatic transmissions at Sharonville?"

I said nothing, and Roger continued.

"The hourly workers are the main road block. The UAW figures it has us by the balls because they know how badly we need these transmissions. They hold back production. They sabotage production. They file grievance after grievance to tie us up with paperwork. The hourly want to control the plant. They fuck us up at every turn. There is a war going on out on that floor. Sometimes it flares up, other times it dies down, but it never ends. It is a battle for control. The hourly are like the Viet Cong laying in wait for a chance to strike at us. But it is *our* job to call the shots. We are management. It is *their* job to do what we tell them – they are labor. Now I don't know what kind of people you managed at

P&G, and I don't care because you're not at P&G anymore. But at Ford the hourly are the bottom of the barrel. There are drunks out on that floor. There are dope addicts out on that floor. There are lazy bastards out there that would cut your throat in a New York minute. Our biggest problem is keeping up with assembly plants in four states and Canada with the lowest quality work force in the United States. Do you know how we do it?"

I was surprised and engrossed with Roger's diatribe. I watched him intently, but didn't dare answer.

He continued, "We do it by enforcing the contract. We have a labor contract with the UAW that spells out in great detail exactly what each man's job is, and exactly how much he will produce in an eight hour shift. We control them by putting the paperwork to them when they break the rules that the UAW has agreed to. The one thing that we have them by the balls is their jobs. These sorry pieces of meat make more money than any other factory workers in the world. They will fuck with us. They will hold back production. They will do as little work as they can get by with. But they do not want to lose their jobs. They straighten out and fly right when we bring out the 4600s."

I said, "I don't want to sound stupid, but what is a 4600? I have heard that term all day long from Ed and Larry. But nobody explained to me exactly what a 4600 is."

Roger said, "That's okay. You don't ask, you don't know. A form 4600 is our formal disciplinary paper work. The contract calls for progressive discipline. When a man breaks the rules, the first 4600 you give him is a written warning in the presence of his union representative and a labor relations rep. The second 4600 you give him docks his pay. The third 4600 is a day off with no pay. The fourth 4600 is three days off with no pay. Then you move up to a week, two weeks, three weeks, and then termination. When the pedal hits the metal, they don't have us by the balls. We have them by the balls. You want to see a man work his ass off? Get him up to the last stage on the 4600 progression. He will be to work early, will never leave his machine, and will work right up to the whistle. Not many men out on that floor can afford to lose a job that pays like Ford pays. Let's move on to my second question. Do you know why I hired you?"

I said, "Well, I imagine my MBA and P&G experience had something to do with it."

Roger's piercing eyes twinkled, and he said, "No. Your education and experience had nothing to do with why I hired you. College degrees and previous jobs don't mean jack shit to me. Not to degrade those things, but the sad fact is nothing you have ever seen or done can prepare you for what you will face out on that floor. What I need is a foreman with a lot of balls, not a foreman with a lot of brains. I hired you because when I read your resume something jumped off the page and grabbed me. Do you know what it was?"

I was fascinated, and clueless, since I spent a lot of time preparing my resume. Roger continued.

"It was the section of our application that asks for a brief description of your personal history. You wrote about growing up dirt poor, growing up hard, about having to work at a very young age, under bad conditions, to help support your parents."

I said, "I struggled for years to pay for a good education, but you hired me because I used to be poor?"

Roger smiled, leaned back in his chair, and said, "No. Not because you used to be poor. Because of what it took for you to rise above being poor. Your resume told me here is a man who fought his way up from the bottom without any help. Here is a man who understands that in life everybody has a club. How far you get in life depends upon how hard you can swing your club. The guy who can swing his club harder than the people trying to beat him down makes it to the top of the hill. The fact that you got away from the coal mines, and earned college degrees, and were good enough to be hired by Procter & Gamble tells me you got the balls to swing your club better than people that try to knock you down. It tells me you have a lot of guts. It tells me that you are a man who will not let anything get in the way of reaching your goals. It tells me that you are a man who knows what it is like to be on the bottom of the heap and not have any money. It tells me that you are a man motivated by money. Ford needs men that are motivated by money. I hired you because I think you have the balls to run 258 and you will do it because of all the money we will pay you to do it. I hired you because there are hard men out on that floor, and I need a hard foreman to deal with them. I need a foreman that is like a junk yard dog. I need a foreman that has an invisible sign on his back that says fuck with me and you will pay a price. I need a foreman that can take the lowest scum in Cincinnati and make me the torque converters that I need to keep this plant humming. I think you can do it. Now get back out to 258 and run me 2400 torque converters."

Roger pulled more papers out of his drawer and started reading them as though I was not in his office. I was not sure if the meeting was over or not.

Then he looked up and said, "You still here?"

I got up and went back to 258.

As I approached my desk, it looked like 258 was running like a Swiss watch. But there was a bicycle leaning against the desk, and a man standing beside it. He was obviously not a worker because he was wearing a clean, pressed white shirt. As I got closer I saw a circular emblem on the pocket that said UAW 863. His eyes followed me as I approached.

He said, "You the new foreman of 258?"

I answered that I was.

He said, "I'm the Wop."

"Excuse me?"

"Did I stutter? I said, I'm the Wop. I am the lead committeeman for Zone 3. I got a call from one of your PR Burrs at the end of 258. I have been waiting here for about fifteen minutes for you. I don't like to wait for foremen; Foremen wait for me. But everybody in 258 knows you were in Little Napoleon's office getting your ass chewed out for losing Fairfax."

The Wop was about my height, but much heavier. His belly protruded over his belt like an overstuffed feed sack. He had coal black hair peppered with grey. I guesstimated him to be about 45 years old. Thick black hair protruded up through the opening on his short sleeve shirt and covered his arms. He was dark complexioned.

He said, "Your PR Burr claims you refused to call him a committeeman. Is there any truth to that? Did you refuse to call a committeeman for your PR Burr?"

I answered, "Well, yes and no."

The Wop shook his head in disgust and said, "Holy shit. You been at Ford for, what, three hours, and already you have learned management double talk. What the hell kind of an answer is yes and no? You either did, or did not refuse to call the man a committeeman. There ain't no use for you to deny it. There are three other men that heard you refuse to call me. But before I turn loose all hell on you, I want to hear it from your own mouth."

I said, "Look, I am not trying to double talk you. The man did, in fact, ask me to call a committeeman. He even said, 'Call the Wop.'"

"But you did not call me. Why is it that you didn't call me when a man properly requested that you call me according to the articles of the labor agreement? Why did you refuse to call me?"

"I didn't say I would not call you. What I said was that I was not doing anything until the man went back to his job and unloaded the converters. We were on the brink of losing Fairfax. In fact, we did lose Fairfax because the men weren't unloading the south line."

He frowned and shook his head, "But you did not call me. Why?"

"Well, for one thing, I didn't know if the guy was jacking me around. I mean, after all, the term 'Wop' sounds like a derogatory racial term. But besides that, I had no idea what a committeeman is, and no one ever explained how to call one."

The Wop flinched with a look of shock, and took two steps backwards as though he had suffered an agonizing blow.

In a painful voice he said, "Did I just hear you say that you do not know what a committeeman is, nor do you know how to call one? Tell me that is not what I just heard you say. Tell me it is all this fucking noise that made it sound like that is what you said."

I said, "No, you heard me right."

His face drained of blood and turned white with rage just as Ed rounded the corner from the ZE34 racks. He ignored the committeeman and addressed me.

"How come the Wop is out on the floor? The Wop ain't sposta be out on the floor unless we got a problem."

The Wop, whose face turned from ghost white to beet red shouted, "Oh, yeah, we got us a problem, all right. We got us a big fucking problem!"

Ed said, "What kind of problem do we have?"

"Well, Ed, seems like Ford Motor Company went and hired a new foreman for a big ass pivotal department like 258, AND DID NOT TRAIN HIM ON HIS CONTRACT RESPONSIBILITIES, LIKE WHAT A FUCKING COMMITTEEMAN IS AND HOW TO

CALL ONE WHEN AN HOURLY MAN PROPERLY REQUESTS THAT HIS COMMITTEEMAN BE CALLED!"

Ed, never flinching, coolly looked at me and said, "What in the hell is the Wop blabbering about?"

I said, "Well, one of the guys unloading asked me to call a committeeman."

"So?"

"So I don't know what a committeeman is, let alone how to call one. You never said anything about a committeeman. At P&G we were non-union. You never said anything about exactly what a committeeman is, or how I am supposed to call one when one of my men requests it."

Ed's jaw dropped, tobacco juice ran down his chin, and he said, "You refused to call a committeeman for one of your men?"

I nodded yes.

The Wop looked smugly at Ed, evidently satisfied that I had come clean and admitted my shortcoming. His face resumed its normal tint. Ed scrunched up his face and looked at me with total disgust. The Wop rocked back and forth on his feet, gloating, and no one said anything.

Then the Wop said, "Look, Ed, you know me. I am a reasonable man. I understand your situation. You got a new foreman. Things are fucked up like Hogan's goat, as usual. You didn't have time to properly train him and instruct him on everything that he needs to know. I'm willing to overlook this serious violation of the labor contract. I'm willing to go and talk to your PR Burr and smooth things over. I'm willing to talk him out of filing a formal grievance."

Ed looked at the Wop with deep suspicion and said, "Provided?"

The Wop shrugged his shoulders and said, "Provided you forget about the Barney incident in 257 and retract his 4600. The Barney incident never happened."

Ed's voice exploded above the noise and he yelled, "Never happened? Shit! We got that sorry son of a bitch dead to rights. He cut wires on the broach. 257 was down for two hours. We are up to the last step on the 4600 progression. Barney gets fired."

The Wop said, "Or so management claims. You have no witnesses and only circumstantial evidence. *Somebody* cut wires on the broach. We do not know who. Barney happened to be nearby when it was discovered. If you fire Barney, we'll grieve it all the way up to the Detroit Mafia.

They'll fuck around with the paperwork for a full year. Then Barney will be reinstated with complete back pay. You know it and I know it, and Barney knows it. But, hey, you want to give Barney a year off with full pay, it's up to you. I can take this failure to call a committeeman all the way up north, too. It's a serious violation. The shit will hit the fan because the Men From Up North are sick and tired of getting grievances because of the incompetent management at the Sharonville Plant. You and Ed and Roger can explain why you put a green foreman out on the floor with practically no training and he committed a grievous violation of the contract. It will be further evidence of piss poor judgment in Zone 3. It's all up to you. The Barney incident never happened, and your new foreman didn't violate the contract. Or we can take both cases up north. Which way do you want to go, Ed?"

If looks could kill, I would be a corpse, as Ed, through clenched teeth, said, "The Barney incident never happened. My new foreman did not violate the contract."

The Wop smiled smugly, looked at me, and said, "You see, management and labor can work together. We're all reasonable men."

Then he got on his bicycle and rode toward the back end of 258. That is when the rage and fury poured from Ed's mouth like an erupting volcano.

He screamed, "Don't you NEVER, EVER admit to a committeeman that you was wrong. You admit that you made a mistake and them lousy bastards will hold it over your head until the day you die. You don't make mistakes. You're management. If you did it, it was the right thing to do. The union can argue until hell freezes over, and Roger will back you up. We don't make mistakes. You got that?"

I said, "I got it."

Ed said, "You know what you just cost us? You cost us the chance to get rid of one of the worst pieces of shit that ever come down the pike."

"But the Wop said he would be reinstated anyway, with back pay, and you apparently agreed. Otherwise you would have let him grieve it."

"Yeah, but the son of a bitch would have been out of the plant for close to a year. It would have been worth it. I agreed to his terms because of what you done."

"Look. I can't do things right unless I have a chance to learn how things are done around here. This so-called training program is a farce."

"I don't want no excuses. I can pay some hillbilly to give me excuses all day long. Roger hired you to run 258, not make excuses."

As Ed was insulting me, I became aware that something had changed in the environment. Then I realized what it was. The noise had decreased tremendously. 258 had ground to a halt. All the machines stopped. Men started walking off the job.

Ed glanced at his watch and said, "It's lunch time. Them sorry sumbitches get twenty minutes for lunch. It's now 11:30. At 11:50 this department better start back up and run full. Not 11:51 or 11:52 – 11:50! I want your ass right here at this desk at 11:50 to make sure this department starts back up on time. They have been screwing us all morning. But we will get a day's work out of them if it kills me."

Ed gave me one last dirty look, spun around, and headed up the aisle. I got the distinct impression that he intended to get revenge on my entire department because he lost the confrontation with the Wop. I looked at my watch. Three minutes had already passed. I had seventeen minutes to find something to eat, wolf it down, and get back to 258.

I remembered seeing a vending area not far from the zone office, and I hurried to it. It had a sandwich machine, a candy bar machine, a soft drink machine, and a coffee machine. It also had two picnic tables, and two large trash cans overflowing with a cloud of flies above each can.

Hourly men sat at the two tables, eating, talking and laughing. When I walked up all conversation ceased and I could feel six pairs of eyes on my back as though I was a foreign invader. One guy nodded his head at the black grease on my white shirt, and they all laughed. I got a coke and a sandwich and headed back to my desk. Seven minutes had passed.

I sucked down my lunch and noted that 258 had four minutes to get back to work. I waited. At 11:49 there was not an hourly man in sight. At 11:51, 258 was devoid of workers. At 11:55 I saw Ed storming out of the blue grey mist like Frankenstein. He started shouting while he was still 20 feet away.

"They are fucking your brains out. What do you intend to do about it? Every minute that 258 isn't running is five torque converters Ford ain't never going to get. That is five cars that Ford is never going to sell."

I said, "What do you want me to do about it, Ed?"

Ed looked at me like I was completely retarded and said, "When your people don't start up on time, you rack their asses. You lay the paperwork to them. These people have to learn that you are not going to take any shit from them."

I said, "Well, okay, but you are going to have to walk me through this process the first time. Don't forget, I have only been at Ford for about five hours."

He shook his head in disgust and said, "Where is your clipboard? What kind of a foreman doesn't even have a clipboard? You go to the office and get a stack of 4600s off of Larry's desk. Put them on your clipboard. Note the time each man came back to his job. Get your relief man, take him to operation 10. You call the Wop and tell him you are holding disciplinary hearings in the corner office for late lunch returns. You call Labor Relations and tell them the same thing. Then you have your relief man relieve the first man on operation 10. You take your operation 10 man to the office. You tell him you are taking disciplinary action because he returned late from lunch. You write that on the 4600 and sign it. You ask the man if he has any questions. Then you tell him if there are any further violations of the labor agreement, further disciplinary action will be taken, up to, and including, termination. You tell him to sign the 4600. Then you give the 4600 to the Wop and the Labor Relations man to sign. Then you say this hearing is concluded, and you tell your man to go back on the job. You put your relief man on the next job, you bring that guy to the office, go through the same thing. Repeat that until every swinging dick in 258 is wrote up. You gotta show these people you got the stones to handle 258. If they ain't afraid of you, they ain't going to work. It's just that simple."

The first man from operation 10 was the big black guy with the red bandana that had warned me about industrial accidents. When the relief man replaced him, he refused to look at me, and we walked in silence to the corner office. As we threaded our way through the forest of machines, employees hooted and hollered.

One guy yelled, "Whatcha gonna do when they come for you, bad boy, bad boy."

Employee 8942 flipped him the finger and we kept walking. When we got to the corner office the Wop was there, as well as a mousy looking guy with a blue shirt and a black necktie, whom I assumed was from Labor Relations.

Before we sat down at the table the Wop turned to the Labor Relations representative and said, "I want to consult privately with this foreman before this hearing begins."

He meekly responded, "You have that right under the contract."

The Wop and I stepped outside and behind a large machine that was either broken or not running that day, and we could hear each other without shouting.

He had a tolerant, fatherly look on his face; smiled cynically, shook his head, and said, "You know, Bob, I had you pegged as a reasonable man that I could work with. Not like these pieces of crud that Ford calls management. They don't belong in a factory. They belong in jail. Maybe I was wrong. I hope not. You look like a smart guy. The word out on the floor is that you have a couple college degrees, so you ain't no dummy. You have to be smart enough to see what Ed and Larry are trying to do to you. Both of them are scared shitless of you and men like you. Young, bright, educated men that grew up in an enlightened era when the working man was not treated like a piece of garbage. Ed and Larry know that sooner or later even the Detroit Mafia will come to the realization that their day has passed."

He paused, slowly shook his head back and forth and said, "They're still using management practices from the 1930s – treating working men like a dog on a leash – acting like if you wear a necktie your shit didn't stink. Do you know how many bright, energetic young men have come to Ford and been pushed out, fired, or frustrated out the door by the likes of Ed and Larry?"

I patiently looked at him, listened, without responding and he continued, "If those kinds of men are allowed to get a foothold in management, Ford would think nothing of shit canning guys like Ed and Larry and replacing them with men like you who have enough sense to work with people. Their job survival depends on getting rid of men like you as quickly as they can. Don't tell me you don't have enough sense to see what they are doing?"

He put his hand on my shoulder like a professor enlightening a doe-eyed new student about the ways of the world. "They want to turn the men in 258 against you from day one. They know that production is determined by the men on the floor, not by the clowns in management, or by the rules in the labor contract. They know these men can run you

2,400 converters every single day, if they want to. But if they hate your guts because of what Ed and Larry told you to do, you will be damn lucky to get 1,000 converters.

"If your production is bad enough, they can fire you right away, like they have so many others. But if you gain the respect of the men, and they start running the hell out of torque converters, then somebody Up North might say, 'Look at 258! Production has jumped way up. Let's take a closer look at that new foreman.' That's when Ed and Larry will have some sleepless nights.

"Now, don't get me wrong. I have nothing against Ed and Larry. They are managing the only way they know how, but they are dinosaurs. The world has changed completely, but they will never be able to change. They have busted their asses for Ford, and I respect that. But their day is over, and all they can hope to do is hang on long enough to draw a pension."

The Wop looked at me knowingly, trying to get a read on me. He said, "Let me work with you, Bob. I can get the men in 258 on your side. But you have to work with me. When Ed comes up with this shit, let it pass right over your head. If they say 'jump' and you say 'how high,' the men in 258 will see you as a puppet. They hate puppets, and they hate Ed and Larry."

He shook his head and warned me, "Look. Do not follow through on these disciplinary hearings. You don't have to. Ford has assigned you to run 258. Ed can advise you, but he cannot compel you. He can ream your ass, but 258 is *your* department, not his. He can evaluate your performance, but he cannot tell you step-by-step how to handle each situation as it arises. That is your job."

I listened intently as he pleaded his position, knowing that every word he said was true. He was visibly getting himself worked up as he pointed toward the factory floor and continued, "These men aren't animals. They aren't prisoners of war. They are middle class working men trying to support their families, send their kids to school and pay their bills. Do you know what it's like to stand in front of a machine for eight hours, repeating the same operation over and over and over, for thirty years? Do you know what it is like to try and swallow your lunch in 20 minutes so you can get back to a machine, and then have the likes of Ed and Larry try to get you fired because you took five minutes longer than you were supposed to? You have to show these men that you know they are human beings and that you aren't just a puppet of the front office.... So what do you say, Bob? Will you let me help you? Will you go back in that office and tell Labor Relations that the disciplinary hearings are cancelled?"

I looked at the Wop, knowing full well that he was right, and said, "I'm sorry, but this is my first day on the job, and I cannot risk being a rebel. I will follow through on the hearings."

The Wop shook his head, shrugged his shoulders, and said," Okay, but when 258 gets fucked up, and nobody will work with you because they hate your guts, don't say the UAW didn't try to put you on the right path."

The mousy Labor Relations guy seemed relieved that we were back. I got the impression that he did not feel comfortable sitting alone in the office with employee 8942. I had the man's file in front of me, and noted that his name was Ronald Ponaber.

I said, "Mr. Ponaber, the purpose of this disciplinary hearing is to take action against you for returning late from lunch."

Ponaber ignored me, looked at the Labor Relations guy, and said, "This motha fucka used my name. I don't want no fucking foreman using my name. I ain't a man to Ford Motor Company. I'm a number. Tell him to use my number, or I ain't going to pay no mind to him."

The labor rep said, "The foreman is instructed to use the employee's last four, rather than his given name."

I continued, "Employee 8942, you returned late from lunch today. If there are any further violations of the labor contract, further disciplinary action, up to, and including, termination, will be taken. Do you have any questions?"

"Hell no, I ain't got no questions. But you can take that 4600 and shove it up your ass, because you won't be at Ford long enough to take any further disciplinary action against my black ass."

I signed the 4600 and pushed it over to Ponaber to sign.

He pushed it back across the table and said, "I ain't signing a damn thing."

The labor rep said, "It's noted that employee 8942 refused to sign his 4600."

I pushed the 4600 across the table to the Wop, who said, "I will not sign this unfair and unjust disciplinary form."

The labor rep pulled the 4600 across the table, signed it, and said, "It's noted that the employee's committeeman refused to sign the 4600."

I said, "That concludes this disciplinary hearing. Employee 8942 return to your job."

I went back to 258, had the relief man fill in for the second stock handler on operation 10, and escorted him to the corner office. He was an average size white man. His hair was scraggly and grew over his ears as though he had not been to a barber in a decade. He had a full beard and several rotted teeth. His face had a distinct pink tint.

He was not hostile like Ponaber. In fact, he seemed on the jolly side. When I got close enough for him to hear me above the deafening noise of Zone 3, the odor of booze was almost overwhelming.

When the relief man took over his job he said, "Gittin my ass wrote up, am I?" Then he laughed.

As we walked up the aisle, somebody yelled, "You better sober up before he gets you to the corner office."

He laughed again and said, "New foreman, writing my ass up."

His name was Searle. I went through my lines.

He said, "Gittin my ass wrote up," laughed, and signed the 4600.

The Wop said, "I will not sign this unjust and unfair disciplinary form."

That was duly noted by the labor rep.

The third employee had a gigantic belly and a big mustache.

When I asked if he had any questions he said, "No, I got no questions. A man has to give a shit to have questions. That piece of paper don't mean jack shit to me. I don't care nothing at all about getting wrote up. Fact is, it gets me away from my machine for a few minutes. But I ain't signing no papers."

It was during the seventh disciplinary hearing that Larry opened the door and said, "I need to see you outside – Right now."

I stepped outside the corner office and Larry said, "Jesus H. Christ, man. Department 258 is falling apart. We ain't getting converter one out of that bitch. And where is the foreman? He is sitting on his ass up in the corner office."

I said, "But, Ed told me to write up every swinging dick in 258. That is what I am doing in the corner office."

Larry said, "Don't give me no excuses. Get your ass back to 258 and get the son of a bitch running." Then he stormed away.

When I turned around the Wop was standing behind me.

He said sarcastically, "I take it the disciplinary hearings are over?"

I said, "Yeah, I guess they are."

The Wop said, "Welcome to the wonderful world of Ford Motor Company, where the excitement never ends. But you made out okay. You only have seven men in 258 who hate your guts. Who knows, maybe you can still turn it around and hang on to your job."

Then he walked away shaking his head in disgust.

When I pulled into my driveway that night I knew my wife would want to know how my first day on the job went. She had been totally against me taking the job, and I knew that as long as I worked at Ford I would have to fight a two-front war: My wife and Department 258.

When I opened the door, my two-year-old son Richard yelled, "Daddy's home!" just like he had every night when I worked at P&G. But I was in no mood, and Richard was confused by my failure to fuss over him which had been a nightly ritual since the day he was born.

My wife appeared out of the kitchen and I knew she sensed that my mood was less than ideal.

Then she said, "Oh my God. What is that black stuff all over your new shirt? Look at your shoes. You are leaving huge black footprints all over the floor!"

CHAPTER 3:
WAR ON THE FLOOR

I arrived at Sharonville dressed differently that second day. I wore a flannel shirt, steel tip work boots with oil resistant soles and blue jeans. I would not be destroying any more expensive clothes in Department 258.

Ed had instructed me to be on the floor no later than 7:15 a.m. I was to get the skinny on which machines were up, which machines were down, my supply of torque converter components, and what the day's production schedule was to be. I was told to look for, "A fat, ugly, light colored coon with a nose that covers half his face, chomping on a pipe." His name, I was told, was 'Hi Yella.'

It seemed like an odd name.

When I asked Ed to repeat, he said, "Did I stutter? His name is Hi Yella."

After I got the line up from Hi Yella, I was instructed to stand at the time clock and check off each man's name as he clocked in. Then I would know if every job was covered, or if I had a short crew.

Since the men in 258 were still nothing more than a blur in my mind, and I had no clue about which machine each man operated, I decided to simply count the number of men clocking in and then count the number of operations and machines. If there was a difference, I would know that I had a short crew.

I looked around 258, but did not see anyone meeting the description that Ed had given me, so I went to the time clock. I planned to say good morning to each man and try to associate his face with the machine that he ran.

I said, "Good morning" to the first man that clocked in, and he shot me a look like I was crazy.

The second guy said, "Fuck you! Any day you gotta come to work at this place ain't no good day."

The third man spit on the floor, gave me a dirty look, and walked away. That is when I saw the man that had to be Hi Yella.

I walked over to him, extended my hand, and said, "You must be Hi Yella."

He almost bit his pipe in half and growled, "Wadju call me?"

I said, "Hi Yella. I just assumed that you were Hi Yella, because Ed...."

"That fucking hillbilly told you to call me Hi Yella, didn't he?"

"Yes, he did."

"He's a racist son of a bitch. He is trying to get you fucked up with people. He does that with every new foreman. He thinks it's funny. But I don't think it's funny. Yeah, I am Cajun. So what? Don't be calling me no Hi Yella. My name is Brad. You got that?"

I said, "Yes, I got it. I'm sorry Brad. The only thing I had to go on was what Ed told me. I certainly had no intention of insulting your race."

Brad shrugged and waved it off. He said, "Don't worry about it. I know the way that son of a bitch is. I could tell you stories that you would not believe about how he tried to get me fucked up. You gotta watch people around here. A lot of them will do their best to get you fucked up. But I won't. You deal with me like I'm a man, and I will try to help you out. I know what you're up against, believe me."

Then Brad said, "Okay, here is what you got. Welder 3 is down. It is waiting on an electrician. The south automatic balancer is down, waiting on a machine repairman. The north Inteco is running, but not very good. It's this damn humidity. High humidity beats the hell out of the electronics on the north Inteco. The south Inteco is exactly the same machine, but humidity don't hurt it. Go figure.

"The south line is set up on Fairfax. You got to run the hell out of that line. As of 15 minutes ago, we only had 400 Fairfax ahead of assembly. The north line is set up on twelves. Keep running twelves until you get 600. They need 600 more for the Lincoln Continental run. After that, they need eleven and a quarters. Change the north line to eleven and a quarters as soon as you pump out 600 twelves."

He pointed randomly down an aisle and said, "Keep your eye on 257. They got a war going on and the people are fucking their brains out. Ed made the foremen write up three guys. It's a funny thing how machines start breaking down when they start fucking with people. 257 hasn't produced enough impellors to keep one of our minor assemblers going, let alone four. What you got to do is get the hilo to shuttle partial racks of impellers to operation 10 to keep it running. 257 is running so bad that if you wait for a full rack, your monorail will be half empty by the time it gets here. But once you change the north line to eleven and a quarters you'll be okay because we have a good float of eleven and a quarter components ahead of operation 10. You got any questions?"

Did I have any questions? He had to be joking. My brain was spinning. What is an eleven and a quarter, and how do you change over to it? What does it mean that the north Inteco is not running good? Is it running, or not, and what do I do if it isn't running? How long do I have to wait for an electrician for the welder and a machine repairman on the south balancer? What happens if they don't show up?

I looked at Brad with a stunned, dumbfounded expression, and he said, "Okay then, I'm out of here."

He grabbed his clipboard and disappeared into the hazy mist of Zone 3. I was left standing in the middle of the oil soaked aisle like an infant abandoned on somebody's doorstep.

I stood there for a moment, thinking about torque converters. Ed never mentioned there were different kinds of converters. But evidently there are Fairfax, which are different than twelves, and eleven and a quarters. It made sense. There are various kinds of Ford vehicles, why wouldn't there be different kinds of torque converters? A fork truck, which is apparently called 'a hilo' nearly ran me over, and I jumped out of the way.

The hilo had a half full ZE34 rack of what looked like very heavy army helmets, but each one had a four inch, shiny looking pipe sticking out the top. I took a wild guess that those were impeller housings, since the rack was only half full. The hilo driver sat the rack at operation 10, spun around, and headed up the aisle. I followed him, theorizing that I could pinpoint the location of department 257, which I assumed was the destination of the hilo, and also where impeller housings are produced.

I did not have far to travel. Department 257 was the next department behind 258. The hilo got an empty rack, pulled up and sat it down in front of a guy leaning against a roller conveyor, looking at the pictures in a Hustler magazine.

The hilo driver turned off the key and leaned back in his seat with an expression of utter, total boredom. Every now and then one or two of the army helmets with pipes rolled down the conveyor, and the other guy sat his magazine down and stacked them into the rack.

Further up in 257, beside an oily, green metal desk much like the desk in 258, I could see a group of men standing in a circle. Among them were Ed, Larry, the Wop, a guy with a red jacket, and another guy with a white shirt and UAW emblem. The noise was too overriding to hear what they were saying, but it looked like a big argument judging from the body language.

Roger cruised slowly past the group in his orange golf cart, like a general overseeing a battle. I looked at my watch. It was 7:35 a.m. I took my clipboard and stood by the time clock again. Most of the men clocking in simply ignored my cheerful, "Good morning," acting as though I wasn't even standing there.

Ponaber muttered something about a "white matha fuck college boy."

The drunk had bloodshot eyes, looked at me, laughed, clocked in, and walked away.

Each of my three set up men, who were the only ones that Ed had introduced me to, sort of, grimly nodded as though they were entering a funeral home. When the clock clicked on 8:00 a.m., according to my count, I was one man short and decided to walk through 258 to see which machine did not have an operator.

I did not have to look very hard. There were only three minor assemblers. I looked back up the aisle to 257, where, evidently, the verbal brawl was over, and each participant headed in a different direction. Ed was walking in my direction with something folded over his arm. It was red.

He handed me a red jacket that had FORD emblazoned on the one breast pocket, and SUPERVISOR emblazoned on the other.

He pitched the jacket to me and said, "Put this on. If you are going to be a foreman, everybody gotta know you are a foreman. What do you have in 258?"

I said, "Thanks a million for not telling me the midnight foreman's name is Brad."

Ed grinned and said, "What the hell. Everybody calls him Hi Yella behind his back. We only got a handful of nigger foremen. Everybody has a name for each one of them. They call him Hi Yella, course they don't do it to his face."

I said, "One of my minor assemblers is absent. The third welder is down and needs an electrician. The south automatic balancer is down and needs a machine repairman. The north Inteco is not running well. I am running tight on impellors because of the trouble in 257. I'm supposed to change over the north line to eleven and a quarters after I run 600 twelves."

Ed said, "Okay I'll get you a borrowed man from the labor pool. Have you been to the outpost yet?"

I said, "What is the outpost?"

Ed shook his head and said, "Christ, don't you know nothing? You got two machines down and one that is running half-assed, and you ain't even been to the outpost yet? What kind of a foreman are you? Come with me."

I let Ed know that I was getting fed up with being expected to know all the details of a complex manufacturing operation when I had no real training.

He said, "Take it easy. The best way to learn stuff is to jump right into the fire and figure things out. It don't do you no good to sit in some classroom reading books about all this shit. You got to be out on the floor, in the thick of it. That is the only way you're gonna learn. That's how I was trained. That's how every foreman is trained. Ford don't waste money on people sitting in classes reading books and shit."

We ended up at some dirty green desks, all lined up, on the other side of the monorail. Each desk had a box of what looked like punch cards. At the top of each desk was a clipboard dangling on a chain.

Ed said, "This here is the Zone 3 Maintenance Outpost. When you need a machine worked on, this is where you come. What you do is fill out one of these cards. You put 258 on the card, and what machine is down. If you need an electrician, you put the card in the slot on the first desk. If you need a pipe fitter, you put the card in the slot on the second desk. Each kind of maintenance man has his own desk and his own clipboard. Your set up man will tell you what kind of maintenance man you need. If you want to find out how long before you are going to get a maintenance man, look on the clipboard. As he finishes each job, he signs off on it. That will tell you how many jobs are ahead of 258. Let's look at the clipboards. See? You are next in line for both an electrician and a machine repairman. Now I will go to the labor pool and get you a man for your minor assembler job. You go back to 258 and make sure we ain't getting fucked by nobody."

About ten minutes later Ed came back to 258. But he did not have a man from the labor pool. He was walking with a woman, apparently from the labor pool. She was the first woman I had seen at Sharonville, other than the clerk in the salaried personnel office, and Roger's secretary.

Ed said, "This here is Grace. She will fill in for your minor assembler."

Then he nodded to Grace and walked away. There was a distinctive difference in how Ed regarded Grace, as opposed to how he regarded the hourly in general, and he used her first name. This was totally out of character for relationships between management and the hourly, as best I could tell, and it surprised me.

Grace said, very pleasantly, "What job do you want me to do?"

I said, "I need a minor assembler. Have you ever assembled torque converters?"

She said she had not, but if I would show her how, she would be glad to assemble them. It was refreshing to talk to an hourly employee that did not seem to detest me. But then I realized that I did not know how to assemble torque converters. Ed had never explained that to me.

I said, "This will sound really stupid, but I don't know how to assemble converters. This is only my second day at Ford. No one really explains anything to me."

Grace laughed and said, "Welcome to Ford Motor Company. I have been here for 12 years, and it has always been the same. I feel sorry for you, being hired right off Sharon Road with no idea what the heck is going on. Don't let them bamboozle you. Don't give them the satisfaction of getting so frustrated you quit. They love to get a new foreman to the end of his rope and have him storm out of the plant. They think it's funny. Why don't you ask one of the other assemblers if he'll show me how to assemble torque converters? Then you can watch. That way, both you and I will know how they get assembled."

I asked minor assembler number four if he would train Grace on assembling converters, and I would listen in. He gave me a hard stare, as though he could not believe I was asking such a thing.

Then he took a long drag on his cigarette, flicked the butt on the floor, and said, "What do I look like, a fucking teacher? It ain't in my job description to train nobody. Get the Wop down here."

I went to my desk, checked the earpiece for grease, and called the union office. In less than five minutes the Wop rode up on his bike, slid across the oil, put his kickstand down, and said, "What did you do now?"

I explained the problem and the Wop said, "Give me a minute with the assembler."

It only took the Wop a few minutes, and Grace and I shot the breeze by my desk.

He came back and said, "Okay, he will train Grace, but he does not want to be bird dogged by a foreman. If you want to be trained on assembly, get somebody in management to do it. It isn't the job of an hourly man to train his boss. His boss is supposed to know the man's job."

Then the Wop hopped back on his bike and disappeared.

Grace went to the assembly station and I walked toward the back of 258. The calibration man was working on the north Inteco, but the Fairfax line was backed up completely to the welders. The set up man and machine repairman were both looking at the south balancer and shaking their heads.

The men at the end of the department were idle because no converters were coming down the conveyor belts. I was on edge because I knew that if that south balancer did not get running soon I would lose Fairfax and today would be a repeat of yesterday. I caught a glimpse of Roger's orange golf cart swinging past 258. He looked at all the men standing idle, gave me a disgusted look, and headed toward the zone office.

The set up man walked over to me and said, "This baby is going to be down for about three hours. It has to have the hydraulic pump replaced. You want me to run them straight through, don't you?"

I repeated, "Run them through? Help me out here. I don't know what you mean."

The set up man grinned and said, "Yeah, sure. How would you know? You're brand new. What I mean is I can lock up the gate on the balancer, and let the converters run straight through."

I said, "But then the converters wouldn't be balanced, right? The balancer is down."

He said, "That's right. They would not be balanced."

"But we can't run unbalanced converters, can we?"

"No, we can't. If I was foreman, what I would do is put two men on the standby balancer and have them balance manually until the automatic is back up."

I said, "But the south standby balancer is a one man machine, unless I misunderstood Ed's training. How can we have two men run a one man machine?"

The set up man said, "That's right, it's a one man machine. The work standard calls for one man to run it for eight hours, balancing all the converters kicked out by the automatic, up to 259 converters. If the man works steady, all he has to balance is 259 converters because that is eight hours work. But if you go that route, you will lose Fairfax. So if I was foreman, and of course I'm not, I would put a second man on the standby. I would have one man balance steady for a half hour, while the other takes a half hour break. Then they would switch. The standby balancer would never stop running. We have a good chance of not losing Fairfax if we do it that way, running off standard with two men."

I said, "If you were foreman, where would you get the other man from? We don't have any extra men, do we?"

"Sure we do. We have two burr hands that are always off standard. You use them anywhere you need them. You can assign a burr hand to work half hour on and half hour off on the standby."

I said, "Okay, let's do it."

The set up man said, "Well, we can, if that is what you want. Tell us what you want and we will do it. You're the boss."

The entire back end of 258 was within ear shot and could hear our conversation because no machines were running.

I said, "All right, lock the gate up on the south balancer. Who is the standby balancer operator?"

A guy said, "Yo, that would be me."

I said, "Okay, we will be running off standard, a half hour on and a half hour off. Where are my burr hands?"

Two guys that were standing together both put their hands up. I pointed at one and said, "You work on the south standby."

He said, "Okie Dokie, boss."

The men went right to work, and as I was heading back to my desk the north automatic balancer, which was being adjusted by the north set up man, started shooting fire and sparks. The converters were moving on both lines despite the south balancer being out of commission.

When I got back to my desk the welder set up man was waiting for me. All four welders were shooting showers of sparks, which was a good thing.

He said, "I hear we are supposed to run 600 twelves and then switch over to eleven and a quarters. Is there any truth to that?"

I said, "Oh, crap. I forgot about that. Yes, we are. How many twelves have we run so far?"

The set up man pulled a piece of paper from his coveralls and said, "Well, as of two minutes ago welder one had a count of 108, and welder two had a count of 114. So that means we still have 378 to go before we make the changeover. But if I was foreman, which I ain't, I'd be getting ready for that changeover right about now. If we got everything ready we can make the switch without hardly missing a lick."

I said, "Oh yeah? Well tell me this, if you were foreman, how would you go about making that changeover to eleven and a quarters?"

The welder set up man said, "Well, if I was foreman, the first thing I would do is flag down the hilo driver and tell him to stage components for an eleven and a quarter run at operation 10. I would tell him we would need to start hanging eleven and a quarters in, oh, about an hour. Next thing I would do is go to the ass end and tell the north set up man to get ready to change the jaws on the turnover, and change the Inteco and automatic balancer to eleven and a quarters. Then I would tell my two north assemblers to work down their set ups on their assembly table, and get ready for the changeover. Next I would tell my two stock handlers to get ready to quit hanging twelves and get set up to hang eleven and a quarters. Then I would check my welder counts and back count the monorail to make sure there were enough impellor housings, turbines, and cover plates hung to make my 600. You got enough components to run 140 converters on the monorail. After I back counted I would show my operation 10 people the last hook to hang twelves, and the first hook to hang eleven and a quarters. After that I would tell my welder set up man, which is me, to watch for the first eleven and a quarters coming up from the assemblers, and change the welders when that last twelve got through each one."

The welder set up man looked at me and said, "But then again, I ain't the foreman. You are."

I grinned at him, nodded my head, and tracked down the hilo driver.

The changeover went without a hitch, and 258 was running like a Swiss watch, even with the south balancer down. I knew that my men were holding out a peace offering to me. They were showing me that they could make 258 run well, so long as I was not an asshole, and I kept the front office off their ass. They were showing me that my function was to get them what they needed to do their jobs and protect them from management.

It was clear in my mind that the key to good productivity was to absorb all the abuse from Ed, Larry, and Roger like a sponge, and protect my men from that abuse. As I stood and watched 258 running smoothly, and contemplated the message in it, Ed appeared, looking deranged.

He said, "Roger just jumped my shit about 258. He says your whole department is sitting on its dead ass."

I calmly looked at Ed and shouted above the noise of 258 running full, "Maybe Roger needs to take advantage of our great Ford eye care benefit and get himself a pair of glasses."

He said, "What the hell are you talking about? Roger don't wear glasses."

I said, "Let's take a walk through my department."

We walked through 258, and Ed had a suspicious eye as he saw every man working, both lines running full, and no one breaking any rules. The disappointment on his face was totally transparent. I was certain that he fully expected to find multiple shortcomings and haul me back in front of the human skeleton. We turned and walked back toward my desk. Ed seemed desperate to find something that I had done wrong. But he could not.

He spat a stream of tobacco juice, walked away clearly disappointed, but stopped after five or six steps, spun around and came back. "You was supposed to change over to eleven and a quarters. You ain't changed over. You are going to shut Lexington down tomorrow because they won't have no converters."

I pointed up to the monorail, where the first eleven and a quarter components were just reaching the first minor assembler. Ed looked up, grunted, gave me another angry look, and disappeared into the smoky haze of Zone 3.

As soon as lunch was over, I saw Roger's orange golf cart driving past 258. He was looking at his watch. I was looking at my watch, too. My department started up precisely at 11:50 a.m. Roger drove within two feet of my desk, looked through me as though I was not there, and kept going up to 257 where he slowly cruised past, looking at his watch. An hourly man quickly shoved his Playboy behind his machine, and went back to work.

I was feeling smug, like the front office had tried to nail me, and I had won. But my over confidence did not last long. At the back end of 258 someone was waving both arms in the air to get my attention. He was wearing the red jacket of management, and I hurried to the back.

He said, "Are you the 258 foreman?"

I said that I was.

He said, "I am day shift QC Foreman. We got a problem on the Fairfax line. Did you know that every other converter is locked up?"

"No, I did not," I said, feeling a bit distraught. "In fact, I don't know what locked up means."

He made a grunting noise and said, "That figures. Foremen always act dumb when it comes to quality. Locked up means the converter will not rotate internally. If it will not rotate internally, it's scrap. Since every other converter is locked up, that should tell you that either one of your two south line assemblers is assembling wrong, or you got a welder problem."

Just then a young man with an oily rag hanging out of his pocket pushed a hand cart up to where we were standing. The hand cart had a Fairfax torque converter laying on it that had evidently been cut in half with a band saw.

He said, "I found the problem. The stator is being assembled upside down. That is what made the converters lock up. One of your assemblers is putting the stators in upside down."

I hurried to the minor assembler stations and watched one of the regular assemblers putting in stators. Then I watched Grace putting in stators. Grace was assembling them upside down. I asked her why she was assembling them incorrectly.

Grace explained that she was assembling the way she had been instructed. I asked assembler number four why he had told Grace to put the stators in upside down.

He said, "Oh shit. Did I show her wrong? I thought I had shown her right. But then again, like I told you, I ain't no fucking teacher. I ain't paid to do your job. Get my committeeman down here."

The Wop spoke privately with the assembler, and then came over to my desk.

He said, "Your man on number four assembly table made a mistake. If you look at a stator and you don't know stators, it's real hard to tell the top from the bottom. He has been assembling for seven years and the job is second nature to him. He has never had to explain every single detail of assembly to anyone. That is the foreman's job. It was an honest mistake."

I said, "Was it an honest mistake, or was it payback for the 4600 I put on him yesterday?"

The Wop shrugged his shoulders and said, "That is something that we will never know for sure. But here is what we do know; the men in 258 are working with you incredibly well. They have your department chugging away like the little engine that could. Don't be foolish enough to lose their cooperation. This department could be barely running, if you get my gist. Now you can write that man up because you're management and you can do anything you damn well please, but I am here to tell you that a 4600 for a man who tried to help his foreman by doing part of his job, but doing it incorrectly, will never fly. I will take it all the way Up North if I have to. It will be overturned by the Detroit Mafia, and, once again, the Sharonville management will come out looking like bumbling idiots."

It did not take Ed long to show up and tell me precisely how many cars Ford would never sell, due to my incompetence. Then we were sitting in Roger's office. A few minutes later Larry showed up and plopped his bag of bones down on the chair next to me. Nobody said anything. Roger looked at his watch, and continued with his paperwork.

Then a nondescript guy that looked like a stereotypical bureaucrat from a grade B movie came in and sat down. His name tag said John Becker, Salaried Personnel.

Roger cleared his throat and said, "This management disciplinary hearing will now begin. The purpose of this hearing is to take formal disciplinary action against Foreman Dewar. Foreman Dewar failed to instruct a borrowed employee on the proper method of assembling Fairfax torque converters. As a result, more than 100 torque converters had to be scrapped. In addition to the high dollar loss that Ford will have to absorb as a result of Foreman Dewar's failure, the loss of those torque converters has reduced our precariously low float ahead of the Fairfax assembly lines. Foreman Dewar, do you have any questions or comments on this disciplinary action?"

I said, "Yes, as a matter of fact, I do. First of all, the total amount of training that I received in Department 258 lasted precisely 39 minutes. The main instructions that I received involved watching men like they are institutional inmates, and write them up when they break rules. I never received any instructions whatsoever about how to assemble torque converters."

John Becker jerked his head toward Roger and said, "Is it true that Foreman Dewar did not receive any instructions about how to assemble torque converters?"

Roger looked at Ed, who was squirming in his seat like a school child caught in mischief.

Ed said, "You know what that floor is like out there. I ain't got time to take and hold a foreman's hand. I can't show him every damn thing there is out there. If I did that, the rest of the zone would be going to hell in a hand basket. If I stay in one department too long, I get my brains fucked out in all the other departments. I have to keep moving from department to department."

John Becker repeated the question, "Was Foreman Dewar properly instructed on how to assemble torque converters?"

Ed said, "No, I never did get to that. I was going to, but I never did get to it."

Roger gave Larry a look that could kill. Larry shot a disgusted glance at Ed, who was looking down at the floor.

John Becker said, "This disciplinary action against Foreman Dewar is rescinded. If we do not train our foremen how are our foremen supposed to train the hourly?"

Then he looked at Roger and said, "I hope you will not be wasting my time on any more of this nonsense." Then he got up and left.

Roger looked at me and said, "Get back out on the floor."

When I got back to 258 it was running full blast. The south automatic balancer had been repaired. My men looked at me as I walked through the department, but there was a different expression on their faces. Some of the hate and distrust was gone. My willingness to absorb the wrath of the front office had reinforced my image. At the end of the shift my numbers were only a few converters short of quota, and Ed had no comment as departed for the day.

On the way out of the plant I was startled by an hourly man who seemed to pop right out of the forest of machines. I estimated him to be in his 50s. He had a three-day growth of beard, a protruding stomach, and a head as smooth as a cue ball.

He stepped right in front of me and said, "You know none of this matters, don't you?"

I said, "Excuse me?"

He said, "This place doesn't matter. We are only here for a short time. All that matters is that we serve the Lord. Praise Jesus. Follow Him. He was sent to save us from our sins. On the last day he will raise us up to sit at the table of the Lord forever. Yay though I walk through the valley of the shadow of death, I will fear no evil. If He is with me, who can be against me? Praise Jesus."

Then he handed me a plain white business card that had the entire Lord's Prayer printed on it. He disappeared into the endless line of machines as suddenly as he had appeared, and I never saw him again.

As I continued to the parking lot, I reflected on the day's events and felt good about what I had learned about my job and Ford Motor Company on my second day as a foreman in Department 258.

CHAPTER 4:
BAD TURBINES AND COCKTAIL HOUR

By the end of my third month at Ford, Department 258 was running better than anyone could remember. Day after day, week in and week out, I made my numbers, regardless of machine downtime, component shortages, or harassment from management. But I had a secret.

I knew that the American worker will perform magnificently if given the tools to do the job and the freedom to perform. I knew this from growing up in the Appalachian coal fields, observing my father, uncles, neighbors, and others who labored in the mines and mills to support their families.

I knew the way to get the men to produce was to protect them from the layers of management above me, and make sure they had everything that they needed to do their jobs. I became a mother hen, protecting her chicks. But it was a two-way street. My men protected me also. They called it, "watching my back and covering my ass."

They knew I was a threat to Ed and Larry, and that they would go to extreme lengths to get me fired. The men in 258 made sure no rules were broken that could trigger the demand for 4600s. They hated the entire management group at Ford Motor Company, and they ran excellent production as a message to the front office of what they can do if they have real managers instead of jail wardens.

A foreman like me was an alien at Ford, and I had to be expelled in order to protect and perpetuate the system that had changed very little since the days when Henry Ford walked the factory floor.

My men set up an early warning system. One man at each corner of the department scanned the mist for Ed, Larry, or Roger's orange golf cart. The minute one of them was spotted the word was passed, and when they got to 258 every man was at his machine, wearing safety glasses, and torque converters were clanking against each other on the conveyor belts. Department 258 started on time, took the correct breaks and lunch periods, and there was very low absenteeism.

But the unwritten rule at Ford was if you were not generating 4600s, you could not be doing your job. How could you be a foreman if you were not riding herd on the cattle called hourly employees? That is why I started getting nervous the day both Ed and Larry showed up in 258.

They walked slowly, as if strolling in the park on a sunny Sunday afternoon. They carefully observed everything, like a doctor giving a whole body physical exam. I stood at my desk watching them. They stopped by the balancers, and watched the back end of the department for a full 15 minutes. Then they came to my desk.

Larry spoke first. He said, "Looks like 258 is running like a top. Same way it ran yesterday."

Ed chimed in and said, "Yesterday? Hell's fire, it has been running like that for a month or so."

I nodded my agreement and said, "My crew knows how to make converters."

Larry said, "Knows how to make converters, Hell. There is some shit going on here. I don't know what it is. But I do know that 258 don't run like this. It never has. There has to be some shit going on. I don't know what the fuck you are doing out here. But I intend to find out. Oh, yes. I will find out."

With that Ed and Larry turned and left.

Within an hour my phone rang. The Wop was on the other end.

He said, "I just heard that something is gonna go down in 258. I don't know what it is. But I just saw Roger, Ed, and Larry go into Salaried Personnel for some kind of meeting. Best I can tell from the grapevine, something is gonna go down in 258. I thought I would put a bug in your ear."

I thanked him for his concern. Over the past three months I had been able to work with the Wop to head off trouble and keep 258 running well. He had been a much bigger asset than anyone in management. My working closely with him really rubbed Ed and Larry the wrong way. The UAW was supposed to be an enemy, not a confidant.

I was on high alert for the next couple of days. But nothing happened. It was the third day that I found out what Larry meant when he said he was going to find out what was happening in 258.

He had scheduled a total labor relations audit of my department. That meant having four grim faced bureaucrats at my desk as soon as I arrived at work. They had clipboards and stop watches and reminded me of Special Forces troops raiding an enemy post.

One of the bureaucrats shadowed me like a puppy dog. He said nothing, but he timed me and jotted down each function that I performed. The other three bureaucrats fanned out in 258 like an army patrol in Vietnam, writing down what every man was doing and how long it took. They compiled copious notes asking each and every employee his last four, his job classification, what he was doing and why.

They noted the precise moment the machines stopped for breaks and lunch, and the precise moment that they started back up. My shadow noted on his report that I took 9.3 minutes to walk to the vending area to purchase coffee and a sandwich. He noted that I spent 14 minutes in the men's room, and it was not during an authorized departmental break. He noted that I went into a stall, shut the door, pulled my pants down, and sat on the commode.

At the end of the shift the four labor relations bureaucrats met, and in hushed conversation compared notes. There was a shaking of heads and some kind of agreement. Then my shadow came to my desk and said the results of the audit would be communicated to me by a higher level manager. That communication did not take long.

The next morning, as I was standing at the time clock taking my head count, Larry walked up, took the clipboard out of my hand, and said, "You won't need this. Ed is going to run 258 today. You and I have a meeting in Roger's office. Right now. Head on over there. I will be there as soon as I can round up Ed and assign him to run 258."

When I got to Roger's office he was reading a multi-page document labeled:

AUDIT, DEPARTMENT 258, SHARONVILLE TRANSMISSION PLANT, FOREMAN: ROBERT J. DEWAR.

He did not look up when I arrived, and I took a seat. After a few minutes Larry walked in and dropped his bag of bones across from me. Roger laid the report down, folded his hands on his desk, and, in his typical 'I am the king and you are a piece of crap' mode, looked right through me and began to speak.

"Foreman Dewar, this is an interesting audit. Department 258 is running very, very well. But anybody can get good production if they compromise the authority vested in them by Ford Motor Company, and collaborate with the hourly."

I said, "Collaborate? The last time I heard that word was in Boot Camp, and we were being instructed about how to behave in captivity. They talked about collaborating with the enemy."

Roger nodded grimly and said, "That is a good comparison, because that is what you are doing in 258. You are collaborating. You have given up your right to be the boss, and are letting the hourly run your department. This is not acceptable. If the hourly are running your department, why do we need you?"

I said, "You would not need me. You wouldn't need Ed or Larry, or yourself, either. Not if Ford was managed with some degree of professionalism. A company is a team. It is a big team with a big goal. That goal is producing high quality products to service their customers. The team is not broken down into two groups of warring enemies. The enemy should be other companies competing for the same market. The team should focus on how to beat the other companies, not how to beat each other. The term collaborate has no application when you talk about a department working to make its numbers. Everyone should cooperate with each other to get the job done. That is what I am trying to do in 258."

Larry's skeletal jaw dropped open, and I wondered if he was having a stroke.

Roger gripped the report so hard that his hands turned red, and he said, "Did I just hear you say that we are not professional in Zone 3?"

I said, "I am just making an observation, based on my education and experience. I try to apply what I have learned to making my numbers in 258. I thought you hired me to make my numbers."

Roger snarled, "I do not give a rat's ass about your education and experience. I told you that when you were hired. You are not sitting in front of me because you have failed to make your numbers. You are sitting in front of me because you have compromised your management rights."

He stood up, hovering over his desk, leaning in toward me his face contorted and his tone filled with contempt. "If we yield our right to manage, by letting the hourly run our show and ignore the labor contract, then we can never get our management rights back because we have set a precedent. If Bob Dewar, at the Sharonville Plant, sits back and lets his people run his department, then that will have implications for every department at every plant where Ford has a contract with the UAW. We cannot have a deviant foreman, no matter how good his production."

He eyes were piercing as he stared at me, pausing; he inhaled a deep breath and sat back down. "We like your numbers. We want you to keep getting those numbers. But you should not be getting your numbers because you think you have some kind of team out on that floor. You should be getting your numbers because you damn well MAKE them get the numbers. The hourly are not our partners. They are our employees. Do you understand?"

I starred at Roger and asked, "Can you tell me specifically how I have compromised my management rights?"

Roger said, "Certainly, that is what the audit has told me. You have four PR Burrs unloading converters, two on the north line and two on the south line. The contract calls for those PR Burrs to stand and unload converters for their eight hour shift. Yet at any given time you have only one PR Burr on each line, doing the work of two men, while the other PR Burrs are fucking off some place. Then the other two PR Burrs come back, relieve the first two, and they go and fuck off some place."

Roger's voice was filled with rage and disgust. "Do not pretend that you do not know that this is a violation of the labor contract. If one PR Burr is absent from his job on each line, why have I not seen a 4600 on each of them? As a matter of fact, why have I not seen a single 4600 from you after your first day on the job? Are you telling me that there has not been one single contract violation in 258 for three months?"

I asked Roger if the goal was for the PR Burrs to get the line unloaded, or for me to control the PR Burrs.

He slammed his fist down on his desk and yelled, "The goal is for you to supervise your men the way the contract specifies, and make your numbers. That is the goal."

I looked at Larry, and then at Roger, and said, "Have you ever stood on your feet for eight hours unloading 40 pound torque converters? At the end of the day their backs are aching, their legs hurt, and their feet are killing them. One PR Burr on my north line is 47 years old. After an eight hour shift of unloading converters, he can barely walk. But if they can work for a half hour, even if they are doing the work of two men, and then go to the break area and sit for a half hour, at the end of the day they are not completely and totally worn out. They still have some life in them to take home to their families."

I looked at Roger and then Larry and emphasized, "I made a management decision to alter the work method so that it would be more comfortable for the PR Burrs. They are happier, and they never fail to do their jobs. They help me out in other ways because they appreciate me altering their work method. When they get older they will not have back, neck, and leg problems. I thought my job was to use some common sense and management discretion to get the job done."

Roger threw his head back in utter frustration and said, "Who in the hell do you think you are? Who gave you the right to change job descriptions that have been hammered out by the highest level managers and UAW officials? I do not give a flying fuck about their backs, necks, or legs. I give less than a damn how comfortable their jobs are!"

He flew up from his desk and started pacing the room. "If Ford wanted them to be comfortable, it would say so in their job descriptions. It does not say anything about comfort level. We give those people the best damn medical benefits known to man. If they have back, neck, or leg problems they damn sure can go to a doctor and it will cost them nothing."

Roger scowled, hovered over me and pointed his finger just inches from my face. "You have no right to authorize a violation of work standards. Did I say anything about common sense when I hired you?... No, I did not! Did I say that you would have management discretion to run 258? No, I did not. What did I say?"

His black eyes starred through me, and I looked back without responding. "I said I hired you because I thought you had the balls to stand up to those sorry bastards and make them do their jobs the way Ford and the UAW agreed that they would do their jobs. Ford does not pay people to be comfortable. It pays them to do the job that they are assigned."

Roger's voice was quivering. It was the first time that I had ever seen him display such emotions. One of the things that set him apart from the other managers was his quiet, professional demeanor. He paused, recovering himself and sat back down, then asked if I had a problem with my eyes. I told him that I had 20/20 vision.

He said, "Do you? For a foreman with good eyes, there are a lot of things in 258 that you do not seem to be seeing. For instance, there is a checkerboard set up on a bucket between the two automatic balancers. There is a stash of Playboy and Hustler magazines in your set up men's tool boxes. Have you ever seen them?"

I said, "Of course I have."

He said, "Is that a fact? And yet no 4600 has crossed my desk. Now why is that?"

I said, "That is because they do not play checkers or read magazines when the balancers are not running well. Ford pays them to keep those incredibly sensitive pieces of equipment running. That takes knowledge, skill, and experience. When those two balancers are running, their jobs are to monitor the gages and watch for malfunctions. They play checkers and read magazines, but they are also monitoring their machines."

Roger said, "Do you authorize the playing of checkers and the reading of magazines on company time?"

I responded, "Yes, I do. My job is to make sure they are doing their jobs. If the balancers are running, and we are making converters, they are doing their jobs."

Roger said, "Let me ask you this. Could they also monitor the machines while sweeping the floor, or can they only monitor the machines if they play checkers?"

I smiled and said, "If I assign a highly skilled man to a lesser task, it would be a slap in the face. Why would I assign my highest skilled men to do something my lowest skilled men can do? Would it make sense to assign Ed and Larry to clean offices when they are not making management decisions? Of course it would not. It would be an insult."

I could tell that Roger was barely controlling his emotions. I was challenging the basic foundation of Ford's management policies. In my MBA training, I learned that a function of management is to strive for constant improvement by questioning everything. That was also stressed in my P&G training. But it went over like a lead balloon at Ford.

Roger said, "How does the wearing of safety glasses square with your common sense approach to managing? Is it common sense to make your men protect their eyes? If so, why are there sections of department 258 where you do not require your men to wear safety glasses?"

I nodded and said, "Let's be honest here, Roger. Wearing safety glasses is mostly a tool for management. When all else fails, a foreman can always catch a man not wearing his safety glasses. Yet in at least 80 percent of this plant there are no eye hazards whatsoever.

"For example, in 258 the only place that has eye hazards are near the automatic balancers and the welders, which shoot out hot sparks that could blind a man. I absolutely require men that work in the vicinity of those machines to wear safety glasses at all times. But in the rest of the department, which comprises fully 60 percent of 258, there are no eye hazards."

I could tell Roger was becoming angrier by my response, but I continued. "As a matter of fact, wearing safety glasses in those areas creates both a safety and a productivity hazard. The air is foul. It is full of oily mist. Your safety glasses are constantly getting so dirty that you have to stop every 15 minutes and wipe them off in order to do your job. This is a drag on productivity. I personally nearly got run over by a hilo because I was cleaning my safety glasses and not looking when he spun around the corner."

Larry had a blank look on his face, like a deer caught in headlights. He had just heard a foreman tell the highest level manager in Zone 3 that most of the rules that were considered gospel were nothing more than tools to beat people down, and that Ford management was a gang of bullies. He had just heard the lowest man on the management totem pole challenge that sacred document, the labor contract. A clear liquid leaked from his fake eye, and he turned his good eye to Roger to await his response to this atrocity.

Roger stared at me for a few seconds. Then said, "Let me understand this completely, Foreman Dewar. You believe that you have the right to use common sense, rather than the labor contract, to manage Department 258. You feel that you have the discretion to abrogate the contract if it would make your men more comfortable. You feel that you have the right to authorize men to not wear safety glasses in areas designated by yourself. You feel that the wearing of safety glasses, which is an established rule in every Ford facility the world over, and even the president of the company wears safety glasses on his visits, is really nothing more than a tool to discipline hourly workers. You believe that you have the discretion to approve of men playing checkers and reading magazines on company time, if, in your opinion, they are meeting their job requirements. Is that an accurate summary of your management philosophy?"

I looked at Roger and said, "You hired me to run 258 and make my numbers, and that is what I have done."

Roger stared at me for a full half minute as though he was not sure what to say or do next. Then he said, "This meeting is over." I left his office and went back to 258.

My department was total chaos. Ed was running around like a chicken with his head cut off, screaming at people. More than half the machines were down. When Ed turned his back my men mocked him, gave him the finger, or pumped their hips back and forth as in simulated intercourse. For a minute I felt sorry for Ed. But it was only for a minute.

When Ed saw me he screamed, "Get this fucking department running. These lousy bastards won't do nothing unless I tell them, then they act like they don't know what I mean. Get these converters moving. When I come back out here you better have this son of a bitch running, or you better have me a stack of 4600s."

He headed for the zone office like a dog with his tail between his legs.

When Ed disappeared into the mist, my three set up men came to my desk. They knew that I had been in Little Napoleon's office, and they wanted to know if I was going to get fired.

I said, "Who knows? But it wouldn't surprise me. They don't think that I am enough of a hard ass."

They shook their heads in disbelief, and went back to their jobs. Within a half hour all the machines were running.

Lunch break came and went, and I had not been called to Salaried Personnel to be terminated. Just as I was wondering how long Roger would take to process my termination, Ed popped out of nowhere. He never mentioned my meeting with Roger or how poorly he had fared in trying to run my department.

He just said, "Have you seen any QC people?"

I replied that I had not.

Ed nodded and said, "That's good, because they are all supposed to be in a meeting."

Then he beckoned a hilo, who was following him down the aisle with a full load of turbines in a ZE34 rack. The hilo swung into operation 10, sat the turbines down, put the hilo into reverse, and peeled down the aisle.

I recognized those turbines. Everyone in Zone 3 knew about them because Roger had gotten into a pitched argument with QC. QC had rejected nearly 10,000 turbines because they had been stamped out of coils of steel that had not been heat treated. They were rejected because the lack of heat treatment would allow metal fatigue to set in, and the turbines would fail before the transmission had 20,000 miles on it. It was a budgetary nightmare for Zone 3, which would have to absorb the cost of scrapping 10,000 turbines.

Ed said, "Tell your operation 10 men to stop hanging regular turbines and start hanging these turbines. I want them all on that monorail before that QC meeting is over."

I said, "I can't put these turbines into converters."

Ed said, "What did you say? Don't you hear good? Didn't I just tell you to get those turbines hung?"

I replied, "Ed that rack has a reject tag on it."

Ed reached over, ripped the reject tag off, and said, "No it don't. Get them turbines hung." Then he started to walk away.

I said, "But Ed – "

He spun around and said, "Get them fucking turbines hung, and don't give me no shit."

I stood and watched the turbines going around the monorail, through the washer, and to the assembly stations. A ZE34 rack holds 375 turbines. I was watching the beginning of 375 defective transmissions. I was watching the birth of 375 defective Ford vehicles. I had just been forced into a conspiracy to cheat 375 Ford customers.

It suddenly became crystal clear to me – Ford Motor Company is going to fail. You cannot run a company like this and stay in business. Sooner or later it will catch up with them.

I don't know how long I stood there, as if in a trance. I felt dirty, like a criminal. What I had just been ordered to do disgusted me. My trance was broken when I realized that the shift was nearly over, and I had to get my numbers together. But before I could, I saw both Ed and Larry walking toward me.

Ed checked the ZE34 rack and smiled when he saw that all the defective turbines had been hung. Then he and Larry walked over to my desk. They both seemed uncharacteristically jovial.

Ed grinned and said, "Tomorrow is Sunday. You ain't scheduled to work tomorrow."

I said, "Why would 258 not work tomorrow? We still are barely ahead of assembly on torque converters."

Larry chimed in. I had never seen the human skeleton smile until that moment. He said, "Oh, 258 is working, all right. But you ain't."

In my mind I felt that this was a low ball way to terminate a man, even for Ford Motor Company. I had expected a formal termination in Roger's office, and an exit interview with Salaried Personnel.

Larry continued, "Your ass is being transferred to the midnight shift. Hi Yella has been bitching about being stuck on midnights for years while we hire young white foremen and put them on the day shift. He is making noise about discrimination. He's getting on the bandwagon with all them other niggers. He claims he's talking to an attorney. Roger don't want to fight all that government shit. So he's flipping Hi Yella to days and sending you to midnights."

Ed added, "Now we will see how all them management skills you got play out on midnights. You know, all that shit about building a team, working with your people, making it more comfortable for them. Shit like that. Midnights ain't days."

Ed laughed so hard I thought he might swallow his chew of tobacco, and I was concerned that Larry's fake eye might pop out and roll across the floor because his body was convulsing with laughter. They were both enjoying this very much.

Larry stopped laughing long enough to say, "No, it ain't. Midnights ain't days." They were still laughing as they disappeared into the haze.

I thought to myself that at least my long term plan of accumulating enough money to break free of economic bondage was still intact. In fact, going to midnights came with a 10 percent shift differential, and every penny of it would get invested in the future of my family.

My private thoughts were interrupted when Ponaber showed up at my desk. Oddly enough, he had become one of my best employees after he apparently concluded that I was not the same breed as other Ford foremen.

He said, "You turned out okay man. But you cost me a lot of money."

"How did I cost you money, Ponaber?"

"I had a lot of money riding on your ass being gone in three weeks. You done made it as a foreman, and I lost two week's pay betting against you. Ain't that some shit? But now they went and exiled your ass."

I said, "Exiled my ass. What are you talking about?"

"You been exiled to midnights, man. Little Napoleon don't know what to do with you. If he cans your ass, the Detroit Mafia will be asking how come he got rid of a foreman that got the best production 258 ever had. But if he leaves you here, other departments are going to say how come I got to wear safety glasses? Some guys in 258 don't have to wear safety glasses. He is between a rock and a hard place, know whatta mean? So he done sent your ass to midnights. You been exiled."

I said, "How do you know that I have been transferred to midnights? They just told me five minutes ago."

Ponaber slowly shook his head and said, "Man, you *still* don't know what is going on at Sharonville, do you? The hourly always knows shit before the foremen know it. You want to know something, ask an hourly man, don't ask a foreman. Come on, man. I want to buy you a drink before you get exiled. You go to midnights, you will need a drink. You will need a whole lot of drinks."

I followed Ponaber as we weaved our way across aisles and past lines of machines. We ended up on the far side of the gigantic Press Room. We confronted a massive wall of ZE34 racks stacked 20 feet high. All of them had red reject tags dangling on wires.

I had heard about the graveyard of rejected parts, but I did not know the location. It was a quality control dumping ground. When QC rejected parts, they were stacked into racks and sent to the graveyard.

On paper the rejected parts were all scrapped. But that was only on paper. In reality they were sent to the graveyard to be stored. When machine downtime or a departmental war dried up supplies of components, the foreman went to retrieve what was in the grave yard to keep his department running. The hourly had a saying that there was no such thing as a rejected part at the Sharonville Transmission Plant.

Ponaber walked all the way to the wall where there was a narrow passage between the wall and the immense row of rejected parts. He squeezed through the opening, and I followed.

We ended up in a large open area surrounded on all sides by the wall and the gargantuan stacks of rejected parts. It was like a big room, invisible from the outside. Incredibly, it was a saloon.

Ponaber grinned and said, "Welcome to the Red Dog Saloon, man."

There were two full size refrigerators stocked with beer and whiskey. There was a radio playing country music. There were a number of ZE34 racks turned upside down for tables, and chairs pilfered from offices. One of the tables had what looked like a hot poker game in progress. There was a bartender with a cash register, and cups of nuts sitting on each table.

I turned to Ponaber and said, "How do you get away with this? What if Ed or Larry stumbles on this? What if Roger finds it?"

Ponaber shook his head and said, "Man you know how to get converters out of 258, but you don't know jack shit about how things work around here. We got us a silent partner. Let's just say Little Napoleon ain't nobody compared to him. Ain't nobody gonna stumble on nothing, because they already know about the Red Dog."

He looked at me sideways, "But they *don't* know about it, if you get my drift. Ain't nobody in management gonna see nothing or hear nothing, and they ain't gonna come nowhere near the Red Dog. Let's just say it would have a negative impact on their job, and let it go at that. Let's get a drink."

I still could not fathom how a saloon could be run right in the plant. I said, "How are these men able to be away from their jobs. Don't their foremen know they are not on the job? I just don't get how you can do this."

Ponaber shook his head like someone explaining something to a child. He said, "No, man, they ain't on their jobs. They already done clocked out. Ain't no foreman gonna be missing them. But after they clock out, what they gonna do then? Go home and listen to the old woman bitch about how they ain't never home? Listen to her go 'you gotta fix this, you gotta take care of that'? Hell no. They already done put up with enough shit at Ford. They come here to the Red Dog, relax a little, have a coupla drinks. A man gotta get away from all this shit to keep his sanity, man. You got to slow down. A man that just works and goes home, what kind of man is that?"

The bartender looked at my red jacket. Then he shot a questioning glance at Ponaber. Ponaber said, "Don't sweat it, man. Bob is okay. Let's have two Buds."

I gobbled up the Red Dog Saloon with my eyes as we waited on our beer. Ponaber seem pleased at my amazement that the Sharonville Transmission Plant had a saloon and someone in top management was a silent partner. Ford was a curious place indeed.

We sat at an overturned ZE34 rack where an hourly man nursed a mixed drink. He had not taken his eyes off me since I squeezed through the opening.

When we sat down he lit up a Marlboro and said, "You are a foreman, ain'tcha?"

I said that I was. I could tell that he was half way to happy valley by the smell of his breath and the way he slurred his words.

He said, "I don't like foremen. I ain't never liked foremen. You know why?"

I took a swig of my Bud and said, "No, I do not. But I have this strange feeling that you are about to tell me."

He said, "Yeah, I'll tell you. Foremen are pricks. You can't never trust a foreman. You know how long I have hated foremen? Forty years, that is how long."

Ponaber said, "Pelltrie, quit living in the past, man. Bob here ain't like them foremen you keep talking about. He has been to college and everything. That was back when you was a kid. Things change. You have to let go, and move on, man. You can't let things keep eating at you."

Pelltrie ignored Ponaber and continued, "I grew up in Detroit. My Dad worked for Ford. That was back in the thirties, back when times was hard. Not like today, where everything comes easy. There was no union. Henry Ford ran Detroit like Al Capone ran Chicago. When Henry Ford said 'jump,' the mayor, the cops, the judges, they all said 'how high' and 'when do you want me to come down?'"

Pelltrie took a drink, sat the glass down, took a long drag on his cigarette, and continued, "Ford had people that watched you all the time. He figured everybody was out to get him. He had a special department, called the Service Department. But they didn't change your oil and check your tires. Every foreman wanted to get picked for the Service Department because it paid better and they didn't have to do too much except watch people and scare people. A lot of times they had to beat people up, if Henry Ford told them to.

"The Service Department kept a lid on things. There was a lot of unemployment. People were hungry. If you had a job, you was damn lucky. If you worked at Ford, you was double lucky because Ford paid better than anybody else. But Ford was a bad place to work. Ford was a real bad place to work.

"If Henry Ford figured you for a union man, he would have the Service Department take you out back and beat the shit out of you. People put up with it because it was a job. There was snitches. If a man thought he could get ahead, or make his job more secure, he would snitch on his own brother. Sometimes it meant you could feed your kids instead of letting them go hungry.

"I was only eight years old. But I will never forget that night if I live to be 100. A knock came on the door. My mother opened it and three foremen from the Service Department pushed their way in. There were only certain kinds of foremen that Ford picked for his Service Department. A lot of them had been to prison. Some of them had been in World War I. They were hired thugs. Ford wanted men that did what they were told and did not ask any questions.

"The Service Department had been told by a snitch that my Dad was stealing tools from the plant and selling them to get extra money. They ransacked our house, but they never found any tools. My Dad never stole anything in his life.

"Two of them held my Dad. The third one said, 'Where are the tools?' Dad said he didn't have no tools. The guy punched him in the gut and said, 'Where are them tools?' Dad said he didn't have no tools. The guy kept punching him until he slumped on the floor. The next day Ford fired him. But he never took no tools. We barely had enough to live on. If you got fired at Ford, you could not get a job anywhere."

Pelltrie drained his glass, sat it down, and said, "But I got back at Ford. I have been fucking their brains out since they hired me 28 years ago. I run bad parts. I fuck up machines. I never, ever run my full quota. I figure that in another couple years me and Ford will be even. Then I will go back to Detroit and visit my Dad at the cemetery and tell him he can rest in peace now."

He stood up and said, "You wanted to know why I hate foremen. Now you know."

Then he staggered toward the opening, squeezed out, and left. I never saw him again.

Ponaber searched my face for emotion. He seemed pleased by what he saw. I had heard similar stories from my father about how the coal companies treated people during the depression. But I never heard a personal story that was that vivid. The Red Dog Saloon was giving me an education about Ford Motor Company.

Someone else was squeezing through the opening. It was Grace, the woman from the labor pool. She saw us, grabbed a beer, and sat down at our table.

Ponaber drained his bottle and said, "Look, man, I gotta split. My old woman accuses me of stepping out on her when I come home too late. Stay here as long as you want. The drinks are on my dime. Good luck on midnights. You are going to need it. Later, man."

Grace took a drink of her beer and said, "So what do you think of Ford?"

I said it is a job. "A man has to work."

She nodded and said, "Yeah, it's a job. I have been here for 12 years, and it has been a trip, I can tell you that."

I said, "You've been here 12 years and are still in the labor pool? I thought the labor pool was mostly for new hires. After they get some seniority under their belts they bid on a regular job."

Grace said, "Yes, they do. But that is not for me. I do not want a regular job in this plant. Honestly, the thought of running the same parts, on the same machines, over and over and over for years and years makes me ill. I like variety. I am a people person. I like to move all over the plant, doing different jobs, and meeting different men. Every one of them has a story, you know. And most of the stories are sad stories."

I said, "Sad stories? What do you mean sad stories?"

Grace said, "Stories of divorce. Stories of troubled kids and broken homes. When you work at Sharonville it becomes your life. It can eat you alive. You work seven days a week. The way they are around here, you go home with your stomach in knots and your fists balled up. Some men turn to booze. There are men in this plant that can't face Ford without being high on drugs. It is sad.

"Sure, you make a lot of money. But you have no time or energy for the rest of your life. What about your family? What about your kids? Don't they deserve a piece of you? But how can you give it if Ford squeezes every last drop of life out of you? So your family takes all that big money and they buy things to try and replace you. But things can't replace a husband. They can't replace a father.

"I like to move around the plant and meet men because I can give them comfort. Sometimes a man does not get any comfort at home. Every person is entitled to a little love and comfort in their life. Don't you agree?"

I said, "Sure. I guess so."

Grace said, "Are you married, Bob?"

I said, "Yes, I am. I have a little guy, too. Richard will be two in November."

Grace said, "Well that is real nice. I hope that Ford does not destroy your home life, Bob. I hope your wife understands what it is like at Ford. Promise me this, if things ever start to get bad, you know, between you and your wife, you look me up. I can help you."

I looked at my watch and said, "Okay, I'll do that. But I came to Ford for a specific purpose, and when I have achieved that purpose, Ford and I will part company. Believe me no corporation is going to get the best of me. I can promise you that. But I have to go now. Tomorrow night I start on midnights. I have to retrain my body to sleep during the day and work during the night. That should be fun."

I squeezed through the opening and headed for the parking lot, pondering how Ford could possibly remain competitive with such abysmal factory practices. It seemed doomed for failure, like the collapse of the Roman Empire.

CHAPTER 5:
NIGHTMARES BEGIN AT MIDNIGHT

My body refused to shift gears. When I pulled into the parking lot at 10:30 p.m., I was aching for sleep. As I turned off the ignition and started getting out of my car to head to the midnight shift, I noticed something I had not noticed before. As I looked through the cyclone barb wire fence that separated the salaried and hourly parking lots, I saw an immense motor home that took up two parking spaces in the hourly lot. Why would somebody drive to work in a gigantic motor home?

I paused and looked at the RV. A front tire was flat, and one back tire was very low on air. There was a pile of decayed leaves under the vehicle. That trailer had been there for a long time. There were lights on inside. I settled back in my seat to ponder the motor home.

An aged and tired looking man came out of the plant, walked across the lot, looked around, and then knocked on the door. A woman in a sheer red negligee greeted him at the door, and they went inside. I immediately recognized the woman – she was Grace.

Later I would learn that giving comfort to hourly men was a profitable sideline, and Grace was a wealthy woman. She had no living expenses. Her home was parked on Ford property. A silent partner in upper management protected her home from probing eyes.

Grace worked seven days a week at Ford and seven nights a week in her motor home. She owned an apartment building, stocks, bonds, and a gas station. Grace also dispensed other services to Ford men. She gave financial advice. Grace had already broken free from economic bondage, and I wondered why she continued to work at Ford.

I looked at my watch, got out of the car, and went into the plant. The most striking thing about the men on the midnight shift was how they moved. They walked like zombies. It reminded me of the horror movie I had seen as a kid, "Night Of The Living Dead."

Working midnights disrupts your circadian rhythm, which is a 24-hour cycle cued to light and darkness. It regulates everything from heart rate and hormones to digestion and alertness. The natural flow of life involves working during the day and sleeping during the night. People on midnight shifts live oppositely from the rest of humanity. The effect on their body is shocking when someone from the normal world first enters the world of the midnight shift.

My management training prepared me for the increased social and emotional problems suffered by people working the midnight shift. They function like lonely nocturnal animals, cut off from normal community activities. They are socially isolated, alienated, and always exhausted because the quality and quantity of sleep is never adequate. They often drown their sorrows in booze or drugs.

While pursuing my MBA I studied the special stresses placed on people who work the midnight shift. In the thirteenth century, European guilds forced governments to outlaw work during the night, because it did so much damage to village life and the nuclear family. Midnight shifts were absent from the entire European continent for 400 years. It did not appear again until the colossal amount of production required by the Industrial Revolution necessitated factories to work around the clock. As I headed for the Zone 3 office I pondered whether corporate America was moving society forward or pushing it backward.

I was on the lookout for Screaming Jim. Jim was the midnight shift general foreman, and I wasn't looking forward to working for him. Screaming Jim was a legend at the Sharonville Plant because his volatile temper got him expelled from more than one zone. He was a cross between a screaming lunatic and a mad man. Even at Ford Motor Company, where outbursts of rage were normal management interactions, Jim was a misfit.

But Ford finally found a job that Jim could do — running the midnight shift in Zone 3. An uneasy truce had been achieved. As long as Screaming Jim stayed in the office and left people alone, the hourly would produce. Well, sort of. The midnight shift always produced far less than the day shift or the afternoon shift.

Sluggish hourly men, half asleep, went to their machines like mechanical toys whose batteries were nearly out of power. Any excuse at all was cause for a man to shut his machine down. Even the machines on midnights seemed listless, and everything moved as if it were in slow motion.

But if production got too low, Screaming Jim would be unleashed from the office like a rattlesnake striking from beneath a rock. His face would turn bright red, and a large blood vessel that always looked like it was ready to explode bulged from his forehead.

He would rant and rave, and write up the first man he saw.

Everything possible was done to keep Screaming Jim safely tucked at his desk in the office. A delicate balance had been unofficially negotiated between the foremen and the hourly. The hourly would produce enough to satisfy minimal standards, and the foremen would keep Screaming Jim off the floor.

On my way to the zone office I walked through 258 and stopped abruptly at operation 10. I was shocked to see that all the turbines sitting in racks, waiting to be hung, were rejects from the graveyard. I had unwillingly conspired to cheat 375 Ford customers on my last day shift.

By now every torque converter that I produced would have a defective turbine, until all 10,000 turbines were safely hidden in C-4 transmissions. Nothing more would be heard about them until transmissions started to fail. But that would be beyond the warranty period, and thus of no concern to Ford Motor Company.

It was common knowledge that on the midnight shift rejected parts were easier to feed into the system. Management was much thinner on midnights and there were fewer quality inspectors. Quality control inspectors were not held to a quantitative standard, as were the hourly workers. Their job was to inspect whatever was produced.

On midnights an inspector might show up by the middle of the shift, or he might not show up at all. If he did not show up by the end of the shift, someone would go to his stall in the men's room and beat on the door. The inspector would be sound asleep on a makeshift cardboard bed on top of the commode with his head propped up on one side of the stall, and his feet on the other. Each inspector staked out his own stall, and everyone knew where he could be found should he be needed.

The production foreman could not turn in his numbers at the end of the shift unless a quality inspector had signed off on the production report. If the inspector could not be located, the foremen forged his signature. No one closely examined quality control signatures, as long as someone signed the report.

When I entered the zone office, Screaming Jim was working on a crossword puzzle.

I said, "I'm here to replace Brad in 258."

Without looking up, Jim said, "What's the name of a river in Egypt that has four letters?"

"Nile. It's the Nile River."

Jim said, "How do you spell that?"

I told him.

He said, "Ah ha. You got it. They said you was a college man. I wanted to see how smart you was. Okay, here is how I work. You get me my numbers, and I stay off your ass. You run 258 and I sit at my desk and I don't fuck with your people. But if you don't get me the numbers I need to keep Larry and Roger off my ass, I will be on you like stink on shit. You don't want me on your ass. You think Ed was a prick, you ain't seen nothing until I get a hard on for you."

Screaming Jim continued his welcome speech to the midnight shift, "You know the ropes out on that floor. But there is one thing that I want to tell you. I heard that you done real good on days. But that shit ain't gonna work on midnights. We ain't got no teams on midnights. On midnights people know what numbers I need, and they get them for me because they know what happens when I don't get my numbers. Now get on out on that floor, and I don't want to see your ass again until you are standing in front of my desk with the numbers I need at the end of the shift."

Jim went back to his crossword puzzle, and I headed out the door. But before I was out of the office Jim said, "Oh, yeah. There is one other thing. Keep your eye on Quillen. He's seeing green men again. He's been seeing them for more than a week, so I called Rollmans. They're ready for him, but don't call them unless the other PR Burr starts to bitch because he ain't gettin' no help unloading."

I said, "Seeing green men? Call Rollmans? I don't know what you are talking about."

Screaming Jim seemed annoyed because he was concentrating on his crossword puzzle. He said, "Talk to your south balancer set up man. He'll clue you in."

I knew the south balancer set up man, Langley, and I shuddered to think that he would be working with me. He was not like the set up men on days, which were a tremendous aid to me. Langley was a militant black man who seemed to detest the entire white race. Everything that happened, in Langley's mind, was a result of the white man trying to subjugate the black man. I headed to the back end of 258 to find out about the green men.

Fairfax converters were backed up all the way to the south welders because the south balancer was down. It seemed to be down a lot more on Langley's shift than it was on the other two shifts.

My day shift set up man often complained because Langley would purposely leave everything out of adjustment when he left in the morning. It was his way of striking a blow for the oppressed black man against the white set up man, the white foreman, which was me, and the white management in Zone 3 day shift.

Langley's head was stuck inside the south balancer, and he had a wrench in his hand. I saw the hate on his face as I approached. I wondered what sort of evil white people had done to Langley to fill him with such hate. I was a white foreman, replacing a black foreman, as his boss.

I said, "Do you need any maintenance men on the balancer, Langley?"

He spun around and said, "Call me Mr. Langley. My name ain't Langley to you. It is Mr. Langley."

I repeated, "Do you need any maintenance people? I can go to the outpost if you do."

Langley laid his wrench down, wiped the grease from his hands, and said, "If I need maintenance people, I will tell you I need maintenance people. I know the balancers better than any fucking white boy pulling a tool box on wheels. Since I didn't tell you that I need maintenance that means I don't need maintenance."

I nodded and said, "Okay. Screaming Jim said something about green men and a PR Burr. He said I should ask you about it."

Langley said, "He's talking about that fucked up white boy with the red hair."

He motioned with his head, and I looked in the direction indicated. I saw a tall, heavy set man with red hair smoking a cigarette and walking in a distinct circle in the aisle. There were cigarette butts scattered all around him.

Langley continued, "That's Quillen. He's one fucked up white boy. He sees little green men, supposedly riding on the converters as they come out of the balancer. Nobody else sees them, just Quillen. The little green men talk to him. Then he has to go out into the aisle and walk around in circles until he figures out what they want him to do. He always does what they tell him. I've seen that crazy son of a bitch walk around like that for two hours, smoking cigarette after cigarette, trying to figure out what the little green men want him to do. Ain't no telling what the goofy bastard will do."

I said, "How did Brad handle this?

Langley seemed pleased that I would take my cue from how a black foreman had dealt with Quillen.

He said, "The only time Brad did anything was if the other PR Burr got tired of unloading the whole line by himself, or if he started some kind of shit, like screaming and throwing stuff around. A lot of times he just stops walking in circles and goes back to work, muttering to himself. But sometimes he does wild shit. If he starts doing crazy shit, Brad always called Rollmans. They send a couple guys out to get him. He stays at Rollmans for a couple weeks, and then comes back. He's normal for a while. But then he starts to see the little green men again, and the shit starts all over."

I said, "What is Rollmans?"

Langley said, "Rollmans is a nut ward. A lot of people from Ford make a trip or two to Rollmans. If you stay here long enough, you'll end up there. Now get out of my face so that I can get the south balancer up and running."

I stood for a minute to watch Quillen. He was lighting up another cigarette, after tossing a butt on the floor. His face was intense, like a battle was going on inside his head, and he was clearly having an argument with himself. There was no doubt in my mind that this was a seriously disturbed employee. I looked at the other PR Burr who was Quillen's co-worker on the south line. He was leaning against the conveyor with his arms folded in front, watching Quillen. I went back up to my desk.

The front end of 258 had not started yet. I looked at my watch. We had already lost over fifteen minutes production. This slow motion business on midnights was beginning to get on my nerves. I liked to see my department rolling when the shift started. The monorail was still motionless and the two stock handlers were examining the reject tags on the racks of turbines.

I walked from ZE34 rack to ZE34 rack, ripping off reject tags. Then I looked at the stock handlers and said, "Start the monorail and hang the parts."

One of them shrugged his shoulders as though he did not care what he hung. All he wanted to do was get his eight hours in and get the hell out of the plant.

I felt a twinge of conscience as I ripped off reject tags. But I knew that I could not change the way Ford Motor Company operated. If I tried all I would do was put a noose around my own neck. I had learned at P&G that survival in the corporate world meant not making waves and going with the flow. In a way, I was like the stock handlers waiting to get the hell out of the plant. I just had a longer time horizon.

The monorail started. I put my list of employee names and last four on my clipboard. My first objective was to get to know each man and what job he did. So far Langley and Quillen were the only two men with whom I could associate a name with a face.

I looked at the front end of 258. Welders one and two were firing. But there were no sparks coming out of welders three and four. Parts were making the return trip on the monorail. That meant that assemblers three and four were not building converters. I walked over to their work stations.

Assemblers three and four were both black men. One was young I guessed in his mid-twenties. The other was older, possibly forty or so. The older one was sitting on the ZE34 rack that held his stators. The younger one had his hand on the older one's shoulder as though he was consoling him. They both looked up when I approached.

I said, "How come you guys are not building converters?"

The younger assembler said, "Man, Jackson, he ain't feeling too good. He is sick as a dog."

Jackson, whom I assumed was the older black man, looked up at me. His eyes were completely blood shot and he reeked of booze.

I said, "Is he sick, or is he drunk?"

Jackson looked at me as though he did not comprehend who I was or what I had just asked. Then he cradled his head in his hands and closed his eyes. In twenty seconds he was snoring.

The younger black man, who was evidently trying to protect Jackson said, "Man, I need to talk to you. Can we go over by your desk?"

He shot a resentful glance at assemblers one and two, who were both white, and said, "This ain't nobody's business but ours."

As we walked toward my desk, assembler one yelled, "Jackson is drunk again."

Then in a mocking tone he added, "Do he MaMa know? She gonna git that wooden spoon after him."

Assembler two yelled, "OH, NO."

Then both white assemblers laughed hysterically.

When we got to my desk the black assembler made an urgent plea. He said, "Look, man, you got to cut Jackson some slack. He got all kinds of troubles right now. Man, his life is all fucked up. His boy just went to jail. They caught him with a buncha dope. His daughter is knocked up. She is fourteen. Yesterday he found out that his old lady is banging the guy down the hall while he is in here working. He went and got shit faced. He ain't been to bed for two days. Give the man a break. Don't be whipping out no 4600. Let the man go home. In a couple days he'll be okay."

I thought on it for a minute. Then I assigned one of my two burr hands to assemble at Jackson's table. When both south welders were firing I went to my desk and called the union office. The midnight committeeman was standing in front of me within five minutes. He wanted to know what the problem was, and I told him. He shook his head in frustration, and said, "Not Jackson again."

I said, "Look, let's not play any games here. We both know that I can get Jackson fired right now with no questions asked. But I won't, because I'm a reasonable man. I want to work with my people, not fight my people. I do not take lightly a man losing his job, even if he deserves it."

The committeeman said, "I appreciate that. The Wop told me you were a good man, and we would be able to work with you on midnights."

I continued, "Here is what I am going to do. I am going to walk to the back end of 258 right now. When I come back to my desk, and see that I have a vacancy at assembly table three, I will assume that Jackson never showed up tonight. I will report him as absent. The ring in on his time card was a mistake. Someone else rang his card in by accident. I never saw Jackson tonight. You and I never had this conversation."

The committeeman nodded appreciatively.

I turned and walked toward the back end of 258. After a few steps I turned and said to the committeeman, "You owe me."

Then I continued, and stopped in front of the south automatic balancer. Langley was wiping his hands again, and I had no doubt that he was fully aware that Jackson was as drunk as a skunk. I folded my arms in front of me and looked at Langley. Then we both watched the committeeman helping Jackson stagger toward the exit.

Langley looked at me. Then he went to his balancer, made a few adjustments, pushed the two green buttons that had to be activated simultaneously for the balancer to run, and yelled, "CLEAR," which warned everyone that the gigantic machine was about to start up. The south automatic balancer ran flawlessly for the remainder of the shift. I turned and walked back toward my desk.

The welder set up man was leaning on the corner of my desk. He had bloodshot eyes and looked like he had been sleep deprived since his teenage years. He pulled out a pack of Lucky Strikes, lit one up, and tucked the pack back into his coveralls.

Then he said, "You are going to run this show the same way Brad did, ain't you?"

I said, "The same way Brad did? What do you mean?"

He shrugged his shoulders and said, "Brad let the niggers get away with anything they wanted. He catered to all the niggers. If you was a white man, you didn't stand a chance. You never knowed it, but that coon on the south automatic balancer set your ass up every night. You tell me you didn't notice that the south balancer was fucked up every morning when you came in? The niggers around here will do anything to fuck up a white foreman."

I said, "Yeah, I knew we had problems with the south balancer nearly every morning. But my set up man on days is one of the best, and he always had it running a few minutes after the shift started."

The set up man smirked, took a long drag on his Lucky, and said, "Sure he did. But he didn't do it just to cover your ass. He did it because you're white. The niggers gang up on white foremen around here. Whites have to protect whites, or where are we going to be? The niggers keep creeping up and creeping up. Pretty soon, if you are a white man, you are going to be flat fucked."

I said, "Well, I don't know anything about all that. I don't see white men and black men. All I see are hourly workers. They are all the same to me. One is no better than the next. One will not get something that the other will not get. That is how I run things."

He said, "Yeah, sure. But you got to remember that white men have rights, too. Niggers ain't the only ones that got rights. You see all this shit on the news, about discrimination, stuff like that. But you know what I see? I see a bunch of niggers that figure they are owed a free ride because of what happened a hundred years ago. I didn't have nothing to do with all that slavery and lynching niggers and shit. Yet I am sposed to get fucked over because I'm white?"

He turned to walk away, and then he turned back toward me and said, "What I'm trying to tell you is you don't want to bend over backwards to help the niggers because most of this department is white. They got eyeballs. That is all I am going to say."

As he walked away I thought to myself how great this was. I had a race war, a boss who belonged in an asylum, a department that can barely stay awake, a drunken assembler, and a man who talks to little green men riding on converters. Oh, yes, I would have no trouble building a good work team on midnights.

But at least 258 was running like a scalded dog. The hiss and spitter buzz of the welders and the clanking of converters was music to my ears. The monorail was making the return trip completely empty, which meant that every part hung on operation 10 would end up in a finished torque converter spit out to the PR Burrs.

I felt myself drifting off. My eyelids did not want to stay open. I looked at my watch. It was 1:30 in the morning. I had not slept since Saturday. My body had not been able to switch gears and sleep on Sunday afternoon. That was the only time that I had to spend with my wife and son, and I'll be damned if I was going to spend it in bed. I checked my pocket for quarters and headed for the vending area.

The first cup of coffee, if you could call it that, was only half filled by the machine. It was light brown and had a vague resemblance to the taste of coffee. The second quarter caused an even lighter colored liquid to squirt out of the machine. But no cup came down, and it went straight down the drain. I put in my last quarter, a cup plunked down and filled with water. I gave the machine a vicious kick, hurt my foot, and hobbled back to 258.

The south line PR Burr was leaning on my desk. He said, "Man, Langley has that south balancer running balls out. I am going as hard as I can, but I don't have no big red 'S' on my chest. Know whatta mean? I can't keep that line unloaded all by myself. You got to get me some help."

I said, "Don't tell me Quillen is still walking around in circles trying to figure out what the little green men want him to do?"

He said, "No, he ain't walking around in circles. He's sitting on the floor pounding his pud."

"What?"

"Quillen is sitting in the middle of the aisle jacking off. Either get me some help or call me a committeeman and give me a pass to go to the nurse. I think I pulled a muscle in my shoulder."

I hurried to the back end of 258. Quillen had his coveralls pulled down, and was lying in the middle of the aisle masturbating and laughing like a mad man. Men from other departments had shut their machines down and came to watch the show. The entire back end of my department was shut down to watch, and torque converters were backed up on both the north and south lines. A man was taking bets on how many more times Quillen could masturbate.

It was definitely time to call Rollmans, and I headed to the zone office to get the number from Screaming Jim. I could hear Jim's enraged voice ten feet before I got to the door. He was berating the Press Room foreman at the top of his lungs when I went into the office.

When I walked in, Screaming Jim's face was lit up lit a Christmas bulb and his famous forehead vein looked ready to blow. He was screaming something about paying men to work, not to sell coffee on Ford's time. When he took a breath I tried to get his attention, but he turned his wrath on me. The Press Room foreman seemed relieved to be out of the line of fire.

Jim bellowed, "Are you fucking blind? Can't you see I am busy?"

Then he redirected his anger back to the Press Room foreman, who had had enough of his verbal abuse, and started screaming back at him. I wondered if it would come to blows, but I did not have time to wait and see. I had to get my masturbator to Rollmans. I thought that the union might have the phone number, since Quillen had been talking to little green men for some time now. I hurried back out to the phone on my desk.

The committeeman was already there. He said Rollmans number, and the name of the guy that I needed to talk to were both in the union office. He hopped on his bike like the Lone Ranger mounting Silver, and sped off into the mist. That is when I heard the siren.

It was mounted on a converted golf cart that had a stretcher on the back and flashing red lights on the top. A security guard was driving and the midnight shift nurse was in the other seat. The emergency cart was spinning around corners and sliding on the slick wood block floor toward the back of 258.

The nurse jumped out of the cart with her first aid kit and ran over to Quillen.

When she saw that he was naked from the waist down and was masturbating, she turned away and said, "Oh, my God. I am not going to touch that filthy man. He is not injured, and he is not sick, and I am not a psychiatrist."

She turned and started walking back toward the plant hospital.

The security guard called for backup. The crowd that had gathered seemed disappointed that the show was over. They clapped and tried to cheer Quillen on. But two more security guards showed up, lifted Quillen up, pulled his coveralls back on, and laid him on the stretcher. He had a dazed, confused look on his face. Then he fell asleep. Foremen from adjoining departments rounded their men up, and the show was over.

The two men from Rollmans showed up, escorted by another security guard. They instructed the driver not to turn the siren on because it would wake Quillen up and they would have to put him in a straight jacket.

After all the excitement was over everyone went back to work. They had seen this movie before. Still, it broke the tortuous monotony of the midnight shift, and shook people out of the stupor of semi-sleep they were in while they ran their machines. Production actually perked up after the Quillen incident and I briefly toyed with the idea that some distraction like this, every night, might even be good for production because it woke people up.

I was totally amazed that Screaming Jim did not show up during the entire incident, since everyone in Zone 3 was aware of the entertainment going on in Department 258. I went to the office for my ritualistic end of shift ass chewing, and to turn in my numbers, but Screaming Jim's desk was vacant.

Four other foremen were in the office, and appeared relieved that Jim was not. The paperwork was on Jim's desk and each foreman, in turn, was writing his numbers on the report. I had never seen this done before.

I asked the foreman in front of me where Screaming Jim was. He looked at me like I should know the answer to that question.

Then he said, "He is tied up in the Press Room with all this bullshit about the coffee pot. If this shit keeps up, that coffee pot is going to flat out shut this plant down."

CHAPTER 6:

THE COFFEE POT WAR

Screaming Jim started the Coffee Pot War. Roger gave him full support because he always backed up his general foremen whether they were right or wrong. Nearly everyone agreed that management was right, but as usual, it was also stupid. The war could have been avoided if Screaming Jim had simply not seen Big Mo's stand the same as management never saw The Red Dog Saloon or Grace's bordello.

The demand for coffee was greatest on the midnight shift. Yet by midnight, or shortly after, the vending machines were out of everything from chewing gum to candy bars to coffee and cigarettes. Sharonville employed nearly 5,000 men, and the vending machines were the only source of snacks, food, drinks, and cigarettes. Ford had a cafeteria, but it was only open for lunch. An outside supplier restocked the vending machines every morning, just as the midnight shift was ending.

Big Mo saw opportunity here. He was from the hills of Eastern Kentucky and came north looking for work when the coal mines played out and poverty settled on the mountains like morning dew. Ford hired him because of his mechanical aptitude, not because of his education. Big Mo only had an eighth grade education, but he could keep machines running while college trained engineers scratched their heads in bewilderment. He could also make machines not run, if he had a mind to.

Big Mo was not an educated man, but, as the saying went, the hill people knew how to 'shit and git' to make a buck. When Big Mo spotted a money-making opportunity, the devil himself could not keep him from being all over it.

He was an imposing man, and some feared him because of the way he looked and the way he spoke. He weighed at least 250 pounds and had a scraggly beard that reached the top of his chest. He was a man of few words, probably because he was hard to understand. Big Mo spoke in a peculiar southern mountain accent, and people usually had to have him repeat things two or three times before they knew what he was saying.

If he had been content to simply sell hot coffee for ten cents a cup on the midnight shift, the Coffee Pot War would have never erupted. His five gallon coffee pot, creamer, sugar, plastic spoons, and Styrofoam cups were safely tucked in a gap between two Bliss presses. Screaming Jim rarely left the office and it is unlikely that he would have spotted men lined up to buy fresh, hot coffee.

But Big Mo saw expansion potential, and that was his downfall. Why should he sell only coffee? Why not add cigarettes, cold drinks, potato chips, and candy bars? How about magazines? He had a captive audience, and it was an article of faith that the men at the Sharonville Transmission Plant read Playboy, Hustler, and Sports Illustrated.

There is no agreement about exactly how Big Mo got the lumber to build his vendor stand. Some claim he smuggled it into the plant, one board at a time concealed in his coveralls. Others say he found wood from crates that Ford had discarded.

It was not Big Mo's full service vending stand, complete with a counter and cash drawer that ignited the Coffee Pot War. It was an enraged general foreman from Zone 2 who stormed into Screaming Jim's office shouting about men from his zone shutting their machines down so they could walk over to the Press Room and shop. Why was Screaming Jim fucking up the Zone 2 numbers and getting that general foreman's ass in a sling?

The night that Big Mo got busted is legendary at Sharonville. Screaming Jim tore around the north 1600-ton press like The Charge of The Light Brigade, and thirty men grabbed their purchases and scrambled to get out of his way. Jim's blood vessel expanded and contracted with each heart beat, as his rage escalated while he examined every square inch of Big Mo's vending stand.

He went to the Press Room foreman's desk, shoved him out of his way, and picked up the phone. In a matter of minutes five security guards showed up with a hilo. Big Mo's stand was lifted up intact, hauled out back, and trashed in the dumpster. Candy bars, potato chips, cans of coke, and his five gallon coffee pot were run over by the hilo and smashed. Cartons of cigarettes and a stack of magazines were doused with gasoline and torched. The Coffee Pot War had begun. It would be an expensive war for Ford Motor Company.

Exactly what transpired in Roger's office the next morning is strictly hearsay. What is known for sure is that Larry, Screaming Jim, the Assistant Plant Manager, and the Salaried Personnel Manager spent two hours in that office with Roger and periodic bursts of shouting were heard above the noise outside the office.

Screaming Jim was seen leaving the office shaking so badly that he had to stop for a minute and steady himself on one of the I-beams that supported the roof. His face was as white as new fallen snow. If a man like Screaming Jim were to find himself suddenly without a job, it would be a personal tragedy, because he was definitely unemployable anywhere but at Ford.

But he did not get fired. He reported for work on the midnight shift, ready to take revenge on the Press Room. He had been humiliated, forced to admit that he had no knowledge of a full service vending stand built right under his nose and operated on his shift. No one had memory of a greater violation of company policy. Someone had to pay. That someone would be the Press Room foreman.

Of all the departments at the Sharonville Plant, the Press Room is the worst battleground that management could possibly choose. The Press Room is the fountainhead of more than eighty percent of transmission components. Giant coils of steel come in on railroad flat cars and are stamped into planetary gears, valve bodies, links, oil pans, impellors, and most of the other parts that comprise the C-4 automatic transmission. If the Press Room catches a cold, the rest of the plant becomes bedfast.

Much of the Sharonville Plant has machining processes, in which the first machine does one operation, and subsequent machines do other operations. They are all linked until a finished component or sub assembly pops out at the end of the department. But in the Press Room, each press is separate and distinct, and spits out a unique part that is transported to other departments for further machining, processing, or subassembly.

Press operators think of their presses as their babies. With a press operator, it gets personal. They deal with their presses much like old time farmers dealt with their mules. Like a mule, each press is stubborn. Each press has foibles that only the operator understands. Only a man that understands his press can keep it running optimally. On the other hand, a press operator can be at his machine for eight hours, following every rule in Ford's book, and run very little production.

One of the blade presses will run properly only if a large rubber band is attached to a strategic place on the machine. One of the Gilman presses will run only if the operator tears off the back of a book of matches and slides it into a tiny gap in the machine. Most of these machine-enhancing tactics are known only to the operators. There are no rules that say they have to be done, and no instruction book explaining how to do them. Experience based knowledge is what made the Press Room tick.

Department 258 was one of the first casualties of the Coffee Pot War. We began to run out of good quality components by the second day of the battle, because the float ahead of us was thin. I flagged down a hilo driver and he followed me to the graveyard of rejected parts. I culled through racks of impellors and cover plates to find matching egg shaped or round parts.

The problem with egg shaped parts was you had to match up an egg-shaped impellor housing with an egg-shaped cover plate. If one was round and the other egg shaped, the assembler had to beat the two parts together with a lead hammer. That slowed down production and produced questionable quality torque converters.

Both parts are supposed to be round, and are supposed to fit together perfectly and be welded one to the other. The problem with egg-shaped parts originated on the north 1600-ton press, nearly 15 years before, when it was set in place by two industrial helicopters. The concrete pad beneath the giant press was not thick enough and the press sunk, very slightly, on one side. The south 1600-ton press, presumably sitting on firmer ground, did not sink. It ran perfectly round parts.

You could get round parts from the north 1600-ton press if the die setters were allowed to take enough time to shim the dies to compensate for the lack of a perfectly level machine. But they were rarely given the time they needed to properly shim the dies, and the north 1600-ton press ran egg-shaped parts.

Egg-shaped impellor housings and cover plates assembled together and welded made egg-shaped torque converters that met Ford's quality standards. The problem came when round cover plates had to be hammered into egg-shaped impellor housings. The impellor housing was distorted as the assembler beat the round part into it. It left a gap that had to be filled with a gob of weld. These misfit torque converters often leaked before the warranty expired. Ford had no concern for leaks that developed after warranty expiration, but warranty defects always caught the eye of the Detroit Mafia.

When egg-shaped impellor housings were run on the north 1600-ton press they were automatically rejected and taken to the graveyard. Then the press was set up to run egg-shaped cover plates. An attempt was made to run the same number of egg-shaped cover plates and egg-shaped impellor housings, but that rarely happened. The midnight shift got stuck beating round parts into egg-shaped parts.

As I climbed through the racks of parts, trying to match up round with round and egg shaped with egg shaped, the hilo driver leaned back in his seat and took a nap. As I climbed up the wall of ZE34 racks, I was amazed at how much the graveyard of rejected parts had shrunk since the Coffee Pot War began. Foremen were scrounging through the racks of rejects to keep their departments running. I wondered why parts were rejected in the first place when they eventually ended up in transmissions. It seemed like such a waste of time, and the entire quality control department seemed redundant.

Another thing that shocked me was how close the Red Dog Saloon was coming to losing its concealment. If the Coffee Pot War continued on much longer, the entire graveyard would be hauled away to be assembled into transmissions, and the Red Dog Saloon would lie there completely exposed, surrounded by hundreds of red reject tags that had been torn off the racks and thrown on the floor.

After climbing racks and searching until I got to the end of the graveyard, I could not find any round impellor housings. The day shift and the afternoon shift had taken all the juice to make their numbers and I was stuck having my people beat round cover plates into egg-shaped impellor housings. I woke up the hilo driver, told him to fill up operation 10 with round cover plates and egg shaped impellor housings, and I headed for the Tool Crib to check out four lead hammers for my four minor assemblers.

But I could not check out lead hammers. If I carried lead hammers back to 258, I would be doing hourly work, and that would violate the contract. All I could do is fill out a request chit and wait for the hourly Tool Puller to deliver the hammers. The guy in the Tool Crib shrugged his shoulders when I asked how long it would take to get the hammers. I went back to 258.

It was impossible for my assemblers to build converters without lead hammers. Until then, 258 was dead in the water.

I checked my watch when the Tool Puller arrived with the four lead hammers. It was 2:30 a.m. I had lost two and a half hours of production. That equaled 600 torque converters. Ford Motor Company would sell 600 less cars than it would have sold if the Press Room was not in the middle of the Coffee Pot War.

I woke up my four assemblers and handed each of them a lead hammer. They started beating the parts together. One of the cover plates popped out on one side as the other side was beat into place. Each assembler could only build about one half the converters he would have been able to build if he had compatible parts. One assembler smashed his hand with a hammer and had to go to the nurse. Another assembler cut his hand and had to have it stitched. The Coffee Pot War was getting expensive.

By the end of the shift, 258 had produced only 1100 torque converters, which was less than half of the numbers that I was responsible for. I estimated that at least 300 of those converters would leak oil before the warranty expired as I watched the PR Burrs unload converters with grotesque gobs of weld filling the gaps. I had become desensitized to the quality of the products that 258 was producing and simply fell into lockstep with the Ford attitude that any production number is a good production number, as long as it gets past quality control.

At least I did not have to deal with verbal abuse from Screaming Jim. There was no end-of-shift ass chewing since Jim was running around like crazy, fighting the Coffee Pot War in the Press Room. I wrote my numbers on the report lying on his desk, and got out of the plant as quickly as I could.

The next night I was confused when the afternoon shift foreman told me that he had been scheduled to work overtime, and that I was not going to run 258. I was told to report to Screaming Jim in the Press Room. When I got there, all of the midnight shift foremen were milling around with confused expressions.

A clearly agitated and exhausted Screaming Jim walked up and the foremen gathered around him. This was the third day of the Coffee Pot War. Both Screaming Jim and the Press Room foreman had been at the plant for at least 16 hours each of those three days. We could all see the toll that the war had taken on both of them.

Nearly every press was out of commission or running poorly. Departments all over the plant were exhausting the last of their components, and the graveyard had been stripped clean. Foremen had been whispering in hushed tones that in less than two days both Sharonville and Fairfax would be flat shut down, and the Men From Up North would descend on us like Attila The Hun.

There was no telling how many management heads would roll, but Screaming Jim and the Press Room foreman would certainly be among them. Roger was probably a good enough bullshitter to keep his job. He had gotten to be superintendent by manipulating people and numbers to show that nothing bad that happened was his fault. But he was responsible for everything good that ever happened.

Screaming Jim's voice was quivering as he said, "None of you will be running your own departments until this Press Room shit is over with. Your jobs will be covered on OT. You are all assigned to work with me, right here. I want you to spread out all over the Press Room. There is enough of you so that each one of you only has to watch two presses. That will be your only job, watching two presses. I want to see a stack of 4600s on every one of your clipboards."

The foreman from Department 285 spoke up. He said, "Jim, what are we supposed to look for? I ain't never worked the Press Room. I don't know nothing about presses. How am I supposed to know if a man does something wrong?"

Screaming Jim exploded in a burst of rage, "Are you a fucking foreman or not? Do you wear a red jacket? You see a man take his safety glasses off, you write him up. If the son of a bitch spits on the floor, you write him up. They don't know if you know anything about presses or not. All they know is there is red jackets all over the place, and they got clipboards full of 4600s. They will go to work. They will run the presses. All you got to do is let them know you are watching them."

Then Jim looked at the Press Room foreman and said, "Do you know what brought all this shit down on us? That stupid son of a bitch right there."

He pointed at the Press Room foreman. "Do you want somebody to be pissed off at? Be pissed off at him. He let some fucking hillbilly that can't even talk good take and start a fucking business right on Ford property. This whole gawdamn thing is his fault. He is the sorriest excuse for a foreman that I ever seen."

All of the foremen looked at each other. They knew that before this was over, Ford would have to have a scapegoat. Clearly, Jim was setting the stage to lay it all on him. When heads started to roll, everybody knew that the first head to roll across the floor would be that of the Press Room foreman. Each of us knew that Ford was like every other American corporation, and job survival meant being able to point the guilty finger at a scapegoat to save your own neck.

We fanned out into the Press Room as Screaming Jim had instructed. I positioned myself between the north and south 1600-ton presses. I had no idea what I was doing, but I did my best to act knowledgeable. Hourly men were working, walking around, carrying stuff. I could see no rules that were being broken, so I looked on as though I was supervising the operation.

One of the men that was working on the north 1600-ton press shook his head, yelled, "Son of a bitch," and walked over to me. "This damn thing is bottomed out. Are you going to get us the compressor, or am I supposed to tell one of these other red jackets running around with clipboards?"

I said, "Bottomed out, is it?" like I actually knew what that meant. "You wait here. I will take care of it."

It took me twenty minutes to find Screaming Jim. I said the north 1600-ton is bottomed out. Jim was following behind the Press Room foreman like a bloodhound, watching every move that he made.

He turned on the Press Room foreman like a striking cobra and yelled, "I want those sons a bitches wrote up. I want a 4600 on every swinging dick on the north 1600-ton press. Them lousy bastards put that press on bottom."

The Press Room foreman, who looked like he was at the end of his rope said, "How do you know my people did it? They could not have done it. The press has not run yet on midnights. The afternoon shift left it on bottom."

Apparently Jim could not counter that argument and turned away in frustration, disappearing behind the row of blade presses.

I looked at the Press Room foreman and said, "Don't let it bother you, man. It is only a job. The more you let it bother you, the more Screaming Jim will screw with you."

He nodded and said, "Tell me about it. That asshole has been riding me since I started with Ford."

I could smell booze on his breath, and his eyes were bloodshot. I nodded, patted him on the shoulder, and headed back to the middle of the two giant presses.

A few minutes later two maintenance guys showed up with what I assumed was a gigantic air compressor. They hooked it up to the north 1600-ton and watched as the pressure built up. I could hear the press groaning as it began to creep off bottom. That was when I felt someone tapping me on the shoulder.

I turned around to find Big Mo. He said something in his thick mountain accent. He had to repeat it three times before I could understand what he wanted. Finally, I comprehended. He could not load the giant coil of steel on the south 1600-ton because the band cutter was missing. I asked him where the band cutter could possibly be.

He said, "Ahh aready todja. I hain't seen it hatall."

While I knew very little about the Press Room, I knew enough to realize that if the band cutter was missing, we had a very large problem. When the giant coils of steel come in on railroad flatcars, they are banded with very thick, two-inch wide steel strapping. After they are loaded onto the press, those thick bands are cut with a four-foot- long band cutter that takes two men to operate. Every press in the department had to have the coil of steel mounted and the bands cut. If the band cutter was missing, we could not run a single press in the department. I tracked down Screaming Jim.

To my surprise, Jim did not erupt in a manic burst of cursing and accusations. He calmly told me to round up all the other foremen. Then he picked up the phone, called the security supervisor, and said he wanted every available security guard in the plant to report to the Press Room immediately.

By the time I had the other foremen rounded up, the security supervisor was there with seven security guards. Screaming Jim said, "All right, you guys listen up. These sorry bastards did something with the big band cutter. Without no band cutter, we can't get any of these presses running. If we don't get these presses running, this plant will be down by tomorrow."

Then Jim addressed the security supervisor, "I want you to call every security guard in early. We are going to turn this plant upside down until we find that band cutter. I want you to call Roger at home and wake him up. Tell him what's happened. Call every day shift foreman in Zone 3 in early on OT. We will find that band cutter. When we do, the man who took it is in a world of hurt."

Then Jim turned to me and said, "Go down to the Tool Crib. They have an extra band cutter there. Don't take no shit about waiting for a Tool Puller to deliver it. You get it. You carry it back here. Get going."

I headed for the Tool Crib. I filled out the chit. The attendant disappeared among the shelves and bins, and was gone for a good fifteen minutes.

Then he came back and said, "The paperwork shows that we have an extra band cutter here. But the bin is empty. It ain't here."

I pushed past the attendant, ignored his complaint that I was not supposed to come into the Tool Crib, and I searched from one end to the other. There was no band cutter. I hurried back to the Press Room.

When I got to the Press Room it was crawling with day shift foremen and security guards who had been called in early. I almost missed Roger because everyone towered over him. I told both him and Screaming Jim that the spare band cutter was missing from the Tool Crib.

As always, Roger spoke softly and with authority. He said, "As we speak, a corporate jet is flying two band cutters down from Detroit. It is not cheap to fly a jet plane with two hand tools from Detroit. But it is cheaper than shutting down four assembly plants."

Then Roger's cold, piercing black eyes focused on the Press Room foreman, and he said, "So far, the cost of incompetent supervision in the Press Room has exceeded one hundred thousand dollars. If this press room is not running by tomorrow, and we lose four assembly plants, the cost could easily exceed one million dollars."

Roger swung his gaze to Screaming Jim and said, "Jim, I want you to remove the foreman who is responsible for this fiasco. I want all authority and responsibility taken from him. I want him to remove his red jacket. I want him to step back from these other foremen and stand by himself at the desk. He is not worthy of being in the same company as these fine men whose lives he has impacted."

I felt sorry for the Press Room foreman. Everyone knew that when the final report was written on this incident, everything would be laid on him. I had always felt that he was badly out of place in an auto plant. He was a gentle, educated and sensitive man. He had a career in the music field, but financial pressures forced him to take a job at Ford where he made more money. I knew that this job was destroying him.

He was visibly shaken as he walked over to the desk, removed his red jacket, and laid it on the chair. He resembled a small child in day care going into time-out. He stared at Roger with hollow eyes; a man who had just lost his last shred of dignity.

Roger raised his voice to address the foremen and security guards. He said, "Those band cutters are somewhere in this plant. I intend to find them. When I find them I will fire the man who is responsible, and I will press criminal charges against him. I want every nook and cranny in this plant searched. I want trash cans turned upside down and searched. I want every Press Room employee's locker and tool box searched. I want every restroom and break area searched. I want every ZE34 rack searched. I want the car of every Press Room employee searched. Get going, and do not come back until you have the band cutter and the man who took it."

As we fanned out to empty trash cans and cut the locks off Press Room employee's lockers, Roger and Screaming Jim walked over to the Press Room foreman.

Roger said, "You know what I have to do. You can go easy, or you can go hard. It is all up to you."

The Press Room foreman was sobbing, and his body was shaking. He said, "Shut up. How can I hear the music with all this noise?'

Screaming Jim and Roger looked at each other then back at the foreman.

Jim said, "What music? I don't hear no music."

The foreman's body was quivering and he was sobbing louder. He said, "That is the trouble with you people. You never hear the music."

Then he flicked imaginary coat tails up, sat down on the chair, and played an imaginary piano with tears still streaming down his face. He was still playing the imaginary piano when the two men from Rollmans came to take him away.

The two band cutters from Detroit did not get to Sharonville until almost 8 a.m. Every nook and cranny in the plant was searched by more than forty foremen and security guards. Cars were searched in the parking lot. No band cutters were found.

It is strictly hearsay how the Coffee Pot War ended, but enough people agree on what transpired to make me a believer. They say that Roger returned to his office when the band cutters from Detroit were used to load the presses, but the presses still wouldn't run properly. Shortly thereafter the Plant Manager and Assistant Plant Manager went into Roger's office for about fifteen minutes. When they left, the Wop was sitting on his bicycle outside the office.

His arms were folded and he stared at Roger's door. Roger came out wearing his overshoes so he didn't soil his expensive wing tips, walked over to the Wop and without making eye contact said, "If an hourly man on midnights were to sell hot coffee in the Press Room, so long as he did not sell anything else, and he did so inconspicuously, well, we could probably live with that."

They say the Wop smiled ever so slightly and nodded his head. Roger turned and walked back into his office and the Wop rode his bicycle to the Press Room.

Within a half hour the Press Room was running at full capacity. No assembly plants were lost. The Detroit Mafia did not have to visit the Sharonville Plant. On the midnight shift Big Mo had a brand new five gallon coffee pot, creamer, plastic spoons, and Styrofoam cups tucked neatly between two Bliss presses. He raised the price of his coffee to twenty cents to recoup his losses. His coffee business was on the honor system. He had a small sign that said if you take coffee, put twenty cents in the can in front of the pot. Everybody did. It was not healthy to try and cheat Big Mo. A lot of guys put in a buck or two tip. They appreciated being able to avoid the gunk from the vending machines and get a good, fresh brewed cup of coffee.

The missing band cutter reappeared as mysteriously as it had disappeared.

The word on the floor was that the shrink at Rollmans advised the Press Room foreman to contact a good attorney, and he did. They say that four years later he was still on paid medical leave, and that Ford offered him a handsome settlement to make it all go away. He took it, and now teaches music at a high school in Arizona.

The Coffee Pot War was finally over.

CHAPTER 7:
THE DOWNTURN: OPEC PULLS THE PLUG

Everyone knew about the bulging inventory of finished transmissions. You could not miss it. For as long as anyone could remember there had been no inventory float, and Sharonville worked seven days a week, three shifts per day to keep up with assembly requirements. But now racks of finished C-4s filled the warehouse, lined the loading docks, and spilled over onto the oil soaked aisles. Screaming Jim came to 258 an hour before my shift ended.

Surprisingly, he spoke in a normal tone of voice, which was startling as Jim always screamed like a mule skinner bellowing at his team. "Don't leave when the day shift comes in. There is going to be an all-management meeting in the salaried cafeteria. Everybody has to be there." There was grimness in his voice that was more troubling than his typical explosions of rage.

The cafeteria was packed with management. Every seat was taken, and men stood elbow to elbow along the back wall. The Fairfax Plant had been shuttered when sales started dropping like a rock, and the entire Fairfax management group had been reassigned to Sharonville.

A supervisor whom I did not know said, "Men From Up North. Bad shit, man."

When everyone was in the cafeteria, the doors were closed and a security guard posted. The three Men From Up North sat at a table placed in the middle of the cafeteria, separated from the remaining tables. They seemed to be on the prowl, searching the face of each supervisor when he entered the cafeteria. It was reminiscent of gruesome tales from Auschwitz about the grim selection process of those who would live and those who would die.

The meanest looking Man From Up North stood up, then stepped on the table and strutted around, gazing at everyone in the cafeteria. He was short and stocky, had his tie undone, his suit jacket off, his long sleeves half rolled up, and looked like a man about to embark on a monumental task. Then he began to speak.

"Gentlemen, Ford Motor Company has a problem. A major problem. As everyone is aware, the towel heads in Arabia have cut off our oil. We allowed ourselves to become dependent on them, and now they have us by the balls. What is going to happen? Nobody knows. Maybe we will have a depression. Maybe we will go to war. What we *do* know is that the country is sliding into a deep recession right now. We know that tens of thousands of people are losing their jobs. We know that when people lose their jobs and cannot buy gasoline, they don't buy cars. We also know that at Sharonville we have two supervisors for every supervisor slot. We have two General Foremen for every GF slot. We have two superintendents for every superintendent slot. We know that we are very, very fortunate because the policy of Ford Motor Company is to retain management during economic downturns so that we have the skill bank when the economy picks back up."

He paused and looked around the room acting as if he were Ike addressing the 82nd Airborne on the eve of D-Day. "But we also know something that should make every man in this room hang his head in shame. And that is that we have yielded ground to the hourly for years at the Sharonville Transmission Plant. We have surrendered our right to manage by looking the other way as rules were broken. Essentially we have yielded the right to manage to the UAW. If Henry Ford could walk the floors of Sharonville today, gentlemen, tears would fill his eyes and he would puke his guts out. How in God's name has this happened? Why have we yielded the right to manage? The answer is simple. The need for production. It was easier to back off and get our numbers than it was to confront the UAW and live up to our management responsibilities."

He shook his head in disgust looking around the room at all the foremen. "Gentlemen, the disgraceful fact is that we got our numbers not by managing, but by compromising. But I have traveled from corporate headquarters today to tell you this retreat from our responsibilities as managers ends here and now. Today the long retreat of management at the Sharonville Transmission Plant ends."

He moved slowly, holding a hard gaze at each man's face. A lion stalking prey. "Let me repeat that. Today the long retreat of management ends. Today we begin to take back the plant that we have surrendered to the UAW. Make no mistake about it. We *will* make Sharonville a shining example of how Henry Ford made this the greatest of all industrial companies. We *will* retake all the ground that we have yielded! How will we do this? It is the simplest thing in the world. We will enforce the contract. A man will come to work and he will do his job. If he does not do his job, he will be fired. Could there be anything less complex than that? Aw, but *you* know, and *I* know that it is far more complicated than that, now don't we?"

There was a nodding of heads in mass agreement, and mutters of affirmation from everyone in the cafeteria. But then the Man From Up North stomped his foot so hard on the table that I thought it would break, and he shouted, "You're GAWdamn right it's more complicated than that. WHY is it more complicated? Because of you. And you. And you. And you." He pointed randomly at managers and supervisors around the cafeteria.

"You made it more complicated by letting the hourly fuck you over for years. You didn't rack ass because you were afraid they would fuck you out of your numbers. You saw how every time you wrote a 4600 your numbers went down. So you turned a blind eye when your men bullshitted for twenty minutes before they started to work. You said nothing when they disappeared into the shithouse for a half hour to play poker or sleep in a stall. You said nothing when they turned their machines off fifteen minutes before the whistle blew."

A bead of sweat swam down his forehead as he whipped himself into a fury. "Oh, yes, gentlemen. Henry Ford would weep in sorrow because of *your* incompetence as managers! You took the largest automatic transmission plant on planet Earth, tied it with a pretty ribbon, and handed it to the UAW. Everybody in this room turns my stomach. If I had my way every swinging dick here would be headed for the unemployment line!"

He stopped and stared around the room; the pregnant pause making everyone antsy. Managers cast their eyes downward, hoping to not meet his accusing gape. "Unfortunately, I do not make Ford policy. But I *do* evaluate management performance! And I am here today to tell you that each and every one of you WILL do your jobs! You WILL manage this plant. You WILL make your numbers, and every number will be one of the best quality transmissions money can buy. Or you will no longer be employed by Ford Motor Company. Make no mistake about it, a requirement of continued employment at Ford is doing your job precisely as prescribed – that is, enforcing the contract to a T. Is there anyone in this cafeteria who does not grasp this concept?"

There was silence, and the Man From Up North continued, "Good. Then we understand each other. We all understand that we are going to shake up this plant like my grandmother shook the dirt out from the rug when she did Spring cleaning. We are going to get rid of the deadwood at Sharonville. We are going to bite the UAW in the ass and hang on like a junkyard dog. Does anyone here think we have an easy task ahead? I hope not. Because what we have here is war, plain and simple. We have fired the first shot. As we speak security guards are patrolling the perimeter of this cafeteria. The hourly will have no advance warning of our strategy of enforcing the contract rigidly. As we speak all stall doors are being removed from all bathrooms by an outside contractor. The hourly will no longer be able to steal time from Ford Motor Company by hiding in a shithouse stall."

The Man From North nodded to one of his partners who was still seated at the table, and had been examining the facial expressions around the room as each point was made by the man on the table. He took something white from his briefcase and heaved it up to the man on the table.

The speaker held it up over his head and walked around the table like a newly crowned pro wrestler strutting around the ring with his belt over his head.

He said, "Does anyone know what this is?"

No one responded.

"This, gentlemen, is shit paper. Not your soft, smooth shit paper that makes wiping your ass a pleasure. This is rough, coarse paper imported from Turkey. The Turks don't wipe their asses. They sandpaper their asses. We may be required to provide shit paper to the hourly, but by gawd there is nothing in the contract that says it has to be good quality shit paper. The contract does not require us to make taking a shit a pleasant experience. As we speak an outside contractor is removing every roll of soft paper in the plant and replacing it with Turkish shit paper."

He waved and shook the paper over his head in a fury. "From this day forward no hourly man will go to a shithouse unless he has to. To insure that is the case, we will stage shithouse raids and will hit them at random. The hourly will never know for sure if or when we are coming. But come we will with at least three foremen and two security guards. Every man in that shithouse had better have his pants pulled down and be on a commode, or have his dick out and standing at a urinal, or that man will be written up. As of this moment, gentlemen, the shithouses at Sharonville will no longer be bullshit clubs, casinos, or comedy barns. Is there anyone here who does not understand that?"

Nobody uttered a word.

"Understand me on this. From this moment forward, your jobs are to *do* your jobs. This means insuring that each of your employees clocks in at least fifteen minutes before the shift starts. He will not stop to bullshit. He will not digress on the current political troubles. He will not stop to tell jokes, or to brag about whose wife he is banging. He will be at his machine at starting time. Fifteen seconds after starting time he will be running parts. He will continue to run parts until his authorized break time, which he will take, and be back at his machine in precisely fifteen minutes. If he is not, you will put a 4600 on his ass. At quitting time he will run his machine until the whistle blows. Then he will step back so that the man from the oncoming shift can step up to the machine with no loss of production whatsoever. Then, without comment, questions, or bitching, he will clock out and go home. You will insure that this is how the Sharonville Transmission Plant runs, or you will be out on Sharon Road wondering how in the hell you managed to lose the highest paying job you will ever have."

He continued, pacing up and down the table like a general commanding his troops. "You will insure that all components in our transmissions are of the highest quality. Now I know we have let parts that are questionable be assembled into our products. This stops now. If you see a bad batch of components, you will personally see that the entire shipment of components gets sent back to the vendor at his expense. Vendors need Ford Motor Company. Ford Motor Company does not need vendors. They cut each others throats to sell to us.

"Not only will you make your numbers, gentlemen, you will produce the finest transmissions on the market today. Do not take what I am saying lightly. We do not have an easy task. But we have a necessary task. When our task is complete, men will come to work and do their jobs not because they want to – we don't care if they want to or not – they will do their jobs because they will be afraid *not* to.

"Henry Ford once said, 'These men are neither your friends nor your neighbors. They are your employees, and they will do what you tell them, or they will no longer be your employees.' Now...," he paused, looking around the room, daring a foreman to meet his gaze.

"Is there any man in this room who does not feel up to this task? If so, save me time and trouble, and speak up now. I have zero tolerance for weak managers. As we speak there are people in the Salaried Personnel Office with preprinted resignation forms and out processing paperwork. If you do not have the stomach for this job, go to Salaried Personnel, sign the papers, and get off Ford property. We have managers far in excess of our needs, and you can be replaced immediately."

I silently calculated my financial status in my head. It was not good enough. I still had a mortgage, not nearly enough saved to realize my dream of having my own business, a rug rat and a pregnant, nonworking wife. Companies in Cincinnati were not hiring. They were cutting jobs like crazy. I remained in my seat.

There was an out burst from two tables to my left. A man stood up and shouted, "You can take this job and shove it up your ass. Fuck you! Fuck Ford Motor Company. Henry Ford was a no good son of a bitch, just like you. You sons a bitches ain't gonna use me as a pissing post. I had enough of your shit."

He stormed out of the cafeteria, pushing the security guard away from the door. Everyone grinned. They all knew this man. He was a general foreman with 37 years seniority. When he signed the paperwork he would immediately receive full pension and medical benefits for the rest of his life. It is easy to be arrogant when you have nothing to lose.

The Man From Up North watched the old GF exit the cafeteria without comment, and his expression never changed.

When the door slammed shut he said, "Anybody else? Any other spineless, ball-less supervisor who cannot handle this job?"

He waited, watching, the room filled with thick, silent tension.

"Nobody? Good. Then everybody here is ready to go out and run this plant like Henry Ford would have wanted it run. Gentlemen, go out and manage the Sharonville Transmission Plant. That is all."

We filed out in silence like men leaving a wake, each supervisor disappearing into the forest of machines that was his area of responsibility. My shift was over, and I headed for the Salaried Parking Lot. But before I got to the door I saw Roger's orange golf cart barreling toward me, and Screaming Jim sat beside him.

Roger said nothing, ignoring me as though I was not even there. Screaming Jim, with his signature blood vessel popping out, shouted. "You're on overtime – get over to the Zone 6 office. They'll give you a set of coveralls. Take off your red jacket and put on the coveralls. They are going to do a shithouse raid."

When I got to the Zone 6 office there were two other supervisors whom I did not recognize, two security guards, and the Zone 6 dayshift GF. The GF explained the plan.

"Okay. We want you to take off your red jackets and put on these coveralls. Nobody here will know you because you all are from other zones and other shifts. But if you had your red jackets on, and all three of you head for the shithouse, well, that would give them a heads up. We want them to think you are just regular hourly men until we make the hit."

We slipped out of our jackets and into our disguises.

"Okay, here is how we will do it. Me and you will go in one door," he said pointing to me. "At the same time these two other foreman will go in the other door. Then one security guard will stand at each door as we go in. The guys inside will have no way out. If there is any funny business, I have a dozen 4600s on my clipboard. Okay, let's go."

We walked slowly, as not to arouse suspicion, pretending to be hourly men going to the bathroom. As we got inside I saw out of the corner of my eye a security guard stepping up to the door. The other two foremen were already inside. There was an hourly man on a makeshift cardboard bed overtop a commode, sound asleep. Two other hourly men were sharing a flask of whiskey in the corner. All three were written up by the GF. I went back to the Zone 6 office, took off the coveralls, got my red jacket, and went home.

In the few minutes I ever routinely had to interact with my wife, she noted that I looked particularly beaten down that morning. I nodded and proceeded to bed. I did not want to put my burden on her. It was me who decided to take the job at Ford, against her advice. I would tough it out in silence and not disturb the harmony of my home with my troubles at Ford.

Shortly before 10:30 p.m. that night, I was abruptly awakened by a nightmare that periodically re-occurred throughout my childhood. It stemmed from one my father's recounted stories of the brutal strikes of 1927.

It was a story I never forgot, but it had been many years since the nightmare returned. The '27 strike was the most massive industrial strike in American history. It started with the railroads, and then spread to the coal mines and the steel mills. The National Guard was called out, and mounted Coal and Iron Police patrolled the coal patches, carrying Billy clubs and rifles. They looked for any sign of union activity and had the power and authority to bust heads, evict families, and even kill people.

It was the shooting of the school kids that chilled my blood and haunted my dreams. It happened in the Bruceton Patch of Pittsburgh Coal Company, which housed miners that worked Montour No. 10. Kids came home from school, waving papers to take to their mothers. They were crayon drawings of Christmas trees, Santa Claus and reindeers. But the Coal and Iron Police had been alerted that union leaflets were going to be passed out. They yelled for the kids to stop, but the children were terrified of the Coal and Iron Police so they started running. They ran until they were cut down in a hail of bullets.

Their massacre was perfectly legal. They were on company property. They failed to obey the orders of the legal authorities, who mistook school papers for union leaflets. The incident never even made it to trial.

No crime had been committed. Company police were doing what they were paid to do.

My father described this incident to me when I was six years old, and for years after it replayed over in my mind, plaguing my sleep. But today, the nightmare had changed. The face on one Coal and Iron Policeman was making me physically ill. In all the other nightmares their faces were blurred, but now I could clearly see one of the perpetrators – It was me.

The dream was so vivid and so repulsive; I awoke with my stomach feeling numb and soured. I went to the bathroom to throw up, but once I was fully awake, the feeling passed.

It was time to get ready for work and face Screaming Jim. The never-ending war in 258 was waiting for me.

That evening, Jim was in fine form when I arrived to work just before midnight. He seemed like a jungle predator lusting for blood. He had some sort of pent up rage against the world, and this was a chance to take it out on the hourly. Evidently Jim was exactly the kind of manager Ford wanted.

He assembled all the Zone 3 midnight foremen in the office and paced back and forth like Bobby Knight in the last three minutes of a tight game.

"You guys know the game. I ain't gonna give you no shit, and I ain't gonna take no shit when you come in at the end of the shift. You better make your numbers, and you better get me some 4600s. You was at the meeting. Your jobs are on the line. My job is on the line. Now get out there and run your fucking departments, and don't come in with a buncha excuses in the morning."

The message that Ford was at war with the hourly had spread through the plant like a fire storm. When a man had to go to the bathroom his eyes darted from side to side like a prey sensing a predator nearby. He tensed up, reluctantly went in, took his leak, and got the hell out before a hit squad of foremen with 4600s showed up.

I stood at the time clock, checking off each name as the man clocked in. We regarded each other with caution, like two wrestlers circling in a ring. They knew what I had to do in order to keep my job. From now until sales picked up – the signal of the end of the war – it would be a game of cat and mouse. I knew, and they knew, it was nothing personal. That was just the way things were at Ford.

I was thankful I had never been able to penetrate the thick veil of distrust between management and the hourly that existed on the midnight shift. It is easier to fire a man that really *is* just a number.

My welder set up man walked up behind me. I did not look at him. Management and the hourly showed disrespect for each other by never making eye contact, but by talking loud enough that they knew the other could hear without recognizing him as a human being.

He said, "Lotta shit coming down. Won't be over 'til sales pick up."

I continued checking off names and said, "Yep."

He said, "If I was foreman, what I'd do is try to nail the dead beats that nobody likes. That way you ain't gonna piss off your good people. You fuck with your good people, they *will* get your ass fired. Everybody in 258 knows where you live, too. Just something you should know. Another thing – best not to fuck too much with the niggars. They stick together. You nail a niggar, every niggar on midnights figgers you a racist. Play it cool. Do what you hafta do and no more. Everybody knows the shit coming down on your ass from the front office."

I did not respond as he walked away. He was communicating that everyone knew this was not personal, and everyone wanted to still have a job when the war was over. It was just another Ford plant-wide war. I knew I had to have my set up men on my side. I also knew that they had to appear to be on the side of the hourly, even as they tried to help me.

There were no absentees and nobody was late. In a gut busting Ford war the hourly know how to cover their asses and not give any excuse for a write up. I tucked my clipboard under my arm and walked through 258. Every man was at his machine. Every man was wearing his safety glasses. The balancer set up men had put away the checker board and porno magazines. No rules were being broken. Every man's eyes followed me as I walked through the department. They knew I had to feed 4600s to Screaming Jim, and they were like sentries at the ready, waiting for the war to begin.

Even though every machine was manned, there were no converters coming down the line. I got a sick feeling in my stomach. These men knew this game better than I ever would. These were not the simple mechanical contrivances from the days of Henry Ford, when a worker was like a dog on a leash with no opportunity to strike back. These were incredibly complex combinations of electronics, mechanics, pneumatics, hydraulics, and electrical connectors, all tied together like a jigsaw puzzle. A slightly incorrect adjustment here, a mouthful of water spit on an electrical panel there, a minor bump here or there and machines could be down for hours. Engineers could not figure out what caused the problem. Men not breaking any rules and having sandpapered asses do not produce a lot of torque converters.

At the end of the shift I lined up in front of Screaming Jim's desk like a whipped dog, with the other midnight foremen.We all knew that the only way to avoid being degraded, cursed, humiliated, and threatened would be to run peak efficiency and write up half the men in your department. The foreman in front of me starred down at his feet like a child being browbeaten by an outraged father. Then it was my turn.

Screaming Jim snarled, "Gimme your numbers."

"900"

"Don't fuck with me. What are your numbers?"

"900"

"Are you telling me that Ford paid top dollar for a P&G hotshot, put him in a department where we have a two-million-dollar investment and the highest paid factory workers in the world, and you produced less than half of the converters you were supposed to produce? Is that what the fuck you are telling me?"

"Yep"

"How many 4600s you got?"

"None."

"Aw Jesus Christ. Don't come into my office and tell me you made 900 torque converters when you was sposta make 2,400, and you ain't got one single fucking 4600! Tell me why I should not fire your ass. Tell me why I should let you come back in here at midnight tonight, fuck up 258, run no fucking production, and not write up one gawdamn single hourly man?"

Screaming Jim's face was beet red and contorted. I thought his blood vessel may actually burst.

I said, "Well, Jim, I was looking for a job when I came to Ford. I can look for another job if that is what you want."

Jim picked up a pencil sharpener, tossed it up against the wall, and screamed, "GET THE FUCK OUT OF MY SIGHT YOU SORRY PIECE OF SHIT!"

I left the GF office and it was the foreman's turn behind me to get his daily beating. I could hear Screaming Jim yelling above the noise of the machines until I was well away from the office.

The next night Screaming Jim herded all the foremen into his office. Outside the door was a group of about fifteen foremen milling around, looking uneasy, and I did not recognize any of them.

Jim, in his routinely enraged decibel level, said, "Aw right, Listen up. Roger got a new plan. We ain't making no numbers, and we ain't getting no 4600s either. So here's what we are gonna do. Roger says the problem is they can fuck our brains out because we are spread too thin. You watch one man, twenty-five other men that you ain't watching is fucking you. So all you gotta do is watch *one* man. I am assigning additional foremen to each department. Fairfax foremen. You will still be in charge.

"Them Fairfax foremen will report to you. You will spread them out in your department. Have each foreman watch only four or five guys. But you, you are gonna watch just one guy. You will not take your eyes offa that guy. You will stand by his machine and watch every move he makes from the time he clocks in. He goes to take a shit, you go with him and stand there until he is done. He goes on lunch break, you follow behind. I got a stop watch for every foreman. The sumbitch you are watching takes more than thirty minutes for lunch, you rack his ass."

He talked with a scowl, inches from our faces, looking each foreman straight in the eyes to ensure everyone was clear about the expectation.

"Roger says we are going to find out exactly how these people are fucking us, and we are going to find out now by watching one man at a time, the entire shift. That way he can't fuck us without you seeing it. So if you don't make your numbers, and you ain't got no 4600s, when all you got to do is catch one man that you been watching for eight hours, and you got three or four other foremen, don't even bother to come to my office. At quitting time go to Salaried Personnel, sign your resignation letter, and get off Ford property."

I started feeling sick to my stomach as I left the office. I had dug coal on my belly a mile underground when I was fifteen. I had lived in a tarpaper shack with no indoor plumbing. I had known the terror of being on an aircraft carrier shadowed by a Soviet sub during the Cuban crisis. I always thought I could stand up to anything in life. I thought I could take anything that Ford Motor Company could throw at me. Maybe I had been wrong.

How could I have anticipated anything like this? Maybe I had overrated my toughness. Maybe the Man From Up North was right. Maybe I did not have the balls to do this job. Not because I wasn't tough enough – because I had a conscience.

Who was I, really? A prison guard? A corporate thug? America's version of Soviet Secret Police? I spent years earning an MBA for a job like this? These men I was expected to try and fire were just working men trying to support their families. Most of them did the best they could under the horrible circumstances of their employment. I shuttered to think what life at Ford would be like if these men did not have a union to protect them from the likes of Ed, Larry, Roger, and Screaming Jim.

As a management person I was supposed to be anti-union, but most often I felt that the union was right to extract as high a toll from Ford as they could, given the conditions Ford created. Truly, management was Ford's worst enemy. Unfortunately, I was part of it.

As the shift wore on, I thought I might be coming down with the flu. I had waves of dizziness. My stomach was churning. Twice I grabbed a machine to steady myself because I thought I might pass out.

I stuck out the shift and was only vaguely aware of the severe reaming Screaming Jim gave me for neither making my numbers nor writing anyone up. By the time I got to my car, my body was quivering and my gut was doing flip flops. I reached for the door handle and great gushes of vomit showered the car door, my legs and feet and the tarmac. That is when I realized I was crying like a baby and my entire body was shaking. This was not the flu.

I had seen a foreman have a nervous breakdown during the Coffee Pot War, and I knew that the same thing was happening to me. I steadied myself and wiped away what I could with my handkerchief. As I got into the car I remembered a conversation I had with Ponaber. He said if I stayed at Ford long enough, I would end up at Rollmans. Not to worry, though, because Ford paid for everything. Sooner or later every manager at Ford ends up at Rollmans.

I started the car and headed for Amberly Village. I made a mental note to call my wife and tell her I would not be home for awhile. I could do it from Rollmans. They never closed.

CHAPTER 8:
ROLLMANS

Rollmans Psychiatric Hospital sits in the middle of the affluent Jewish suburb Amberly Village. The subdued entrance blends nicely with the quiet beauty of top tier landscaping. I pulled into a parking space and went inside.

I headed straight to the men's room and used nearly an entire roll of paper towels cleaning vomit from my shirt, pants and shoes. Then I went to the nurse behind the reception desk who had been watching me.

She was pleasant and soft spoken. She wrote down my information and asked for my Ford I.D. I got the distinct impression that people from Ford were a significant part of Rollmans' clientele because the nurse knew exactly what paperwork to fill out. She had the phone number of Ford Salaried Personnel in her rolodex.

She told me that Ford would be notified and that I should take a seat and relax. I asked if I could call my wife and she pointed to a phone sitting on a coffee table in front of the sofa where I assumed I was supposed to sit.

It only took a few minutes for a doctor to show up. He whispered briefly to the nurse, and then came over to me.

He extended his hand, and said, "I am Dr. Weinstein. Please, let's go to my office."

Dr. Weinstein was short and plump, with a full black beard. I guessed him to be close to sixty years old. He had intense dark eyes, and I immediately felt confident that he was a competent professional.

When we were seated comfortably in his office he looked at the file the nurse had given him and said, "Do you pronounce your name De War or Dewar?"

"Dewar, just like the whiskey."

"Are you part of the whiskey family?"

"No. If I was, I probably wouldn't be talking to a shrink. I'd be sitting on the deck of my private yacht off the coast of France."

Dr. Weinstein laughed and said, "May I call you Bob?"

"Sure. Everybody else does."

He nodded and said, "Tell me, Bob, how can I help you?"

"I'm not sure. I wasn't sure where to go. I knew that I damn well better talk to somebody or do something. People at Ford joke about taking a trip to Rollmans, but I didn't know what it was. Then I found out it was a psychiatric hospital, and sooner or later a lot of Ford people end up here."

Dr. Weinstein nodded and said, "Yes, in fact we do have a lot of people from not only Ford, but also GM and Chrysler. What prompted you to come to Rollmans?"

"Well, I started shaking. I felt like my stomach was doing summersaults. Then I puked all over my car and started crying like a baby. My hands were shaking so badly I could hardly get the key into the ignition."

"What job do you have at Ford, Bob?"

"I'm a front line supervisor in Zone 3. I run the torque converter operation."

Dr. Weinstein nodded, made some notes on his pad, then looked at me and said, "Tell me what preceded the shaking and vomiting incident."

"Well, as you probably know, we are in a bad recession. They are calling it the worst business downturn since the Great Depression. Car sales are way down. Ford has started a war with the hourly. They are *always* at war with the hourly. But this particular war is the worst anyone at Sharonville has ever seen."

"What makes this war worse than the never-ending war against the hourly?"

"Well, for one thing, they don't seem to care about production. They don't need to because cars aren't selling, and they are jam packed with inventory."

Dr. Weinstein said, "If they don't care about production, what do they care about?"

"They are trying to get the plant to run like Henry Ford would have run it if he were still alive. They want men to be like machines, not like human beings with a mind and feelings. What they care about is how many men they can write up and fire. Supervisors are required to present 4600s to the bosses at the end of each shift like Roman conquerors delivering plunder from conquered lands to Caesar. If you don't deliver 4600s there's hell to pay. Ford is trying to get Sharonville to the point that the hourly do their jobs because they're terrorized they'll be fired if they do anything wrong, just like Ford plants were in the days of Henry Ford."

Dr. Weinstein made notes and asked if that was what led up to the shaking and vomiting incident.

I said, "What led to the shaking and vomiting is the new one-on-one plan that Roger has devised. Roger is the Zone 3 superintendent. He reminds me of Al Capone."

Dr. Weinstein shook his head slowly and said, "Tell me about the one-on-one plan that Roger has devised."

"Well, a foreman has a lot of men in his department, spread over many machines and processes. He can't watch all of them all the time. So Roger has decreed that instead of riding herd on the whole department, each foreman will pick out one man, and watch only him. The foreman is required to stick with that man for the entire shift. He has a clipboard and a stopwatch. He stands beside the man while he runs his machine, watching every move that he makes. He follows him on break, and stands there while he smokes his cigarette and drinks his coffee. He follows him to the bathroom and stands there while he takes a leak. He is not to take his eyes off that one man until the whistle blows at the end of the shift. The foreman..."

I corrected myself, "*I'm* expected to find something that the man I'm watching has done wrong before the shift ends, and write him up. Its unacceptable performance for me to follow the man for eight hours and not find something he has done wrong."

I realized that my voice was rising, bitter resentment of Ford flowing out. I started speaking more softly, shook my head in frustration and said, "Working at Sharonville has become a horror show for everyone. Ford is turning good employees into festering bundles of rage that will strike back at the first opportunity. The hourly are just trying to survive now, while sales are down. But they know that sales will not always be down. They know that if they can survive this war until sales pick up, then the shoe will be on the other foot. Ford will be desperate to get production. That is when the hourly will take their revenge for what Ford is doing now. I cannot believe that a giant corporation in the twentieth century could be so stupid."

Dr. Weinstein said, "No, neither can I. Was it the new one-on-one plan that led to the shaking and vomiting incident?"

"Yes, it was. I didn't go into the management field to be a jailer. I earned an MBA. I studied management techniques. I didn't study law enforcement. You have no idea what it is like to take a man who is simply trying to earn a living for his family, and follow him around like he's a criminal, waiting like a mugger in a dark alley to strike at him for breaking some minor rule that Ford dreamed up."

Dr. Weinstein studied me for a minute. Then said, "No, I certainly would not have any idea what it would be like to do that. Tell me, Bob. You have an MBA. That is a very marketable degree. Why do you work at Ford Motor Company? Why don't you get another job with another company that is not trying to run things like its 1920?"

I said, "I had another job. I worked at Procter & Gamble."

"You quit P&G to take a job at Ford?"

"Yes, I did."

"I see. Why did you quit P&G to work at Ford Motor Company?"

"I quit because I didn't fit their mold. Actually, it was more of a mutual agreement that I needed to leave the company. I just didn't see eye-to-eye with them. As a P&G manager you have to become a corporate robot. They control your life around the clock. If you want to advance you have to have a P&G wife, P&G kids, live in a P&G suburb, go to a P&G church, and do P&G things with P&G people. At Ford they only own you during your shift. They don't care about your private life."

Dr. Weinstein made notes, then looked at me intently and said, "At Ford you are a jail guard. The employees build up a terrible rage against the company, and as a foreman, you are *the* company. Tell me why this is better than working at Procter & Gamble."

I leaned back in my chair to get comfortable and said, "At P&G the entire management group is a big, phony club. I went to college to learn complex subjects because I wanted to apply my knowledge to a career. I wanted to advance because I knew how to run things and was a hard worker."

"But that didn't happen at Procter & Gamble?"

"No, it did not. Management at P&G is a fraternity. It's hard to get into the fraternity. Once you get in, your success has absolutely nothing to do with what you know or how hard you work. In fact, the more you advance, the less you have to work. Your success depends entirely on how well they can condition you to become a Proctoid."

Dr. Weinstein raised his eye brow and said, "What is a Proctoid? I'm not familiar with that term."

I was surprised at Dr. Weinstein's response. I thought everybody in Cincinnati, the home and headquarters of P&G, knew what a Proctoid was. They employ more than 15,000 people in the Greater Cincinnati area. The company is like a shadow government that influences everything that goes on, from the state level down to the boy scouts. People snicker behind the backs of P&G managers and tell Proctoid jokes all the time.

I said, "A Proctoid is a man who turns his entire life over to the company to mold and shape like a wood carver turns a block of wood into the piece that he wants it to become. He lets P&G control his entire existence. He is America's version of Soviet Man. His career path is determined not by how much he knows or how hard he works; its determined by how good a Proctoid he becomes. Put me in a crowd of strangers and in a half hour I can pick out the Proctoids."

Dr. Weinstein was silent for a minute, as he made notes and studied me as though I was a new and strange specimen. Then he said, "Describe to me the characteristics of a Proctoid."

I said, "A Proctoid always wears the P&G uniform. He has closely cropped hair, perfectly in place. He always wears a white shirt, never a colored shirt. He has a narrow tie. He may or may not wear a vest, but he most certainly wears an expensive suit, always dark, never light, usually pin stripe. He always wears expensive wing tip shoes, always shined."

Dr. Weinstein said, "But don't other businessmen often dress like that? Don't a lot of people dress like that? In fact, I sometimes dress that way. If you saw me in a crowd of strangers, how would you know that I'm not a Proctoid?"

"Well, I would have to hear you speak. If you were a Proctoid your speech would use distinctive key words. It's called 'P&G Speak.' They accent their words in a characteristic way. Being a good Proctoid is like being in a religious cult. In fact, they are, almost to a man, fundamentalist Christians. P&G Speak avoids controversial subjects, unless the company has clearly taken a position on that subject. If that were the case, you would go on and on, parroting the P&G point of view. If you were a Proctoid you would name drop, as you worked into the conversation your position with the company. In one way or another you would let me know what important position you and your wife have in the church. You would also allude to other organizations of which you and your wife play prominent roles. Your self puffery and P&G Speak would leave no doubt in my mind that you were a Proctoid. With great subtleness, you would let me know that you are a man on the move at Procter & Gamble."

Dr. Weinstein said, "So Proctoids are shallow, mindless robots. Is that your conclusion?"

I said, "No, quite the contrary. P&G hires only the cream of the crop. You can't even get an interview with the company unless you are near the top of your class at a good college. They are very intelligent, well-educated men. So intelligent that they quickly learn in order to succeed in management they must focus their talents on becoming a stand out Proctoid. They quickly learn that P&G gives a man only a couple years to be molded. If he cannot fit the mold, he is dismissed like you might flush your toilet. Cincinnati is replete with managers who have 'left' the company. They could not, or would not, degrade themselves into letting P&G dangle them and their families like a puppeteer."

Dr. Weinstein smiled slightly, seeming somewhat amused by my description as he looked down at this pad and jotted notes.

I continued, "A successful Proctoid has a wife and kids that adapt well to the game. His wife is his mirror image. Her red badge of courage is the number of activities she chairs in the community. There is a hierarchy of wives, just like there is a hierarchy of Proctoids. Proctoid kids have an arrogance that says 'if your Dad does not work at Procter & Gamble, then your family is not as good as my family.' A genuine Proctoid has outward symbols that identify his level at the company. He uses them to communicate to the world that he is moving up. When he gets promoted he changes friends, cars, houses and churches. It is neither appropriate nor acceptable for an advancing Proctoid to retain the same friends and community that he had at a lower level in the organization."

Dr. Weinstein tapped his pen on his pad and studied me intently. "Tell me, Bob. When you decided to study business management, what did you think working in management at a big corporation would be like?"

I said, "Well, I assumed that I would be using the knowledge I had acquired. Why would I beat my brains out to get good grades in math, science, accounting, and all the rest if my success would ultimately depend on how well I could play the game of becoming a corporate aristocrat? To me that is not only degrading, it is an insult. Why don't they teach country club techniques at the MBA level if that is what they want you to become?"

Dr. Weinstein said, "But surely you had some inkling of life in the management ranks. What did your father do for a living? Did he advise you to study management?"

I laughed and said, "My father had a forth grade education. He dug coal with a pick and shovel for 50 years. We lived in a tarpaper shack on the side of a hill. I never knew anyone in my life, other than my teachers, who had more than an eighth grade education. I never saw anybody in management. In fact, I never saw a man wear a suit and tie other than at school, at church and at weddings. I studied management because everybody said that is where the opportunity is. Get an MBA and you have it made, they said."

Dr. Weinstein said, "I see. So you thought that once you became educated you would automatically get an ideal job using the knowledge you acquired in college."

"Yes that is exactly what I thought. What else would I think? Why would I spend years paying my own way to earn two degrees if that was not the case? I could have had some fun in life. Instead I kept my nose to the grindstone to get that education that everyone said you have to have if you want to get anywhere in life. I definitely wanted to get ahead. Living in an Appalachian shack and working in a coal mine did not necessarily appeal to me as a career."

Dr. Weinstein said, "And yet after you got a taste of what management is really like, you jumped from the corporate frying pan at P&G to the corporate fire at Ford. After getting out of college, and learning what the real world is, you must have known about the harsh conditions in the auto industry. I am searching for the logic of that move. I could understand your desire to move to, say, a different profession than management. But quitting P&G for a similar job at Ford puzzles me. Did you think Ford Motor Company would be substantially different than P&G?"

I said, "Of course not. By the time I had gotten my feet wet, I quickly became aware that it really doesn't matter what big company you work for. They are all the same. All that changes are the names and faces. If you want to get ahead, or even keep your job, you have to sell them your soul. You have to discard your dignity, your self respect, and your honesty. I decided that I would have no part of it."

Dr. Weinstein knitted his eyebrows and appeared confused. He was tapping his pen rapidly on his pad as he said, "Then tell me why you took a job at Ford Motor Company."

"I took the job at Ford for the money. I make more money than any other job you can name. I make as much money as a vice president at Procter & Gamble."

Dr. Weinstein smiled cynically and said, "So you sold your soul, your dignity, and your self respect to the highest bidder. How are you different from a rising Proctoid?"

"It's not just the amount of money. It's the ability to choose what I do with the money."

He shook his head and said, "I don't understand. Are you saying that P&G tells you what to do with the money that they pay you?"

"Yes, that is exactly what I'm saying. As you climb the ladder you have to live a lifestyle commensurate with your position. P&G has a rigidly structured social class system. As they promote you and raise your salary it is with the unspoken understanding that you will move 'up' and live like the other Proctoids at your new level. If you don't, you will not fit in. You will not be part of the Proctoid team. When you advance and get a big raise, you buy a bigger car, move to a more expensive neighborhood and join the country club. It is expected of you. It is no longer appropriate for you to swim in the little pond you swam in before you moved up. Your fat raise goes to support your more expensive lifestyle. You have to put on display the benefits of being an up-and-coming Proctoid, like a peacock strutting in a zoo.

"It is a subtle and very real control that they have over your life. The message is you have to keep playing our game, or all of this will be taken away. No matter how empty you feel inside, or how shallow your life has become, you cannot stop. Procter & Gamble has you in a set of golden handcuffs. If you try to stop, your wife and kids, who have become accustomed to a constantly rising affluence, will be devastated.

"The corporation has interned you in economic bondage. They control your life every bit as much as the Soviets controlled the lives of their bureaucrats. Their method of control is money, not terror. The higher you climb, the tighter the grip they have on you. Economic bondage is as brutal as political bondage, but we don't know it because we think we are moving up."

Dr. Weinstein was tapping his pen again. He said, "You are confusing me. You tolerate conditions at Ford so that you can make more money. Yet you do not want a bigger car, bigger house, or membership in a country club. I thought the goal of making more money was so you could spend more money buying nicer things."

I nodded my head and said, "Yes, it is, but only to an extent. For example, I grew up in a shack covered with tarpaper. We had no running water or indoor toilet. Our vehicle was a 20-year-old coal truck with bald tires. But now I provide a nice suburban home for my family. We have a new car, and we take vacations. That is enough. I am not willing to beat my brains out or sell my soul so that we can live in an even bigger house in a snooty neighborhood and associate with phony people that, frankly, I cannot stand. I will not play the corporate game of constantly striving to move up and acquire more and more. I don't have a deflated ego that needs to be reinforced by displaying how much money I have. That alone makes me an outcast in the management class of society. You do agree that in America we have distinct social classes don't you?"

Dr. Weinstein ignored my provocative question and said, "So P&G raises don't belong to you because they are the nuts and bolts of economic bondage. You have achieved a life style that is as extravagant as you wish to live. You went to Ford because you make as much money as a VP at P&G, and you are free to do as you please with the money."

I said, "Yes, that's right."

He said, "Then please explain to me the advantage of making all that money, if you are not going to spend it. You have presented me with a confusing conundrum."

I said, "I invest my money. I invest every dime that I can get my hands on. We live a modest lifestyle, far below what we could afford. My goal is to break free of economic bondage permanently. I want my own business. I want to call my own shots in life. I don't want to bow down before any corporate gods. I don't want to work for anyone but myself and my family. I want to succeed or fail on my own merits, not on how well I suck up to some social climbing boss. I want to be my own man. The so-called security of a job in corporate America has no appeal to me whatsoever. No job at any company has appeal. I don't believe that a man can be free if someone controls his paycheck. Control a man's paycheck and you control the man. I must control my own paycheck. I will do that by running my own business. When I have enough saved to see my way clear, I will tell Ford Motor Company to stick it up you know where, and I will start or buy a business of my own."

Dr. Weinstein studied me like a cardiologist studies a chest x-ray. He said, "So what you are telling me is that leaving Ford before you have saved enough money to strike out on your own is not an option."

I replied, "No, it is not."

He tapped his pen for a few seconds and then asked, "What do you want me to do to help you?"

I said, "Tell me how I can cope with Ford Motor Company. Tell me how I can keep making the big bucks without being driven to the edge of insanity or having a nervous breakdown. Show me how to tolerate the intolerable until I am ready to quit."

Dr. Weinstein slowly shook his head, as though he was beginning to understand me. Then he rubbed his chin and said, "Ford Motor Company reminds me of another place where people were treated like cattle and controlled by fear. It was a much worse place than Sharonville. Yet it shared a disturbing number of characteristics with Ford. Do you know what place it was?"

I shook my head no, and Dr. Weinstein continued.

"Auschwitz, the infamous Nazi concentration camp. Of course Ford is not throwing people into gas ovens, and you can walk out anytime you want. Yet the methods used to control people have uncanny similarities to methods Ford uses. Also, the physical environment of a Ford plant is, in many ways, no better than the facilities at Auschwitz. The reason I know this is because both of my parents were inmates of Auschwitz. Both of them survived. I made a study of how people survived the death camps. I have written papers and have given seminars on the difference between those who survived and those who did not. My advice to you is to adopt some of the methods that people used to survive the death camps. That may sound extreme, but I believe it is one way you can survive emotionally at Sharonville until you have the money that you believe you need."

Dr. Weinstein got up from his chair, walked over to the window, and stared in silence for an uncomfortable several minutes. He seemed to be deep in thought. Then he rubbed his chin, walked back to his sofa, sat down, and continued.

"Let's look at the tormentors at Ford. I am speaking of your managers. Are they inherently evil men? The answer is, like the SS at Auschwitz, some are and some are not. But they are all caught up in the system. Like the SS men, they do as they are told and that is how they survive. Now let's look at the hourly workers. Who are they? Do they not share some similarities with inmates in a concentration camp? Of course they do. They have families to support. They want to earn as much money as they can for their families. They do not risk death, as the people at Auschwitz did, yet they risk a kind of death. That is, their economic security can be taken away from them, and that can be as emotionally devastating as a death. So they allow themselves to be controlled, even degraded, and, no doubt, hate every minute of it.

"Do the hourly people hate you because you do what you are told in order to survive, and thus make their lives miserable? Some of them hate you, because you *are* Ford Motor Company. No matter how you feel personally about Ford, you wear the red jacket of management."

I listened intently. He clearly knew a lot about the inner workings of Ford Motor Company, and the comparison to Nazi concentration camps seemed eerily similar.

He continued, "Some of the hourly will hate you to their dying day because you are the face of Ford. Others will feel sorry for you. None of them will trust your motives. They will perceive that everything you do is to satisfy the demands of management. All of these interacting emotions were true of Auschwitz, and they are true of the Sharonville Transmission Plant. Now, let's look at how my parents took this bubbling brew of madness and found a method to survive."

Dr. Weinstein stared at me intently and said, "First and foremost, they never gave up hope. They knew people that gave up hope; they could see it in their eyes. When a person had given up, they would not live through that day. If you do not have hope, you are finished. My parents had a clear and distinct vision of hope. Their vision was of the day when they would hear the distant thunder of artillery and see the Allied tanks crashing through the gates of Auschwitz. Every day they described to each other what the artillery would sound like. They drew pictures in the dust of the tanks crashing through the gates. They argued with each other about which gate the tanks would crash through first. That vision of Allied tanks was the first thing they thought about each morning, and the last thing they thought about at night.

"Bob, you must have a vision of hope. You must visualize that day of liberation, when the total of your bank account reaches that magic number. Project how much money you need. Calculate the monthly amount you are investing. Divide, and come up with a day when you will reach the magic number. Write that date on a slip of paper. Carry that slip of paper with you at all times. Every day look at the date on that paper. Visualize yourself on that day. See yourself taking your safety glasses off and pitching them into the air. Visualize yourself taking your red jacket off, stomping it into the oily floor, and then taking it to your boss, dripping with oil, and saying, 'take this and shove it, because I am out of here, baby.'"

He smiled as he told me how to visualize my day of liberation. "But that will be your long-term vision that keeps you going. You must also develop a coping mechanism for each day. You must be able to handle each ludicrous situation as it arises, and recover quickly, or you will never reach liberation. Ford will wear you down, and then they will have won. You must never let Ford win. Again I go back to my parents. They coped by developing a highly refined sense of humor."

"Your parents found humor in Auschwitz?"

Dr. Weinstein said, "Absolutely. It was the only way they could survive the degradation and inhumanity. Jewish humor is wry, biting, cynical, even sarcastic humor. I want you to develop your own brand of cynical humor about Sharonville. I want you to laugh at them every day. I want you to take every disturbing, insane incident and see the humor in it. I want you to laugh all the way home after each shift. The Sharonville Transmission Plant is not a tragedy. It is a comedy. Think about it. It is funnier than Saturday Night Live. You have incompetent managers who would probably be garbage men if they didn't work at Ford. You also have the Detroit Mafia trying to turn the clock back to the days of Henry Ford. Throw in the hourly workers who measure their revenge by how much they can sabotage production. Then you have the Keystone Kops, called supervisors, who try to keep a failed system running long enough to draw their pensions. What could be funnier?"

It was sad, cynical, ludicrous and true. Ford Motor Company was one big laugh-out-loud joke. I felt something inside of me release just a little. Dr. Weinstein had made me feel much better. I thanked him and left Rollmans. As I drove home I continued to think about what he said. He was right. The Sharonville Transmission Plant was hilarious. It all depends upon how you look at it.

I reviewed in my mind the various situations that had troubled me. But looking at them from a different angle, and they are comedic. By the time I got to my driveway, I was laughing so hard tears were streaming down my face.

Ford would never again get my spirits down. I would make it to my day of liberation, and laugh all the way there. The joke would be on Ford.

CHAPTER 9:
THE UPTURN

The events at the beginning of the recession were precisely reversed when the downturn ended, and everything returned to the normal at the Sharonville Transmission Plant. Finished transmissions that had been stacked twenty feet high in all the aisles in front of the warehouse began to disappear as car sales picked up. Then the warehouse, which had been chock full of finished C-4s, began to be cleared out.

The dark clouds of economic uncertainty on the 6 p.m. news gave way to patches of sunshine. We were encouraged by a story on NBC about how much the oil embargo had hurt the Arabs. They needed to sell oil as badly as we needed to consume it. They opened their spigots and dropped the price. Oil, once again, was cheap and plentiful, and Americans would have a chicken in every pot.

Smiling Ford executives held a news conference attended by all three major TV networks. Sales were up, profits were up, and, soon, employment would be up. Ford Motor Company had a bright future. It would soon re-open the shuttered Fairfax Transmission Plant near Cincinnati, and 1,800 hourly workers would be recalled from layoff.

But Ford was shocked when dozens of laid off workers refused the recall. This puzzled the company because they paid the highest wages in the state of Ohio. They could not comprehend how several dozen men could afford to turn down their offer of the highest wages available in the market place.

But these men, and their families, made a hard decision that the money could not compensate for the deplorable conditions at Ford, and they would rather be able to live and work like human beings even if they made less money. I knew one of those men.

He came back to say his goodbyes to the men he had worked with on midnights in Department 258. I did not recognize him; he looked like a different person, a new man. He was cheerful and full of life. He was smiling. He was clean and sober. His name was Jackson.

Jackson was shaking hands with each of the men in 258. He extended his hand to both of the white assemblers that had tormented and degraded him. They had dumbfounded expressions as Jackson extended his hand to each of them and told them he wished them and their families the best. Those men had never gotten close enough to Jackson to actually touch him. Then Jackson came to my desk.

He shook my hand warmly and said, "Man, you saved my life. I ain't never going to forget you."

I replied, "What do you mean, I saved your life? I remember you. But I never saved anybody's life."

Jackson grinned broadly and said, "Oh, yes you did. You saved other lives, too. It was your first night on midnights. I was so drunk that I couldn't stand up straight. I don't even remember walking into the plant and clocking in my card. You could have fired me, but you didn't. You covered for me. You were a kind man. You cared enough for a drunken black man to save his job. I never seen no foreman that would do that for a man."

I said, "Jackson, I would have done that for anyone. I believe that there is good in every person, but sometimes it has to be coaxed out. I didn't do anything for you that I wouldn't have done for any other man in 258. If a foreman wants his people to take care of him, he has to take care of his people. I didn't save your life. I just gave you one more chance."

Jackson searched my face with his eyes. Then said, "Nooo, man. You don't understand. I was going to blow you away that night. I had it planned when I heard that you were coming to midnights to replace Brad. I had a Smith and Wesson 38 in my car."

I felt like I had just been sucker punched. I was stunned, silent, and he continued, "I figured what we got here is another white dude with a red jacket gonna come to midnights like his shit don't stink and be down on all the brothers. We lost a good black foreman and they was gonna stick a white foreman down our throats. I done had enough, man. I had enough of white dudes treating the brothers so mean. Now I was gonna get a white foreman? No, I wasn't."

He shook his head, his eyes cast down toward the ground, searching his memory, recalling that fateful day.

"What I was gonna do was come in here and waste all them honkys that done give me such a hard time. I was gonna waste you, man. I was gonna save that last bullet for myself. I figured what do I have to lose? My wife done cheated on me. My boy was in jail. My fourteen-year-old daughter was knocked up. I figured being dead can't be any worse. I figured I would waste all the white dudes and then blow my brains out. I was already in Hell. When I got down there, I figured I would get it all worked out with the Devil himself. I was fucked up, man."

He paused. I didn't know what to say or how to respond to what he was telling me.

"You saved my life. You saved your own life by being a kind man," he said.

I starred at Jackson in utter awe and amazement. "You had a gun that night? I didn't see any gun."

Jackson said, "That's the thing, man. I was so stoned I forgot and left my Smith and Wesson stuck under the seat of my car. When the committeeman helped me out to my car, I was going to bring it back in here and start shooting. But then I thought about it. I said, 'that white foreman saved my job. He didn't have to do that. That white committeeman helped me all the way out to the parking lot. He didn't have to do that. Maybe all them white dudes ain't evil men. How could I shoot a man who just saved my job?' Then I fell asleep.

"I didn't wake up until noon the next day. Then I drove home. I was really shaken up. I came within a hair of killing you, and as many white dudes as I had bullets for, and myself. Every night I get down on my knees and thank the good Lord that I didn't go through with it. You are the reason that I didn't."

I starred into Jackson's face in silence. I was looking at a man who might have made my wife a widow and my little boy an orphan. Jackson had a sincere smile on his face. Then he said, "Do you want to hear the funny part? The funny part is I got laid off when we done run out of oil."

Somewhat disgusted and completely nonplussed by his confession, I tried to remain calm. "It was funny when you got laid off?"

Jackson shook his head and said, "No, not at first. At first I thought now what am I going to do? I got bills, man. I got a house payment. I got two car payments. But let me tell you something. Getting laid off was the best thing that ever happened to me. It changed my life for the better. Me and my wife and kids sat down at the kitchen table and took a hard look around. We done a lot of honest talking. We ain't never talked like we did when we set down at that kitchen table. Do you know what we came up with?"

I said, "What did you come up with?"

"We looked around and we talked. Was no arguing, was no shouting, nothing like that at all. We all knew that we had to do something, and we had to all pull together. Do you know that I got seven televisions in my house? Now why would a family of four need seven televisions? My wife, she admitted that she went out and bought stuff just to get back at me. Our house is plum full of stuff that we don't use. We move it here. Then we stick it there. Then it goes out in the trash. Every time my wife got pissed off, she went out to the mall and spent every dime we had on stuff we never use.

"What we come up with is I was not working for Ford. Hell no. I was working for Uncle Sam. Do you know how much of my money went to taxes? I was working for the liquor store. I was working for the bank and the credit card companies. I was working for the shopping mall. At the same time my wife had to find comfort in the arms of another man.

"You see, man, if you work at Ford you can't be a husband and you can't be a father. Ford guts you like a catfish laying out on the table spread out on newspapers. There ain't nothing left when you get home. My kids didn't get in trouble because they're bad kids. They got in trouble because they were trying to get my attention. Who needs it? I'm telling you, man. Making too much money ain't no good. It don't help your family. It ruins your family.

"Do you know what we do now? We make a family decision on each thing we buy. Do we really need it? Is it more important than spending what money we have on something else? Do you know how much money I make now? One half of what I made assembling converters. But now I got a happy family, and I can look in the mirror at a man, not a hunk of meat that Ford chopped up and cooked."

He continued as if on a pulpit, preaching to a congregation. "I don't drink at all no more. You come to my house, don't expect me to offer you a drink. My wife and me got back together. I forgot about that guy down the street, and she forgot about how I was a mean drunk the whole time I worked at Sharonville. My boy is in drug rehab. He is doing real good. We all are raising my little grandson. My baby girl, she ain't gonna be making no more mistakes. Her Daddy is back."

Jackson shook my hand again, cupping it between both of his hands. He waved to men as he walked down the aisle, grinning from ear to ear. My eyes followed Jackson until the mist of Zone 3 swallowed him up. I thought to myself that I would be as happy as Jackson someday when I had enough money saved to break free of corporate bondage. That is when I realized that my phone was ringing.

It was Screaming Jim. He wanted to see me in the zone office, right now. During the recession Screaming Jim spent a lot of time out on the floor. That was when Ford did not need high production. They needed 4600's. There was a direct correlation between the level of production on midnights, and how much Screaming Jim was out on the floor.

Now that the recession was over and Ford needed high production again, Screaming Jim stayed in the office. No one could verify that he had been told to stay in the office and keep out of the way so we could make transmissions, but that was the rumor. When he came out on the floor, one could almost see production dropping.

Jim looked up from his cross word puzzle and said, "We need Fairfax."

I said, "The south line is set up on Fairfax, and running like a scalded dog."

Screaming Jim said, "That ain't good enough. We didn't leave no float when Fairfax shut down. Them Men From Up North said we might not ever start the Fairfax Plant back up again because it's the oldest transmission plant we got. That's why we didn't leave no float when it shut down. It needs to be replaced."

He leaned in toward me, as if confiding a secret. "Just between you, me, and the door post, there is talk up north about building a new transmission plant. But we ain't got no new transmission plant yet. All we got is Fairfax, and it is starting back up again. We ain't got no converters ahead, so when it starts up, it ain't gonna be able to run. We got 1,800 men coming back, and they ain't got no torque converters to make transmissions. That is why I need lots of Fairfax. I want you to set up the north line on Fairfax too. I don't want that one-eyed son of a bitch coming in here in the morning and bitching because we didn't make enough Fairfax."

I said, "I never heard of running Fairfax on both lines. Do you want me to set up Fairfax on *both* lines?"

Screaming Jim shot a look at me with daggers and said, "You got a problem with your ears, or did I stutter? SET THE FUCKING NORTH LINE UP ON FAIRFAX!"

I went back to 258 and made arrangements for changing the north line to Fairfax. Within five minutes my welder set up man and my north automatic balancer set up man were standing at my desk.

The balancer set up man said, "What the hell are you doing? I been here eight years, and I ain't never seen Fairfax run on the north line."

The welder set up man said, "Bob, I ain't for sure, but I seem to remember that they made that south line for Fairfax, and the north line can't run Fairfax. I could be wrong because it was before I came to 258, but it seems to me they tried to set it up on Fairfax and they couldn't do it, and the line was down for hours while they tried to get it back to running twelves."

I explained to both set up men the need that we had for Fairfax converters because the Fairfax Plant was recalling 1,800 men and we had no float ahead of them. The two set up men shrugged their shoulders and went to work trying to set up the north line on Fairfax.

I watched both set up men struggle with the changeover. It seemed to be a lot harder than simply changing from twelves to eleven and a quarters, or vice versa. As I watched them, my mind wandered, and I thought of all the things that had changed since the recession ended. It was almost as though a curtain went down on a two-act play, and when it came back up, it was a completely different scene.

The most significant change was management's attitude toward the hourly. It had backed off from rigid, mindless enforcement of rules that were mostly written by Henry Ford himself. Now the hourly weren't sorry pieces of meat. Now they were employees that Ford needed to get high production. The shoe was on the other foot. Power had shifted to the work force because they alone determined the level of production, no matter what the clowns of management decreed. Both management and the hourly were aware of the subtle shift of power.

The UAW was guilty of a lot of things, but having a short memory was not one of them. Ford thought that if they backed off, the hourly would forget the days of having foremen raid bathrooms and watch every move they made. I smiled to myself as I recalled a story from my Uncle Jack and was reminded of Dr. Weinstein's advice.

Uncle Jack spent two months in a German prisoner of war camp. He was captured during the Battle of the Bulge when the Germans were sure they were going to win the war. They beat American prisoners, starved them, and let them freeze in the bitter cold. But when they realized that they were going to lose the war, they started being nice to the Americans. They gave them more food and warm blankets. They hoped that when they became prisoners of the Americans, they would forget the harsh treatment. But of course they did not forget.

The hourly men at Sharonville did not forget, either. When Ford had all the bathroom stall doors put back on, and replaced the rough toilet paper with Charmin, the hourly did not forget. When the union grieved cases of men that had been fired during the madness of the downturn, and they won those grievances, and those men were reinstated, the hourly still did not forget. When foremen looked the other way instead of writing men up, the hourly did not forget. Management had sown a lifetime of distrust during the insanity of the downturn.

Each hourly man had his own way of taking revenge on Ford for the agony imposed during the recession. Some men took passive revenge by doing no more than the absolute minimum that they could get by with. Other men took active revenge, such as sabotaging machines and running bad quality. One man dropped a bolt into each torque converter, which made it blow apart like a bomb when it was put on the test stand.

He was one of the few hourly who was apprehended and fired for taking revenge.

My private thoughts on how the flip flop of management had created deep rooted resentment was interrupted by my north automatic balancer set up man.

He said "Bob, can you take a look at this damn turnover? I have adjusted them jaws as good as I can, but they just won't grab them Fairfax converters. The damn things are dropping all over the floor."

I went to the north turnover. The jaws clamped the converter, lifted it up, started to flip it 180 degrees, but then the converter would simply drop out of the jaws in mid air and fall on the floor. I looked closely at the jaws, and how they could be adjusted. Then I looked at a Fairfax converter. There was no way in hell those jaws could be adjusted to grab a Fairfax converter. If I could not get the converters through the turnover, I could not run Fairfax on the north line, even assuming they would run O.K. through the Inteco and the automatic balancer. I headed for the zone office.

Screaming Jim had finished his cross word puzzle and was reading a copy of Hustler, which he quickly stashed in his desk when he saw me walk in. I explained the problem on the north turnover.

He shook his head and said, "Your people are fucking you. They don't *want* to make the changeover because it's too much work. You been around here long enough to know what is what. If they don't want to do their job, write their asses up. You're the hotshot, you figure it out. Now, get back out there and run me Fairfax on both lines and don't come in here in the morning and tell me you couldn't do it. I don't give a shit how you do it. Just do it."

The only way I knew how to do it was to manually carry the converters around the turnover. I went to the labor pool and borrowed three men to bypass the turnover. But then I realized that there would be a problem with that. The converters were red hot. They come out of the welders and go directly to the turnover. I headed for the Tool Crib to get three pairs of long, heavy leather gloves to protect my borrowed men's hands.

I explained to the borrowed men what I wanted them to do, and I stayed and watched. It was a slow, tedious, even dangerous operation. But the Fairfax converters were getting to the next operation, the Inteco. As

I watched, my mind wandered back to my original thoughts about shifts of power during the recession.

A major power shift occurred between Production and Quality Control. Prior to the downturn, QC had very little power. They seemed to be there mostly for show. They would write up reject tags and send parts to the graveyard. But Production would simply pull the tags off and haul the parts back to the line. Most inspectors felt strongly that Quality Control at Ford Motor Company was a farce.

But that changed dramatically during the recession. The Detroit Mafia decreed that warranty defects *would* decline precipitously, or heads would roll at Sharonville. QC managers, supervisors, and inspectors acquired immense power and status. If a part did not meet every quality specification, the entire batch of parts was rejected. The machine was locked out by QC, and could not be run again until it was properly repaired or adjusted to run good parts.

The days of the graveyard being a place where foremen went to get components ended during the downturn. Every rack of rejected parts had to be accounted for. Every rack had a 'Destroy by_____' dated tag, and if destruction did not occur by that date, the QC manager had to explain why, in writing.

During the recession the Sharonville Transmission Plant produced some of the best automatic transmissions ever made in America. Warranty defects on C-4s dropped off the charts. QC people walked with a new dignity. Ford was not selling many cars, but by God every one of them was a good car.

I smiled to myself as I thought how quickly all that changed as the price of oil dropped, the recession ended, and car sales took off. The pendulum swung completely back the other way. Now all that mattered were numbers again. Get big numbers and you are a hero. Bring in bad numbers and your ass is grass. Reject parts. Haul parts to the graveyard. Remove reject tags. Haul parts back to the line. If a man was sane when he started at Ford, he most certainly would be crazy when he left.

The set up man was motioning for me to come to the north automatic balancer. The Fairfax converters were going through the Inteco just fine, but not the balancer. The balancer was stuck in mid cycle. A Fairfax converter was laying sideways on the intake, red lights were flashing, and oil was gushing from a broken hydraulic hose.

My set up man said, "Man, this is a gawdamn mess. Them Fairfax just flat ain't gonna run on this north line, and that is all she wrote. That broken hydraulic main squirted oil all over the electrical panel and shorted it out. This sumbitch ain't gonna run again until we replace that whole electrical panel and the hydraulic line. We are talking at least four hours of downtime here."

Then there was a blood chilling scream. Everybody looked in the direction of the north turnover, and ran toward the screaming. One of the borrowed men had slipped on the oily floor, the scalding converter fell against his stomach, and then dropped on his foot. He winced in agony as we waited for the emergency cart. The nurse opined that the man's foot was broken, and that he would have a permanent scar on his stomach where the red hot weld seared his flesh.

It had been one of the worst nights in 258 since the night I nearly had a nervous breakdown. I had produced only 1,190 converters, despite the best efforts of my crew. But at least I had both lines set up on Fairfax, as per Screaming Jim's instructions. I went to the office for my end of shift bashing.

Both Ed and Larry had already arrived to begin the day shift. Screaming Jim had his production report in front of him. Without looking up he said, "Gimme your numbers."

"1,190. I ran 1,190 converters."

Jim jerked his head up and said, "You have *got* to be shitting me! What in the *hell* happened?"

I said, "Well, it was that north line. It just did not want to run Fairfax. I had to have three extra men to manually bypass the turnover. One of them was seriously injured, by the way. Then one of the Fairfax converters turned sideways in the north balancer intake and tore up the hydraulic system and took out an electrical panel."

Larry walked over to Screaming Jim's desk and said, "Did I just hear you say you ran Fairfax on the north line?"

I indicated that he heard me right.

He said, "Are you a fucking idiot, or what? Everybody and his brother knows you can't run Fairfax on the north line. Why in the goddamn hell did you try to run Fairfax on the north line? The south line was engineered to run Fairfax. We run Fairfax on the south line, not on the north line."

I said, "Well, I didn't know that. All the time that I've been in 258, nobody ever explained that to me. I ran Fairfax because the Fairfax Plant is starting back up and they don't have any converter float."

Larry smiled sarcastically and said, "So you just decided to be a hero and build the float for Fairfax all by yourself, is that it?"

I said, "No, that's not it. My boss instructed me to run both lines on Fairfax because we needed to build up that float before those 1,800 men show up and can't build transmissions because they don't have any torque converters. That is why I set the north line up on Fairfax."

Larry jerked his head around and shot an inquisitive look at Screaming Jim.

Jim avoided eye contact, shook his head, and said, "I don't know what the hell he is talking about. I never told him to run Fairfax on the north line. I was busy with other shit. I didn't know what he was doing in 258. He runs 258, not me."

I felt something inside of me erupt as I lunged toward Jim and yelled, "You lying son of a bitch!"

Jim threw his hands up in front of his face, as if to block a punch, and stepped behind his desk. Two other foremen in the office spun around to see what was going on. I had both fists clenched.

Larry stepped in front of me and said, "Don't make me call security! You go outside the office, right now." I regained control, turned, and went outside. Larry was right behind me.

I was still steaming, but able to calm down. "I can't believe he said he didn't tell me to run Fairfax on the north line. That son of a bitch is a stinking liar."

Larry grinned broadly and lit a cigarette. Then he put his hand on my shoulder and started to laugh. His one good eye twinkled, and he said, "By gawd, I underestimated you. You *do* have some hair on your ass."

Then he shook his head, laughed again, and said, "I thought you were going to take Screaming Jim's head off. You made my day."

Now I was totally confused. Ford Motor Company was not a factory. It was an insane asylum.

Larry stopped laughing, took a deep drag on his cigarette, and said, "I have no doubt whatsoever that Jim told you to run Fairfax on the north line. This is Jim's fourth zone as general foreman. He has never been able to handle any of the jobs he has had. I keep him on midnights because he can do the least amount of damage there, especially if he stays in the office and keeps out of people's way so they can run parts.

"You see, Jim is a good general foreman if he doesn't have to think. You can sick him on somebody, like you sick a junk yard dog on a man, and Jim won't let loose until his teeth meet. But when Jim tries to think, that is when he gets into trouble. He will completely fuck things up, and then lie through his teeth to get out of it.

"Now you take this Fairfax thing. Jim thought he was doing the right thing. He knew that we have no float ahead of Fairfax. But he didn't use common sense. Look, half of those 1,800 men haven't even received their official recall letter yet. How long do you think it takes to get a transmission plant up and running from a cold start when it has been shut down for more than six months? For Christ sake, we will be lucky if Fairfax is running a month from now. Hell, we have plenty of time to build up a float. But now that the north line is all fucked up from trying to run Fairfax, we will lose a lot of production on twelves and eleven and a quarters. That will throw us back into a seven day work schedule and the people up north will piss and moan about blowing our budget."

Larry took out a note pad, wrote something on a page, ripped the page out, and handed it to me. Then he said, "Here, this is my phone number at home. If Jim tells you to do something, and you think it's fucked up, you call me before you do it. I don't care what time of the night it is. People can't work *with* Jim, and they can't work *for* Jim. What they have to do is work *around* Jim. You have been around long enough to know what I'm talking about. I don't have to draw you a picture. You're doing a good job on midnights. Don't let Jim fuck you up."

Larry slapped me on the shoulder, turned, and went back into the office. I stood there for a minute, trying to figure out what just happened. I folded the piece of paper, tucked it in my wallet, and headed for the parking lot. When I walked past 258 I counted seven maintenance men working on the balancer. The north line was dead in the water. The operation 10 men were reading magazines. Two assemblers were sleeping. The other two were talking about how hot the Cincinnati Reds were this year. Ed was arguing with the maintenance foreman and dousing the floor with tobacco juice. Department 258 was back to normal as though the worst recession since the Great Depression never even happened.

CHAPTER 10: AN EQUAL OPPORTUNITY EMPLOYER

Sales grew strongly throughout that year. Sharonville worked seven days a week to keep assembly plants supplied. By the following spring, we could not produce enough C-4 automatic transmissions to keep up with demand.

It was the end of my shift, and I expected the ritual berating that had become the norm in Zone 3, but Screaming Jim, to my surprise, just wrote my numbers on his report with no degrading comments.

He looked up from his desk and said, "Don't go home."

Then he raised his voice so that everyone in the office could hear and yelled, "Don't nobody go home from the midnight shift. We got Men From Up North in the salaried cafeteria. There is going to be an all management meeting. Everybody has to go. There ain't no exceptions."

We went to the meeting as a group. As we left the zone office, the foreman from 251 said, "Oh, shit. Here we go again. What do they want us to do now, take people out back and shoot them?"

But the Detroit Mafia that came to Ohio this time were far different from those who had come to launch the war on the hourly at the beginning of the recession. They were engineering people and labor relations people, and they had flip charts. It was a professional presentation, which surprised me, because I had never seen anything that was remotely professional in Ford management.

The engineering guy started the meeting by explaining the problem that Ford faced. It was a good kind of trouble. Ford and Lincoln Mercury sales had exceeded Ford's capacity to produce transmissions. This would be solved by both a short term capital expenditure and a long term capital expenditure.

The long term capital expenditure involved designing and building a brand new transmission plant. This plant would be state of the art. It would have the very latest technology in transmission manufacture. It would be designed by the best minds at Ford Motor Company, and would be a super efficient plant. It would produce the finest, most gas efficient transmission made anywhere in the world.

Indeed, Ford fully expected to supply such minor competitors as Toyota and Honda with transmissions made somewhere in Ohio, the exact location to be announced at a later date. When this new super plant went on stream, in approximately three years, the aging Fairfax Plant would be permanently closed.

But it was the short term capital expenditure that was most relevant to the Sharonville Plant. This capital expenditure would be known as the 5,400 Program. The 5,400 Program would expand the capacity of Sharonville to 5,400 transmissions per day, up from the current 4,800. It would involve the expansion of some departments, and the addition of certain machines to other departments. It would also involve the addition of 800 jobs at the Sharonville Plant, and that would be the topic of the labor relations guy's talk.

The engineer took a seat and the labor relations guy stood up and set up his flip charts. He talked about demographics. About one half of the people in the United States are women. More than 10 percent are African Americans. Smaller percentages are Asian, Latino, and Native American.

He said, "We live in the latter half of the twentieth century, and the government wants corporations to hire women, blacks and other minorities. Ford is a progressive company, and a good corporate citizen. Therefore, we will endeavor to hire those 800 new employees in approximately the same percentage that their group represents in the demographics."

In other words, when those 800 new employees hit the front door, we could expect to see approximately 400 women, 160 blacks, a handful of Asians and Latinos, and the balance would be white males. The face of the work force would be changing, as older white males retired and were replaced with a mix of other Americans. From a social standpoint, this was only fair, since every American should have a chance to get a job at a company like Ford Motor Company. Did anyone have any questions?

A foreman from Zone 6 asked, "Do you mean that you are going to hire broads to run machines and shit?"

The labor relations guy nodded his head and said, "Absolutely. Female employees will work side by side with men. Ford will be blind to the sex, age, race, religion, and nationality of applicants. As I said, we will do our best to hire people that are a reflection of Cincinnati. How can we ignore half of the population, simply because they are female?"

There was a chorus of groans and utterances of disbelief as this statement was digested.

As we filed out of the salaried cafeteria, I walked slowly listening to comments about what the work force of the future would look like.

One foreman, just ahead of me whom I did not recognize said, "It ain't bad enough that they're going to hire a bunch of niggers, gooks, and spics. I can live with that. But do you know what kind of hell will be out on that floor when they bring in 400 cunts? What happens if all 400 of them hit the rag all at the same time? How will them boys from up north handle that?"

Another foreman quipped, "They won't handle it. *We* will!"

I started walking faster and caught up with the Zone 3 group. Brad was speculating on what life would be like when 400 women were added to the Sharonville work force.

He said, "For one thing, they will be the lowest seniority people, so they will automatically end up on midnights. Midnight guys will bump to afternoons and days. The only reason they are on midnights is because they don't have the seniority to get anything else. Wouldn't you know it? I spent years on midnights, trying to get on days. When I finally get days, what happens on midnights? It becomes a pussy playground. Man, I just can't win."

Everybody laughed. I headed to my car, looking forward to going home. I did not care what kind of employees I had, just so I could keep building my savings until I had enough to break free of corporate slavery.

The following Sunday I opened the Cincinnati Enquirer and saw a quarter page ad that read:

FORD IS HIRING. WOMEN AND MINORITIES ARE ENCOURAGED TO APPLY. FORD IS AN EQUAL OPPORTUNITY EMPLOYER. WE PAY THE HIGHEST WAGES AND OFFER THE BEST BENEFITS AVAILABLE ANYWHERE IN THE MIDWEST

Several weeks passed before anything happened. Then women started to show up on midnights in virtually every department. As the 5,400 Program got off the ground, and new jobs were created, men bid off the midnight shift and were replaced largely by females. Another week passed, and I received my first female worker. One of my burr hands had bid on a new job opening on days, and she was his replacement.

She was standing at my desk, looking wide eyed at all the machines, and in a state of apparent confusion. I wondered how I was supposed to deal with females. Would I have to measure every word? Would they break out in tears instead of cursing profanities? What about the crudeness and vulgarity of the men at Ford? Was it my job to shield women from the harsh reality of the manufacturing floor? How about lifting? The burr hand often had to lift torque converters on and off the line. Would a woman be able to handle a job like that? I went to my desk.

She couldn't have looked more out of place. She said, "Excuse me, sir. Can you tell me if this is Department 258? I saw your red jacket and all. I'm supposed to report to the foreman of Department 258."

I told her that I was the man she was looking for, and she could call me Bob.

She said, "My name is Gladys. Gladys Moore."

I showed Gladys the time card rack, found her time card, and showed her how to clock in. Then I explained that her job would be burr hand, which involved doing whatever I assigned her to do. She would not necessarily be running a machine, although at times she would, if that is what needed to be done. Other times she would move parts, relieve men for bathroom breaks, and so forth.

I yelled for my other burr hand and asked him to show Gladys around 258 and give her some idea of what a burr hand does. It seemed to me that she must not have had any idea what she was getting into when she arrived at Ford that day.

While he was showing Gladys the nuts and bolts of making torque converters, I headed toward the office to talk to Screaming Jim about some major concerns I had about Gladys. As I walked to the office, I heard cat calls to new female workers. By now virtually every department had at least one.

Out of the corner of my eye I saw an attractive black girl waiting for the foreman by his desk in Department 257. She looked like she had been poured into her jeans, and her shirt was just as tight. Men gawked around machines to get a better look.

Screaming Jim was not sympathetic. He said, "Don't come in here bitching about having some woman working for you. You ain't had none yet. All the other foremen have."

I said, "I don't care if she's a woman, a donkey, or one of those little green men that ride converters. My problem is she probably only weighs 110 pounds soaking wet. How is she supposed to unload red hot converters that weigh forty pounds? That is, if she is still alive by the time I need her to unload."

Jim wrinkled up his face in sarcasm and said, "What the hell do you mean, if she's still alive?"

I said, "Well, first of all, she has long hair. Not just long hair, hair that goes all the way down to her butt. There are moving conveyors out in 258. You may not realize that, since all you do is keep the chair warm here in the office."

"Fuck you. So she has long hair, so what?"

"So what if she gets her hair caught in the conveyor, or in a machine? She would be dragged into the machine before anybody got to the emergency stop button. Then there is the issue of her shoes. She's wearing open toed loafers, like she's on a beach. If a converter falls on her foot it will smash every bone. But the main thing that worries me is her dress."

Jim said, "She come to work wearing a fucking dress?"

"Oh, yes. Not just a dress. A dress that goes all the way down to her ankles! What if she climbs the cross over ladder and gets her dress caught in the conveyor? Do you want a serious injury on your watch? How about hot sparks from the welders and balancers? If her hair catches on fire, and she becomes a human torch, am I supposed to squirt her with a fire extinguisher?"

Jim tapped his pen on his desk. This was a problem that was, very possibly, beyond his managerial problem solving capability.

But then he perked up, said, "We ain't got no problem here."

He opened his top desk drawer, pulled out the labor contract, and thumbed through it.

"Here it is, in black and white. All production employees will wear steel tipped safety shoes, safety glasses, and protective clothing. Ford Motor Company will reimburse the cost of said protective work gear. In special cases the department manager will make such decisions and will enforce such common sense safety rules to insure that his employees are properly protected."

He closed the book, stuck it back in his desk and said, "You are the department manager. It's up to you to enforce safety in 258. You go back out there and tell Miss Long Hair to go home, get her hair cut, buy safety shoes, check out coveralls like everybody else wears, and be back in here at midnight tomorrow and ready to go to work. If she don't want to do that, tell her to get a job some place else, and I will requisition you another burr hand."

I asked Jim if I had to call the committeeman before I gave an employee an ultimatum like that.

Jim said, "You ain't gotta call nobody. Until a new hire has worked his thirty day probationary period, and the foreman signed off stating, 'yeah, we want this person to work at Ford,' he ain't in the union, he ain't got no protection, and you can fire his ass anytime you want, no questions asked. It is that thirty first day you got to worry about, because then he is in the union, and you got to fight them bastards to get rid of him."

Gladys had no problem buying safety shoes. She agreed to wear coveralls, so long as she could wear her dress over top of them. She refused to cut her hair. She said wearing a dress and never cutting her hair was part of her religious beliefs, just like not wearing lipstick or any makeup was part of her beliefs. She added that her religion prohibited her from working from sundown on Saturday to sundown on Sunday, because that was the Sabbath, and the Lord God said Thou Shall Rest On The Sabbath.

I stared at Gladys for a full minute, wondering why the Lord God had stuck me with something like this. She seemed to be a sincere enough person, and would probably be a good worker, but wearing a dress over top of coveralls defeated the purpose of the protective coveralls. The hair had to go if she was going to work for me. I would not be responsible for a woman being pulled into a conveyor and, essentially, scalped.

Department 258 had worked a seven day schedule since the downturn ended, and it would continue to work a seven day schedule as far into the future as anyone could see. I had visions of 25 men suddenly converting to a religion that prohibited them from working on Sunday, and me showing up in 258 on Saturday night with no crew. No, Gladys had to go.

She did not seem surprised by my decision. It was my guess that she had gone through this before, at one or more other companies. She pulled out a note pad and a pen and asked me how I spelled my name, and I told her. She put her pen and pad away, told me that I would be hearing from her attorney, because it was illegal to discriminate against a person because of their religion, and disappeared in the direction of the hourly parking lot. I never heard anymore about the incident.

Jim requisitioned me another burr hand, and I was thankful that he was a young black fellow who was a terrific worker. I did not get any more female employees for some time, and that suited me just fine because everyone was aware of the kinds of problems that were being created by adding women.

First, there were the condoms. Some were blown up like balloons and tied to women's work stations. Others were fastened like Christmas decorations. When condoms became old hat, the dirty pictures started. They were taped up all over the plant. There seemed to be a competition on who could post the most obscene pictures. One man spent what must have been a small fortune on a full page picture of a naked woman with her legs spread wide open. He cut it out of Hustler, took it to a photographer, had it blown up to life size, mounted it, brought it to work with him everyday, and sat it at his work station. Men from all over the plant filed past the picture everyday. He had won the competition.

Then there was the shooting in the parking lot. A woman complained to her husband that a man was harassing her at work. The husband waited in the parking lot, shot out the guys back window and two of his tires, and created the biggest news story of the week by being chased for miles by the police. He was caught, put in jail, and fined. While he was in jail, his wife filed for divorce and moved in with the man that was supposedly harassing her.

Foul language in the plant increased dramatically when women were within earshot. Some men got a kick out of seeing their reaction. Then I started hearing things that I had never heard before.

I grew up in the forties and fifties, when women rarely cursed. But now, periodically, I was hearing women say, "fuck this" and "fuck that." I held out hope that the male workers would have their level of decency increased by the addition of women. But instead, the women were pulled down to the level of the men.

I knew that it was just a matter of time before I would get more females in 258, and have to confront the same kinds of problems that most other foremen were already wrestling with. My turn to deal with equal employment opportunity came in early July.

It was a stinking hot summer. Ford had no air conditioning, and people broke out in a heavy sweat as soon as they entered the plant. Heat generated by one thousand machines was added to the sun beating down on the concrete building. The plant turned into a human bake oven. I grabbed a handful of salt tablets from one of the many wall dispensers, mopped the sweat from my forehead, and headed for 258.

She was a very attractive red head about the same age as me, and she was waiting at my desk. When I walked up with my clipboard she said, "Are you Bob?" I said that I was, and she told me she was assigned to work as a torque converter minor assembler in Department 258.

I knew that assembler number one had been accepted into the Skilled Trades training program, and I was wondering who would replace him. Now I knew. She had already been at Ford for a couple months, and knew the basic routine of clocking in. I took her to assembly station one. The assembly stations were in close quarters and cramped. Assembler one had to squeeze past assemblers four, three, and two to get to her work station.

My other three assemblers stood in awe of assembler one, and gawked at her like a kid seeing a Christmas tree full of presents for the first time. They got out of the way as I led my new assembler to her work station. She said her name was Linda. I proceeded to explain to Linda how to assemble converters. That was when it started.

Assembler two had always been a particularly foul-mouthed man. In a voice loud enough for half of Sharonville to hear, he yelled to the assembler behind him, "Yo, Mike. Do you wear underwear when it is this hot?"

Mike yelled back, "Sure I wear underwear. Why wouldn't I?"

"Because of this fucking heat, you dummy. You take me. I don't wear no underwear at all under my coveralls. If I wore underwear, I would have to stop and scratch my balls so much I wouldn't get any work done. Hey, man, do you think them new broads wear underwear? I bet the sweat rolls down between their tits like that big waterfall up there near Canada."

I decided to put a stop to it before it got out of hand. When I finished instructing Linda, I turned around and asked each assembler, as I squeezed past, to come to my desk. When all three were there I said, "Look, fellas, you had your fun. Now knock it off. Just flat knock it off. I do not want to hear a lot of foul mouth just because we have a woman in 258. It is childish, and it is demeaning. How would you like it if men talked that way around your wife, or your daughter? I think you would be looking to punch somebody out. Let's extend some common decency and courtesy to our new assembler. What do you say?"

The three assemblers looked at each other. Then assembler two said, "Well, for one thing, I would never let my wife work at a place like this. If a woman comes to Ford with all these men, you know she is looking for cock. Why else would she come here and take a man's job?"

I said, "Maybe she works here for the same reason that you work here, to earn a living for her family. Every woman that comes to Ford is not on the make. Most of them are here because they need a job. We just pulled out of a bad recession. People need to work. That is why most of the women are here. We do not have to degrade them simply because they need jobs."

They looked at each other again. Then number four said, "Are you saying we aren't allowed to cuss? All you hear around this place is cussing. Foremen cuss, general foremen cuss. How can you say we aren't allowed to cuss?"

I said, "All I am asking is that you show some respect, and keep your foul talk within reasonable limits. We all know the kind of stuff that has happened in other departments, and I do not intend to see that stuff happen in 258. Not on my watch."

Number two had his arms folded in front of him. He said, "Bob, I think you better get our committeeman down here."

The committeeman talked to each of the three male assemblers, glanced at Linda, who had her head down and was building converters, and headed for my desk. I was sure that she knew that I was trying to establish ground rules for behavior in my department.

The committeeman said, "I understand you got a problem with the way your men talk. What is the deal here? Is management trying to control free speech, or is it trying to rewrite the labor contract without consulting the union?"

I said, "Well, let me tell you what happened. Assembler number two is the instigator. He yelled out something about not wearing underwear when I was instructing the new woman assembler."

The committeeman shrugged his shoulders and said, "So? He is allowed to talk about underwear without a supervisor monitoring his conversation with another hourly man. Was he doing his job? Was he late for work? Was he wearing his safety glasses? These are issues you should be monitoring, not whether he talks about underwear."

I said, "Yes, I know. He was doing his job and all that. But then he yelled something about women not wearing underwear and sweat rolling between their tits in this heat."

"Okay. So you think that sweat doesn't roll down between women's tits in this heat? Is that the point?"

"No, damn it and you know it."

"So what is the point? I don't know what is going on here."

I said, "The point is that when a woman works in a department, the men should have enough common decency and human respect to not use gutter language and make her feel uncomfortable."

The committeeman said, "Oh, I see. So you are a moral policeman, and a speech cop."

He pulled out his copy of the labor contract, and in an exaggerated manner said, "Let's see common decency, common decency, common decency. Nope, nothing in the contract about common decency. Now what was that other one? Oh, yeah, human respect. Let's see human respect, human respect, human respect. Nope. Nothing in the contract about human respect. Are you sure you ain't trying to rewrite the contract and not tell anybody about it?"

He stuck the contract back in his pocket and said, "Look, Bob, you and me, we get along good. We ain't got no problems. Let's not start some shit where there ain't no shit to begin with. If women want to come to Ford and take men's jobs, and Ford lets them, that ain't got nothing to do with you and me. Women are not going to remake Ford Motor Company. If they don't like the way Ford Motor Company is, then they don't have to work at here, right?

"As far as you and me, all we got to go on is what it says in the labor contract. If it don't say nothing in the labor contract, then we can't go and make up rules based on what we think is right and wrong. Know what I mean? If women don't like how we talk, then they ought to go get a job some place else."

At the end of the shift Linda came to me and said, "I know what you are trying to do, and I want you to know how very much I appreciate it. But don't go and get yourself into trouble. I'm a big girl. I can take care of myself."

I said, "Okay."

She turned to leave, but after a few steps she stopped, came back and said, "There is just one thing. I can ignore filthy language, condoms and pornographic pictures. But if someone touches my body, well, that will not get ignored."

"Did someone touch you?"

Linda said, "No, they didn't. But you do realize they won't stand aside so I can squeeze by them, don't you? They just stand there, grinning like school boys, waiting for me to squeeze between each one, making full body contact. I am not going to let men get a free feel. I didn't go to the bathroom, and I didn't eat lunch because I will not give them the chance to feel me up. I just wanted you to know. Tomorrow I will go to the bathroom before I start, and I will eat lunch at my work station."

It had never occurred to me that Linda was a virtual prisoner at assembly station one. I decided that I would start the paperwork to reassign assembler positions. I would switch Linda with number four. That way, she would not have to squeeze by anyone going into and out of her work station.

When I walked in the office I was greeted by a chorus of hoots and hollers from the entire day shift whom had just arrived. Screaming Jim had no interest in my numbers. He, along with the rest of Zone 3 management was enjoying the moment at my expense. Apparently, the incident in 258 had spread like wildfire through the entire zone.

Someone yelled, "Here he comes, Captain America, fighting for truth, justice, and the American Way!"

Jim said, "I heard tell you was staking out your claim on that new redhead you got."

Ed said, "Just let your people know you are banging her. Hell, an hourly man got enough respect to back off from the foreman's private piece of ass."

Everyone in the office laughed. I threw my paperwork on Jim's desk and left.

The next night I flipped assemblers one and four, so Linda was at the last station. All three assemblers were upset and demanded to see the committeeman again.

The committeeman said, "Bob, your department is running like a top. Why do you want to go and start some shit at the front end, and fuck up the works? Your three assemblers have been here for years. That woman just came here last night. Why should she be allowed to change everything around? If I have to get all legal on you, I will. The simple fact is if you want to put number four at the number one position, you will have to re-bid the job. Number four assembler is his job. You can't arbitrarily decide that because some woman wants to work there that you can fuck him over and do what she wants."

I said, "Look, the problem is that woman is like a dog in a cage. She can't get out of that work station without squeezing past two, three, and four. They won't step back and let her through. They just stand there, and she has to rub past them to get out. She is an hourly employee, too. What is your obligation to her?"

"Actually, I ain't got no obligation to her. She won't be in the union for eleven more days. She is not entitled to my representation. But let's say she was. My answer would be the same. She got bumped onto assembly table number one. She has to work assembly table number one unless she bids on another job, or unless somebody with higher seniority bumps her off station one. We have to go by the rules, here, Bob. You know that. You can't yank people off the job they got through the bidding process and reassign them. Number four is entitled to that job. That job belongs to him."

The committeeman was right. There was nothing I could do. The system gave those men the right to do what they were doing. At lunch I told numbers two, three and four to get out of my way, and I went to Linda's station to see if she had to go to the bathroom. She thanked me and I led her out of the assembly area. I knew that she was embarrassed by all the attention, and felt like she was causing me a lot of trouble. But it was not Linda, it was the system that was the problem.

I decided to see if I could change the system. I went to see the Labor Relations Manager. It was highly unusual for a front line foreman to go directly to a higher level manager without going through proper channels. But I knew that proper channels had no pathway to solve a new type of problem. All the pathways were geared to white men working jobs with all the ironclad rules spelled out in black and white in a written contract. There was no allowance for flexibility or for a change in the makeup of the work force, which would require new rules.

The Labor Relations Manager folded his hands and patiently listened to me describe my problem. Then he sat back in his chair and said, "I sympathize with you. I really do. I can see that you are a man with a conscience. You should be aware that you are not alone. We are facing these kinds of problems throughout the company because women were never a very big part of the work force. But they are becoming a much bigger part.

"As a matter of fact, there is a labor relations seminar being held at Dearborn in two weeks. They have coined a new phrase 'sexual harassment' to describe what's going on in the auto plants. The big problem is how to deal with it. How do you take a few thousand men, who have a written contract, and add women to the mix while making sure those women are protected and have equal rights? We faced this issue with blacks a few years ago. As the mix in the work force changes, the system has to adapt."

He paused, pondering the dilemma and rounded his desk toward me, speaking assuredly. "But of course a system like we have does not adapt easily, or quickly. Our system has worked well for decades. Ford Motor Company has grown to be one of the largest, most profitable corporations on Earth with the system that we have in place. The system *will* change. But it will change slowly and cautiously. We depend on men like you, who face the fire on the production line everyday, to come up with stopgap solutions, and keep the ball rolling until the system does adapt to the new situation. You are Ford's front line troops, so to speak. You have to keep the battle going until reinforcements can arrive from up north. The cavalry will come. You just have to give it time."

When I reported for work the next night, Screaming Jim was livid. The minute he saw me he shouted, "Who in the FUCK do you think you are? You went over my head. You went over Larry's head. You went over Roger's head. Who in the hell do you think you are? You are a gawdamn foreman on the midnight shift. You ain't nothing. We could hire any hillbilly to do your fucking job. Don't you EVER go over my head! If you are screwing that redhead, that's your business. But when you go over my head to try and get special favors for her, then it *is* my business. You ever do that again, and you will be out on Sharon Road looking through the fence."

I continued to run interference for Linda each lunch period for over a week. It became the talk of Zone 3. Men watched when the monorail stopped so they could hoot and holler when I went in to escort her out of her captive work station. Everyone was aware that the following Monday marked thirty working days and she would be in the union. The foreman from 257 was standing at my desk when I returned from escorting Linda. He was grinning broadly.

He said, "Man, that is one sweet little mama you got there. Are you gonna give her one last interview in your car, after the shift is over, before you sign off on her? You know what I mean." He poked me with his elbow.

Actually, I did know what he meant. Strangely, he was a deacon in the Christian church. Everybody called him the "sneakin deacon" because he lied all the time, and was very possibly the least trusted foreman in Zone 3. His wife, who had wrapped her life around the church, had no idea the kind of man that she was married too. He was famous for giving "last interviews" to newly hired women before he signed off that they were acceptable employees. The foreman had full say. If he said, "nay," she was out with no recourse. That is how the system worked.

Everyone knew the sneakin deacon had given several "final interviews" to females, some in his car in the parking lot, and at least one in the local motel before he would sign off for them to be permanent Ford employees. Some of those women desperately needed the job. Some were the sole support of dependent children. They did what they had to do to keep their jobs.

He disgusted me, and I'm pretty sure he knew it.

I said, "Ron, go back to your department. You have no business in 258."

He shrugged his shoulders and said "I'm just sayin, man. If you ain't getting none now, this is your chance. Once she's in the union, she can tell you to go pound salt. Do you know what I would do if I was in your shoes?"

I took my clipboard and walked away, not interested in hearing what he would do if he was in my place. I signed off on Linda the following Monday, and she became a permanent hourly worker, protected by the labor contract. Whenever possible I continued to escort her out of her work station at lunch time.

Nearly two weeks passed. I was not always able to escort Linda, and sometimes she needed to go to the bathroom when I was not around. But it seemed to work out. I saw her squeeze by the other assemblers several times, and I assumed that the situation had stabilized, and the other assemblers had finally begun to show her some common decency.

I was wrong. Toward the end of a shift I heard men shouting, and knew there was some kind of commotion at the front of 258. I hurried to the assembler stations. I saw Linda swinging her lead hammer with both hands. Assembler two was on the floor. Blood was gushing from his head. His arms were trying to protect his face. Linda was swinging the hammer as hard as she could at his head.

Number three grabbed Linda from behind, and she tried to hit him, but he was able to subdue her. I examined number two while I waited on security and the emergency cart. His eyeball was lying out on his cheek, and blood was pouring from his head. He had lost consciousness.

The trial was almost six months later. Linda testified that she had begun her period, and had to go to the restroom right away. I was at the back end of 258 on a balancer problem. She was embarrassed to have me constantly escort her, and she knew the kind of reaction that got from all the men. So she squeezed out and passed each assembler as quickly as she could, and they did not get much of a feel. She did not want to bother me every time, because she knew I always had a lot of other problems in the department.

On the night in question, she had to get to the restroom quickly, and assembler two thought that was funny. When she tried to squeeze by, he pinned her against the stator rack. Then he put one hand on her breast, and the other hand on her rear end. Linda did not remember grabbing the hammer. It all happened in an instant, and was an involuntary reaction for self preservation.

Linda was convicted of assault with a deadly weapon. Number two lost sight of one eye, and lost his ability to walk without a cane for support. He went on permanent disability.

CHAPTER 11:
QUALITY IS JOB ONE

Ford kept up with the times at its own sweet pace. The quality of C-4 transmissions was inversely proportional to Ford sales. When sales were down, quality was up. But when sales skyrocketed, quality was sacrificed to make the numbers. The only real measure of final quality at Sharonville was the level of warranty defects. If transmissions made it to 12,000 miles or 12 months, they were good transmissions.

Final quality fluctuated with the amount of power granted to the Quality Control Department. When sales were strong and growing, QC was treated like an annoyance that was getting in the way of making the numbers. If a QC supervisor tried to be a hero, and made a stand, production simply went to engineering and got an "engineering deviation" which allowed the use of defective parts in the interests of production. So much for control of quality.

The inconsistency of enforcing quality standards had a devastating impact on the morale of QC inspectors. They truly believed that their work was meaningless and they were there for show, and to be used as scapegoats when there was a quality catastrophe. Why bother writing a reject tag if it is going to be torn off?

An inspector in Department 273 kept records of reject tags that he had written for at least ten years. He would write the reject tag, run in the office and make a copy of it to take home for his files, and then tag up the defective parts. I thought this was curious, and I asked him why he did it.

He said, "You want to know why? I will tell you why. It's because someday this shit is going to hit the fan, that's why. Someday running all this junk is going to blow up in Ford's face. When that happens, the Detroit Mafia will come to Sharonville and fire people left and right. But they won't be able to fire me because I have records that show I rejected this garbage, and they overrode my reject."

His confident answer seemed betrayed by a sense of anxiousness that reasoning with Ford management would be futile. But he continued his self-defense.

"Most inspectors don't give a damn, because they know their reject tag don't mean jack shit. They bring in their Penthouse and Playboys, get coffee from the Press Room, and sit at their inspection tables and 'read the articles'. When they get tired of reading, they go to the warehouse, grab a piece of cardboard, go to the shithouse, make a bed on top of a commode and go to sleep. But I happen to believe that a man should do the job he is paid to do, even if management is too stupid to follow their own rules. My files at home are for protection. They prove that I tried to do my job the way it was supposed to be done."

I was stunned. That QC inspector's intense diatribe impacted me forcefully. As I walked away, something was tugging at the edge of my memory, but I could not put my finger on it. Then I remembered; it was Dr. Dawson's lecture at the University of Southern California. Professor Dawson said that the quality of a finished product is a function of the sum total of the attitude of the people that produce that product. I shook my head as I thought of the sum total of the attitude toward quality at Ford Motor Company. Quality played a very small role, and I felt that, eventually, Ford's attitude toward quality would be the straw that broke the camel's back.

My attitude, on the other hand, was focused on the bottom line, specifically, *my* bottom line. At Sharonville I was known as an "overtime hog." I wanted every dime that I could get. I was anxious to build up my savings because I did not know how many more dimes there would be before Ford went down the tubes. Word spread quickly in Zone 3 that I wanted all the overtime that I could get. I made a point to get qualified in every department in the zone so that when there was an absence I could be called in four hours early or stay over four hours in any department that had a vacancy.

My bank account benefited from the indifferent attitude of those around me at Ford. There was no problem with being able to consistently work twelve hour days. The result is that I got an eyeful on how Ford deals with quality issues as I worked every department in the zone.

One evening I was called in early to the Press Room; there was a problem with metal thin-out on transmission oil pans. It was not a new problem. Sharonville got steel coils from Ford's River Rouge steel plant, a place notorious for producing bad quality steel. When I got to the Press Room at eight in the evening the foreman who had stayed over four hours from the day shift passed on the skinny.

He said, "What we have here is pure garbage. A lot of times a coil of steel will have small sections of metal thin-out. But this coil is thinned out the entire coil and the only other coil we have is the same way."

I watched the press stamp out the oil pans and then picked one up. Like Superman I was able to bend it completely in half with my bare hands, something a normal man should not be able to do.

The foreman shook his head and said, "This shit is so thin that we had a hard time feeding it into the press. Twice it broke off and once it just bent in half. It's too damn thin to feed in properly."

I shouldn't have been, but I was stunned. I estimated that the thickness of the steel was about five or six times the thickness of a roll of aluminum foil that you would buy in a grocery store. I knew that metal fatigue would cause hairline cracks in the pans, and sooner rather than later, oil would begin to leak out of the transmissions. I looked at the finished racks of oil pans. Every single one had a reject tag. The inspector had written a stack of reject tags to put on every rack as it came off the press because he could see that all the pans would be thinned out.

I said, "If everything is being rejected, why are you running the press?"

The foreman threw up his hands and exclaimed, "The GF said to run them, so I'm running them. It ain't my problem. This ain't my department. They forced me to stay over in this department. I'm outta here."

I knew this problem would haunt us all. So I picked up one of the oil pans and headed for the zone office. The GF was doing some paper work.

I asked, "Did you see these oil pans?"

He did not answer. Unswayed, I took the oil pan, bent it in half and laid it in front of him.

"I want to know, do you want me to keep running *these* things?"

The General Foreman picked up the distorted oil pan, looked at it, pitched it in the trash can, and said, "Yep. If we don't, assembly won't have oil pans. I know all about the metal thin-out. It ain't my fault they sent us bad steel. I ain't gonna be the one to shut down assembly. Keep running the oil pans."

I stood there dumbfounded listening to his numb rationalization for accepting unacceptable defects. The time to make a stand for quality at Ford would never come.

He looked at his watch and said, "Jim will be here in three hours. Then it will be his show. If he wants to shut that press down, well, that is his business. But I ain't gonna do it."

I went back to the Press Room to check the count. We had run 8,750 oil pans since the bad steel was put on the press. I had quickly learned that it was pointless to take a stand at Ford Motor Company, so I did like everyone else and just went with the flow. Those 8,750 Ford customers would have to get in line with all the other customers who received defective vehicles.

By the time the midnight foreman relieved me at eleven thirty, the count was 12,945 oil pans. I gave the low down to the midnight foreman. We grabbed an oil pan and went to see Screaming Jim. He looked at the pan, twisted it in his hands, and told the foreman to pull off the reject tags and set the oil pans in the staging area for assembly. I shrugged my shoulders and went to 258 to get my shift started.

At the time, Ford sales were setting new records and nothing was allowed to interfere with production. The quality of purchased components dropped to a new low. Ford pressured parts suppliers to cut costs as much as possible. They cut costs by eliminating inspectors and replacing a 100 percent inspection system with a statistical inspection system, in which every 100th part was checked for quality.

In more cost-cutting moves, Ford decided to switch from aluminum stators in torque converters to plastic stators to lower costs.

My assemblers indignantly asked, "Do you want us to build converters with this shit?"

I looked at the stators. Some were cracked; others had chips in the plastic. Some had loose bearings. They were complete crap. I ordered my four assemblers to stack any plastic stators that were chipped, cracked, or otherwise defective on the floor. I did not want to be responsible for converter failures, even if it was after the warranty expired. I felt that Ford was knowingly cheating customers by building converters with plastic stators. Aluminum stators had been used ever since the first automatic transmission was invented in the late 1940s. But like all great decisions at Ford, quality was sacrificed for efficiency.

Before the shift ended, I had to reverse my decision because there were more plastic stators being stacked on the floor than were being assembled into converters. At least 80 percent of the new plastic stators had some kind of defect that I felt would eventually result in a torque converter wipeout. But concern slowly evaporated.

Exhaustion was common at the plant as we worked seven days a week for months on end. We worked Easter Sunday and the Fourth of July. We worked Thanksgiving, Christmas, and New Years Day. Most of my days were twelve hour days and I was making so much money that my income tax bill was greater than my total salary had been at P&G.

The trade-off was that I was a walking zombie who flew off the handle at any little annoyance. If I sat down for even a minute I was sound asleep like a narcoleptic. I fell asleep at the dinner table. I fell asleep at stop lights while driving. I fell asleep in the middle of conversations. Half the time my kids, which now numbered two, were afraid of me because I was so grouchy. Was this ever going to be worth it, I wondered?

I could only dream of the day I could leave Ford. But that dream kept getting interrupted. One afternoon the phone rang at two o'clock which, for me, was the middle of my night. I barely was cognizant. I heard ringing off somewhere in the distance, then, I felt my wife shaking me. Someone from Ford was on the phone. Someone named Ed wanted to talk to me. I blinked away the sleep and went to the phone.

Ed barked, "Git yer ass in here! The foreman in 269 ain't coming in. His wife can't wake him up. He is breathing funny and moaning. She called the life squad. I want you in 269 in an hour."

Everybody had long felt that the 269 foreman could not last much longer working the kind of schedule we were all forced to work. He was in his fifties and had been at Ford for 28 years. He needed two more years to get his pension. Most felt that he would not make it. They were right. He was dead when the life squad got to his house. His dream of retirement expired with his last breath.

Department 269 was a small department that machined and assembled impellor housings for Pintos. The housings were small and it was a hand build operation. The Pinto torque converter was only ten and a quarter inches in diameter. Pinto sales were declining as quality problems were rampant and everybody at Ford knew that the Pinto was a piece of junk. Profit margins were low, there was a flurry of lawsuits, and nobody cared about the Pinto.

When I got to 269, the foreman who had been forced to stay over four hours to cover the dead foreman was looking at his watch. I was a few minutes late. Foremen who were forced to cover absent foremen in other departments had no commitment at all. They would not have to deal with the consequences of how they had managed the department because it was not their department and it was not even their shift.

My colleague gave me a dirty look, grabbed his clipboard and said, "Okay, everything is running and you got plenty of float ahead of your assemblers. We got trouble with blades not fitting in the shells. I am out of here."

As he walked toward the parking lot I looked at the back end of 269. It did not have a PR Burr unloading the line. It had a quality inspector unloading. I had never seen a quality inspector assigned to do production work. I headed for the back end of the department.

I stopped a few feet from the inspector because I had no idea what he was doing. He would pick up a finished impellor housing, look at it, and then drop it on the floor. Blades would fall all over the place. The inspector would then pick up the impellor with half the blades missing and toss it into a ZE34 rack with a reject tag on it.

I said, "What the hell are you doing?"

He said, "I am doing my job the way I was told to do it. I am supposed to drop each impellor from a height of four feet. If the blades don't fall out, it is a good impellor. If blades fall out, I toss it into the reject rack. I don't give a shit no more. I just do what they tell me."

I looked at the scrap rack. It was half full of impellors with some or most of the blades missing. The blades were scattered all over the floor and in the bottom of the rack. I walked to the front of 269 to talk to one of the assemblers, who I knew, a man named Bandini.

Bandini was an interesting man. He had been a Marine on the second wave that hit Iwo Jima. I was a World War II buff and Bandini's stories of crawling up the steaming hot black sand beach and flushing Japs out of caves enthralled me. I had great respect for men who fought in the war, no matter if they were hourly or not. The respect that I showed was obvious, and those vets showed me respect in return.

I was genuinely curious and asked, "What do we have here, Bandini?"

Bandini said, "Pure shit, that's what we got. These shells must have been run on the north 1600-ton, because they are all cockeyed. On one side the blade slots are real deep. You just drop the blades in, but they are real loose. The other side the slots are real shallow. You beat the hell out of the blades, but they won't fit right into the slots. They bend and they twist, but they won't go down right into the slots."

Bandini's hands were taped, as were the other assemblers. They covered raw, red hands caused by trying to beat blades into holes that were too shallow. There were blood stains on the assembly tables where their hands had bled before they taped them up with masking tape. Ford was literally getting blood and sweat from their workers that went largely unseen.

I went back to the end of the line and picked up one of the housings that the inspector had put in the "good" rack. I shook it, and the blades in the loose half of the housing rattled like a maraca. I had no doubt whatsoever that these housings would result in a converter wipeout. First there would be a grinding sound, and then the car would stop and would not move again.

I put the impellor back in the rack. Why should I care? Ford certainly didn't care. The Pinto was not making enough money and people were suing Ford. The company was a lot more interested in Gran Torinos, LTDs, light trucks, and Lincolns, because that was where the money was. I headed in the direction of the Press Room to see if Big Mo had his coffee pot fired up yet. Big Mo was an overtime hog like me and my guess was that he was in early also.

As I got my coffee I thought back to when this craziness on production started. It was right after the recession. Sales went from the basement to the ceiling in a matter of a couple months. Production pressure was so great that there simply was no such thing as a bad part or a defective transmission.

In my home department of 258, force feeding defective components to the assemblers had resulted in a much higher percentage of locked up torque converters. There was no way to tell what had caused them to lock up unless you destroyed the converter by sawing it in half and examined the internal components. Ford could not afford to lose a converter simply because it was locked up internally. So they invented a machine to unlock locked up converters. They called it "The Expander."

The Expander had a powerful hydraulic pump that hooked up to the hub on the impellor and pumped hydraulic pressure inside the converter. It was much like you would blow up a balloon. The operator would pump up the converter and then check for internal rotation. If it still did not rotate he would pump in more pressure until there was so much slop inside the converter that the parts rotated. The Expander was operated day and night because parts that did not fit together properly in the converter simply would not turn when the inspector put the rotation gage on the converter.

When an expanded converter was set back on the conveyor from The Expander it reminded me of a line of school kids. In any line of school kids you see several normal size kids, and then a big fat boy. There are several more normal kids, and then another big fat boy. Expanded converters were the big fat boys. Their sides had been pushed out so the internal parts would rotate. I always smiled when I watched converters going down the line. There would be a bunch of regular kids, and then a big fat boy. Sometimes one third of the line was big fat boys.

One evening I was called in four hours early to work Department 285, which manufactured cover plates for the torque converters. The foreman had gotten so stressed out over the problem of out of square stud bolts that he had to go home before he had a nervous breakdown.

Each cover plate had four stud bolts welded to it. The four studs were screwed into the transmission, and held the torque converter in place.

Those studs had to be in square, and match up with the four holes. If they did not match up final assemblers would have to force the converter in. This would eventually result in vibration in the car, as a torque converter struggled to work properly when it was forced into holes that did not match its four studs.

Everyone in 285 knew that the inspector had not checked stud squareness for a very long time. The welders were supposed to be permanently adjusted to weld the studs into the correct position on the cover plate. So why bother to check? Just make sure that the welders were adjusted correctly. But no one checked welder adjustment because the inspector was supposed to alert the operator when studs were not in square. Assembly was having a hard time attaching the torque converters because all of the studs were out of square.

A Sharonville showdown ensued. When I arrived at eight in the evening to cover the last half of the afternoon shift, the GF was arguing with the quality control foreman. They could not find the stud squareness gage. How could the inspector check stud squareness if he had no inspection gage? The two managers were shouting at each other as they looked behind machines, under trash cans, behind ZE34 racks, on shelves. The gage was nowhere to be found, and there were accusations and counter-accusations.

"The gage is the responsibility of production because it belongs on the final inspection table."

"No, it's not a production asset; it's a quality control asset. This is the responsibility of QC!"

Never being one to get in the middle of a good argument, I headed for the Press Room to get a cup of coffee. As I waited for Big Mo's pot to perk, I mentioned the missing stud squareness gage in 285. If you wanted accurate information at Sharonville, you went to Big Mo. Everybody in the plant bought coffee and vented. Big Mo did not talk much, but he was a good listener. He knew what was going on all over the plant. He would give his opinion if you asked for it. If you did not ask for it, he said nothing. But this time Big Mo volunteered some critical information.

He said, "Tha hain't a gonna find that gage."

I said, "Really? Why not?"

"Cause t'ain't there, that's why?"

"Where is it?"

"It done got throwed away a long time ago. The inspector, well, he couldn't find no room fer it on the table. Oncest he got his lunch out, got his coffee, got his Playboy, t'weren't no room fer the gage. He tuk and put it by his feet. Then he tripped ever time he got up. Then he said what the hell, we h'aint a usin' this here gage no way, and then he tuk and plum throwed it out."

When I got back to 285 the search was over, but the GF was still eyeball to eyeball with the QC foreman. QC said he was going to call his manager at home. He would make sure that every rack of cover plates was rejected. If production pulled the tags off, he would make sure every torque converter that had an out of square cover plate was rejected. By gawd, he would take it all the way up north if he had to.

The GF looked at me and shouted, "Where the hell you been? You are supposed to be running 285."

I held up my cup of coffee and said, "I have had three hours sleep in the last 36. If I don't have coffee you are going to have to get security to scrape me off the floor."

He shouted, "Just run the fucking department!" Then he headed back to the office.

I looked at rack after rack of cover plates with reject tags. Then I shrugged my shoulders and sat down at the desk. I was supposed to manage this insane asylum? I must be crazy to still be working here.

When the midnight shift came in I passed on the skinny to the foreman, explained about the missing gage, showed him nine ZE34 racks of rejected cover plates, and headed for 258. Mercifully, I had no absences and all the machines were running. I glanced at the rejected cover plates at operation 10.

The stock handler yelled, "Are we supposed to hang these? They got reject tags on them."

I yelled, "Hang them." Then I went back to the Press Room for a fourth cup of coffee.

When I got back to 258 with a steaming cup of black liquid that was keeping my eyes pried open, Langley was at my desk.

He said, "You know that every converter that comes off the line is being rejected, don't you? They got two QC foremen at the end of the line."

I headed for the back end of 258. Langley was right. The QC foreman had been true to his word. He had called his manager at home. The manager called the day shift QC foreman back in. QC was ganging up on us. It looked like it might turn into a full scale management rumble. I knew from the tone of the manager's voice that he intended to stand his ground and had no intension of backing off. I headed back to the office to get reinforcements.

Screaming Jim stormed out of the office. His face was as red as a beet. I could hardly keep up with him as he headed for the back end of 258, full of vein-popping rage.

"Just what the fuck do you think you are doing? You reject these converters and you will shut down Fairfax and Sharonville. You know GAWD damn right you can't do that."

The QC manager said, "You think I can't? Just hang around you fat little fart. None of these converters are going into transmissions. You knew the cover plates were no good before you built them into converters. You build shit, and then put it into converters, which makes the converters shit. Your ass is going to be fired over this."

I looked around. Two managers shouting in each other's face was drawing a crowd. Half of 258 was watching like spectators at a soccer game. There had not been this much entertainment at the back end of 258 since the little green men had told Quillen to masturbate in the middle of the aisle. Money came out of coveralls and bets were placed on which manager would throw the first punch. More bets were placed on which one would win.

Screaming Jim said, "Are you telling me that you are rejecting every fucking converter coming out of 258? Is that what you are telling me?"

The QC manager turned to his foremen and said, "This sumbitch is stupider than everybody says. What do I have to do, draw him a picture?"

Jim turned to me and shouted, "Shut 258 down. Send every swinging dick home. I ain't gonna run converters if they ain't no fucking good." Then he spun around and headed for the office. I was dumbfounded for a minute. I knew that we could not shut 258 down. We had worked for almost eight months without a single day off, and we still could not keep up with the assembly plants.

I hurried to catch up with Screaming Jim and said, "Did I hear you right, Jim? You want me to shut 258 down and send my men home?"

Screaming Jim turned on me like a rattlesnake striking at prey and screamed, "Are you fucking deaf? Shut that son of a bitch down. Turn every fucking machine off. Send every one of your people home. Do it now. If that QC son of a bitch wants a war, he is gonna get one. We will see who gets fired over this."

Then he lurched off in the direction of the office, leaving me to wonder if I would get fired if I shut down a critical department when we already had a severe shortage of torque converters. But he was the boss.

It was no problem sending my people home. They were on the hairy edge of exhaustion. Before the words were out of my mouth they were shutting machines down, grabbing their lunch pails and running for the time clock. They were as happy as fifth graders that had just been told school was cancelled. I listened to the strange sound of silence in 258 and watched my people heading for the door like they were going to a picnic. I stood and watched them until the last one rounded the corner and was out of sight. That is when I thought I heard someone calling my name. I turned around. It was Screaming Jim. He was running toward me waving a piece of paper.

Jim screamed, "Get your people back! Stop them before they get off of Ford property. I got us an engineering deviation. Them converters is good. Get your people back on the job."

I ran toward the door as fast as I could without slipping on the oil slick floor. When I got to the hourly lot I saw a lot of headlights on and a procession of cars headed for the gate. I yelled as loud as I could and waved my hands. But I was only able to head off half of my crew. They came back to 258, but they were not happy campers.

I had enough people to run one line and I chose the north line. We had a better float ahead of Fairfax than we did on eleven and a quarters. I knew that if I did not make at least 1,000 eleven and a quarters the Atlanta assembly plant would be shutting down the next day.

The next morning I was sitting in Roger's office along with Larry and Screaming Jim. Roger spent fifteen minutes telling Jim how incompetent and stupid he was and how lucky he was that Roger felt sorry for him and would not fire him. Then he put a letter of reprimand in Jim's file. Then Roger turned to me and said he was putting a letter of reprimand in my file for failure to run fast enough to get all of my people back on the job. I sat there in silence.

Jim got up and left. I followed. But Larry grabbed me outside Roger's office and said, "Gawdamn it, man, didn't I tell you to call me at home if that stupid son of a bitch told you to do something that you knew was wrong?"

Before I could tell Larry that I had lost his phone number he walked off shaking his head in utter frustration.

When Roger received the report from QC about the missing stud squareness gage he ordered a total audit of every quality control gage in every department in Zone 3. He was shocked to learn that many gages could not be found and most of the ones that were found were badly out of calibration. Some were rusty and obviously had not been used for a long time. Parts in Zone 3 had been manufactured without being properly gaged for accuracy since the beginning of the sales upturn. Most inspectors felt that there was no point to checking them because Ford would use them whether they were good or bad.

Ford Motor Company was getting a bad reputation for quality in the market place. It had a less than stellar reputation for many years, but quality had rapidly gone downhill so badly since the end of the oil recession that it made the news. Articles appeared in *Time, Newsweek,* and *Forbes* about the growing quality problems with Ford vehicles. Heart wrenching stories appeared in newspapers about people who had purchased Fords and had quality problem after quality problem and were unable to get the company to do anything because the cars had exceeded the warranty period.

In Cincinnati, a man wrote "LEMON" all over his new Ford. He put a sign in the back window that read, "Ask me about the quality of a Ford." He drove slowly around the city and up and down parking lot aisles in shopping centers. He parked the car at the gate to the Sharonville Transmission Plant. Eventually, Ford had it towed to an impoundment lot.

At the same time there were many articles about the exceptional high quality of cars manufactured in Europe and Japan. Rating agencies compared Fords to Toyotas and Volkswagen with Ford consistently sitting at the bottom of the charts.

The Detroit Mafia finally decided to do something about the perception of Ford vehicles. They apparently believed that quality was not the problem. The problem was that people perceived Ford as having low quality. They set out to change people's perception by conditioning them to believe that Ford had high quality, much like a farmer conditions cattle to follow the herd. Evidently they believed that if they spent enough money on advertising, people's perceptions could be changed.

Their main advertising thrust was the slogan *"At Ford, Quality is Job One."* They spent tens of millions running these ads on practically every TV and radio station in America. Full page ads appeared repeatedly in major magazines and newspapers. Later advertising slogans were *"Nobody Sweats the Details like Ford," and "Have You Driven A Ford…Lately?"* implying that quality had improved, and you should now switch back from a foreign car to Ford.

But the trickle of consumer dissatisfaction grew into a downpour. Ford decided that they needed a trusted spokesman to assure people that all those horror stories about atrocious quality and service were mere exaggerations. They wanted someone whom was known for integrity and honesty, and was authentic, wholesome, and trustworthy. They chose Bill Cosby. At the time, *The Cosby Show* was the number one family program on television. If Bill Cosby said that at Ford quality is job one, who could doubt him?

Ford had Bill Cosby make commercials at a number of Ford plants. Each commercial showed an immaculately clean factory with smiling hourly workers diligently building high quality vehicles, while Cosby explained their dedication and highlighted the fine equipment they had to work with. He concluded the commercial by stating, "At Ford, Quality is Job One."

At Sharonville, there was a series of jokes after these commercials were aired because everyone knew that they were totally fake. Then it was announced that Bill Cosby would be filming one of the commercials at the Sharonville plant. An area of the plant was chosen and cleaning people went to work. They brought in scissor ladders that extended all the way up to the roof. Outside contractors scrubbed the buildup of filth from the ceiling and light fixtures for a couple days. Then every fluorescent light bulb in the area was replaced, and all the light fixtures were painted. Every machine in the area was shut down, cleaned, and painted. Giant floor sanders were brought in and sanded through the filthy, stinking oil until dry wood was reached.

To showcase the quality of Ford, a C-4 automatic transmission was used. Not one from our assembly line, mind you. Instead, a hand assembled transmission from components that had been individually checked for quality and tested to make sure it was perfect in every way. It was suspended on a newly painted J-hook and spotlighted like a million dollar diamond at Tiffanys.

On the day the commercial was filmed, Ford beefed up security and roped off the area. The transmission had been guarded day and night. Were they afraid that mediocrity would seep into their perfect model? Both Ford and the UAW let it be known that if anyone screwed with the filming of the commercial they would be terminated immediately. Giant fans were hauled in to blow away the oily mist and blue gray clouds of machine dust that saturated the air. All machines in the area were turned off, and hourly workers were herded back behind the ropes. Security guards made sure there was no talking, no moving, and no smoking. There were more white shirts and neckties than coveralls since most of the spectators were people from Detroit.

The crew of actors who would impersonate Ford workers were escorted to the area by security guards. All of them were above average in appearance and they represented a cross section of American society so as to not offend any social segments. There was the middle aged black man, graying at the temples. There were two women, one black and young, one white and older. There were two younger white males and one Asian male. It was a microcosm of America displayed in the commercial, but not at all reflective of actual Ford workers.

All of the actors were smiling like the Cheshire cat in *Alice in Wonderland* and all were dressed in new, crisp work coveralls with the Ford logo prominently displayed. All had new safety glasses, perfectly positioned on their faces. A Ford engineer handed each of them a tool, showed them how to hold the tool, and showed them the area of the transmission they were supposed to look like they were working on.

A commotion behind me caused everyone to turn their heads like guests at a wedding when they play *Here Comes the Bride*. It was Bill Cosby, surrounded by a dozen security guards. They led him to the spotlighted transmission and the camera people showed him where to stand. There was a call for silence and the cameras rolled. Cosby stood to the side of the transmission so the happy, professional workers could be seen performing exceptionally high quality work. He explained how these workers spare no effort to insure that every transmission is built perfectly. He concluded with the well known slogan, *"At Ford, Quality is Job One."*

If only as much fuss had been invested in actually making sure we had parts that could come close to making what they were showing.

CHAPTER 12:
YOUR SAFETY IS MY BUSINESS

I quickly learned that safety rules had nothing to do with safety – they were a disciplinary tool. The philosophy of Ford management was that everything that happens is caused by somebody. Our job was to find them and write them up. The easiest and quickest way to nail somebody was on a safety rule violation.

The UAW kept a sharp eye out for salaried people breaking safety rules because what was good for the goose was good for the gander. A female clerk went from office to office to do filing each day. When she came out of each air conditioned office, into the hot, humid, smoky plant, her safety glasses immediately fogged up, and she could not see.

She only had to walk a few feet to the next office, and there were no eye hazards nearby. But the unbendable rule was if you come out on the factory floor, you wear safety glasses. She placed them on the very tip of her nose, and looked over top, because that was the only way that she could see.

A committeeman happened to observe her and complained to management that she was not really wearing safety glasses because she had them so far down on her nose that her eyes had no protection. Why did management have a double standard on the safety glass rule?

Two labor relations people and two UAW people stopped her as she went from office to office and precisely measured the distance from her eyes to the tip of her nose where her glasses rested. Then they gave this information, via a three-way telephone conversation, to headquarters in Detroit.

Corporate Labor Relations people consulted with top union officials and dug through the labor agreement. It did not specify exactly where on a person's face the glasses had to be placed. It only required that safety glasses be worn on the factory floor. The clerk was in compliance with safety rules.

By the end of the day, hourly all over the plant had their safety glasses perched at the very tips of their noses. The next morning when Roger rode his golf cart through Zone 3 the hourly made extraordinary efforts to insure that he saw them with their safety glasses perched on the tips of their noses, which offered no protection at all to their eyes.

Within a single day it became a competitive game throughout the plant. Bets were placed on how far down on a man's nose safety glasses could be mounted before they fell off. The bet was won by a man who taped his glasses to his nose and ears.

Management rage about this rule loophole boiled down through the ranks. Screaming Jim held a meeting at the beginning of the midnight shift.

He paced back and forth, his vein enflamed, and shouted, "Some of them bastards is going to lose their glasses. When they start moving around and doing their jobs, some of them glasses are going to fall off their noses and hit the floor. When they do I want a 4600 on every one of them smart ass sons a bitches! If them glasses break, I want a second 4600 for willful destruction of company property. They think they got us on this shit, but we will see who got who."

The focus shifted from the safety glass game the very next day. The clerk came out of an office, turned right, and started walking to the next office. What she did not know was that an hourly prankster waited in the shadows between the two offices. When she got in sight he pulled down his coveralls, mooned her, and yelled, "Can you see this, bitch?" She screamed, threw her papers up in the air, and ran into the nearest office.

By the time security arrived the hourly man was long gone. The clerk was so upset that the nurse had to give her something to calm her down, and sent her home for the rest of the day. The next day the clerk met with Labor Relations and the union. Labor relations stated that this was an extremely serious offense, and that when the offender was apprehended, he would be terminated.

The UAW said termination seemed harsh for a man merely playing a prank on a clerk. Besides that, how would the man be identified? Could the clerk give a positive identification on the man who mooned her?

She said, "It was dark between those offices. When he yelled, it startled me, and I didn't get a good look at him. All I saw was bare buttocks sticking out. He was bent over, and his face was in the opposite direction."

The union rep said, "Okay, but did you see a white ass or a black ass?"

"The man was definitely white."

"Did his ass have any distinguishing characteristics that you could identify?"

The clerk squirmed in her seat and said, "I didn't stand and stare at his bare rear end. I ran to safety as quickly as I could."

The UAW rep sat smugly back in his seat, turned to the Labor Relations rep and said, "So management is going to try to nail a man that has a white ass. On the day shift we have over 2,000 men, and most of them are white. Every one of the white ones has a white ass and wears coveralls."

The Labor Relations rep was silent for a moment. Then he turned to the clerk and said, "If we line up all the white men that work in the vicinity of where the incident occurred, have them bend over and pull down their coveralls, could you identify the man who frightened you?"

The UAW rep said, "Hold on here. How do we know the man worked in the vicinity of them two offices? How do we know the man does not work all the way on the other side of the plant? We got no proof of where the man works. If we do a line up, we got to have every white hourly man in the plant lined up. For that matter, how do we know it was a man from the day shift? It could have been a man working overtime from midnights. If we are going to do a lineup here, it has to encompass all possible suspects."

Stunned at the suggestion, tears streaming down the clerk's face, she indignantly said, "I am NOT going to look at a bunch of men lined up with their pants pulled down. Just forget it. Forget the whole thing!"

The UAW rep smiled, nodded to the Labor Relations rep, got up and left the office. The rep tried to console the clerk, but she was not to be consoled. She stormed out of the office and went back to her job. Everyone in the plant knew that she was fuming. The plant buzzed for two days about how upset the clerk was. But all I heard was the sound of opportunity knocking.

I knew that the clerk made her rounds at the beginning of the day shift, collecting all production, quality, and disciplinary records from the midnight shift, and filed them. I knew that she stopped every morning at a certain vending machine for her morning cup of coffee. I was waiting for her, bought her coffee, and we sat down at the picnic bench to talk.

I said, "That was a really ugly incident that you went through."

"I don't want to talk about it. I want to push it completely out of my memory."

"Do you like working at Ford Motor Company?"

She looked at me like I was crazy and said, "Are you joking? I hate this place. I despise working here. But I'm like most everybody else. This is the best paying job that I can find. It has full benefits that I really need. My husband walked out on me, disappeared, and left me with two kids to raise by myself. I need this job and benefits. If I didn't, I would be out of here in a heartbeat."

I took a sip of coffee and said, "Well, that's funny, because I feel exactly the same way."

"You? But you are in management."

"So? I hate this place as bad as you do, and I have plans to quit."

"Really? You're going to quit? When?"

"As soon as I have enough money saved up. I don't plan to work for any other big corporation, either. To me they are all just a pack of legal gangsters. I feel dirty being called a member of management. I have more respect for a garbage man than I do for anyone that wears a suit and tie. No, someday when I have enough saved, I'll be working for Bob Dewar. But you can help me out. I'm keeping track of all the things I see and experience here, but I think people will be interested after Ford goes belly up."

"Ford is going belly up? All I hear is about how much money they are making. Everybody says buy Ford stock because all it does is go up, up, up."

I said, "Sure it does, for now. But they are digging their own grave. They are just too stupid to see it. You see, I want to turn the tables on Ford. You know how they build a case against you with 4600s and progressive discipline?"

She lit a cigarette, and I knew her interest was sincere. She said, "Sure. I file all the 4600s. I maintain all the disciplinary records. When they do a termination, I have to pull out records of all the hearings and take them to Labor Relations."

"Well, I am building a case against Ford, just like they build a case against people. I keep a daily journal of everything that happens. It is only a matter of time before Ford goes down the tubes. The simple fact is you cannot run a company the way they run this one and stay in business forever. Their day will come. When it does, they will be judged in the court of public opinion just like they judge people at disciplinary hearings. They will be judged for the way they treat employees, the way they treat customers, and the junk that they slap together and call cars."

She starred at me in amazement and said, "You know, I have thought exactly the same thing many times. But I never took it any further. I go to a bar, have a few drinks, blow off some steam, and come back to work. But you are actually documenting all this?"

"Yes, I am, and you can help me."

She looked at me sideways, skeptical. "Really? How could I possibly help? I have never written anything. I barely passed senior English."

"No, you don't have to write anything. But you can get me copies of stuff like management memos, quality reports, disciplinary records, anything that will help me paint a picture of how Ford Motor Company was run before it disintegrates like the Roman Empire. People will have a right to know, because Ford employs nearly a half million people. When it collapses, it will take a big part of our entire economy with it, and people have a right to know what happened. I hope to be able to tell them by explaining how Ford managed their car factories. They can put two and two together from that, and figure out why they went down the tubes."

The clerk starred at me wide-eyed and speechless.

I continued, "You can make copies of anything you think I can use, and stick it in my mail slot. Nobody will know what you're doing. But this has to be our little secret. You can't tell anyone at all. You can't tell your friends, your neighbors, or your relatives. If it gets back to Ford, you and I will be terminated, and we will never be able to get another job. Ford will make sure of that. The last thing they want is for the public to get a worm's eye view of the company."

She smiled, and I could tell that I had hit the bull's eye.

Enthusiastically she said, "Can I get a copy of your book when you write it?"

I smiled and said. "Certainly. I will write a personal note on the inside cover about how much you helped me gather information."

"Oh, wow. Sure, I'll help you. I can't wait to start feeding you information."

After that, once or twice a week I found copies of memos and reports in my mail slot, and I started a file at home.

Shortly after the safety glass issue with the clerk, there was a very serious accident at Sharonville. An hourly man lost his life. His head was smashed in a machine like kids smash pumpkins on Halloween. It was the only fatality at the Sharonville Plant that anyone could remember.

Ford ruled that it was the man's incompetence that got him killed. A 4600 was written, for violating a safety rule, and placed in the dead man's file before his file was sent to inactive records.

The fatality took place on the Case Line, which is a machine that is as long as a city block. It takes a solid block of aluminum and shaves, mills, drills, grinds, and bores, and a finished transmission case comes out of the end of the machine. The employee was an electrician. Safety rules call for the power source to be locked out when a machine is being repaired.

But to lock out the machine, the electrician would have had to walk to the end of the machine, where the electrical panel was located. That was 200 feet from where he was working. The operators were at lunch, and the repair would only take a few minutes. So the electrician did not bother to walk back and lock out the panel. His head was inside the Case Line when the operators returned from lunch. They did not know he was inside the machine, and they pushed the green start buttons.

Yellow tape was placed around the machine, investigators swarmed all over the Case Line, and the department was down for over four hours. Blood, fragments of brain and bone had to be flushed out with high power water hoses. Then the electrician's job was posted on the open jobs board. The Case Line was started back up, the 4600 was filed in the dead man's records, and Roger called a Zone 3 meeting.

Even though the accident did not happen in Zone 3, the anxiety in Roger's voice was obvious.

He said, "As you all know, a man was killed today because he failed to follow safety rules. No one can be blamed for his death but the man himself. Even though this accident did not happen in our area of responsibility, we will be affected. In fact, everyone in this plant will be affected."

He looked around the room. We starred at him, as he continued, "First of all, when there is a fatal accident, OSHA will come down on us. Their people will be all over this plant. They will look in every nook and cranny. They will require us to take action if anything half way looks like it is dangerous. They will identify themselves by a name tag and OSHA in big black letters. If an OSHA man has any questions, you will cooperate fully with him. You will be courteous and polite. If OSHA gets a hard on for us because one of you men gave one of their men a hard time, you will personally answer to me.

"In case anybody here does not know what OSHA is, it is an agency of the federal government charged with insuring that work places are safe. If they decide that something is unsafe, they can shut it down. They can levy fines of up to $25,000 per day for unsafe work environments, and a company can't do jack shit about it. Nobody can challenge an OSHA ruling. These people can make a factory so safe that the company goes bankrupt. If any of you has contact with an OSHA man, I want an immediate report. I want your name, who you talked to, exactly what he asked, and exactly how you responded. Do not try to blow smoke up my ass on this. This is serious business."

Roger seemed edgy and more nervous than I had ever noticed him act before. "Obviously, OSHA will not be the only people coming to the plant. We've had a fatal accident. Corporate people will be down here from Detroit. They'll be asking a lot of questions. If you're approached,

I want to know immediately. Of course, you should respond that the accident did not happen in our zone, and you have no knowledge of it."

The first OSHA people reported to the plant before the blood and bones were flushed from the Case Line. They strutted around the plant like cocky little Hitlers. The safety problems that they identified baffled people. Then, when everyone realized that they were serious, it became amusing. OSHA jokes made rounds all over the plant and in the local bars.

According to OSHA, a major safety hazard at Sharonville was the fire extinguishers. They were mounted too high on pillars and supports. Now that Ford employed more than 400 women, and the average height of a woman is less that the average height of a man, Ford had to lower 4,000 fire extinguishers six inches, so that a short woman could get to them in an emergency. OSHA gave the company 30 days to accomplish the task, or be fined $10,000 per day until all fire extinguishers were lowered.

A second major health risk identified was the toilet seats. They were not open in the front. Therefore, it was possible for diseases to spread from private parts touching toilet seats. Ford had 30 days to replace every toilet seat in the plant with an open front seat, or be fined $10,000 per day until the change was made.

OSHA recognized that the intense noise level in the plant presented a major health hazard. They required Ford to set up hearing tests for every employee at Sharonville. The results were shocking. At least 90% of the hourly work force had some hearing loss, with long term employees having lost up to 50% of their hearing. OSHA immediately mandated that Ford require every employee in the plant to get fitted for ear plugs.

Ford immediately made up a new safety rule: anyone caught without their ear plugs in would be subject to disciplinary action.

The biggest single source of noise was the 1600-ton presses. They sounded like artillery barrages on a battlefield. When they were both running, they could be heard a quarter mile from the plant.

OSHA required Ford to design gigantic lead lined folding doors to enclose each press. These folding doors would be closed when the presses were running, and would muffle the sound and reduce the overall noise level in the plant. They were so large, and so heavy that they had to be opened and closed with a hilo. When they were closed, the noise was concentrated, and forced upwards, and wiring and piping in the ceiling vibrated. The vibrations caused the sound to be carried further than it would have had the doors not been installed.

OSHA mandated that Ford set up an employee safety training program. Toward the end of the midnight shift Screaming Jim informed everybody that we had to stay over for a meeting. We were all shocked when we got to the salaried cafeteria and saw a table set up with coffee pots.

A foreman said, "Oh Shit. I ain't never seen them give us coffee. Why do I get the feeling this is going to be one long-ass meeting?"

The Men From Up North were all sitting at one table. One of them got up and identified himself as a Corporate Safety Officer. He droned on and on about safety. Then he passed out articles, and droned on some more. I got a second cup of coffee, and then a third. His voice began to sound like a good night lullaby. Screaming Jim poked me in the ribs as I drifted off.

I shook myself awake, and then started to drift off again. Jim leaned over and told me to kick the 285 foreman in the leg. His head was tilted back, his mouth was open, and he was snoring. I caught myself just before I fell off the chair, and I heard the Corporate Safety Officer say "...and now I will turn the meeting over to Roger, who will discuss the safety meetings in detail."

I was wide awake now, and whispered to Screaming Jim, "What is he talking about? What safety meetings?"

Jim screwed up his face up and spat, "If you would have been listening instead of being in Lala land, you would know. Now keep your fucking eyes open so you know what's going on."

Roger held up a short sleeved white shirt. The front left pocket had an embroidered "Ford" and the right pocket had "Supervisor" just like our red jackets. But the back of the shirt had bold black printing which stated: YOUR SAFETY IS MY BUSINESS.

Roger said, "From this day forward, Thursdays will not be Thursdays. They will be 'Safety Thursdays.' Each and every foreman and general foreman will be required to wear his Safety Shirt on Thursdays. There will be no exceptions. If you do not wear your Safety Shirt on Thursday a letter of reprimand will be placed in your file.

"The purpose of the Safety Shirt is to jog people's memory, and force them to remember to work safely. Each foreman will hold one safety meeting a month. This safety meeting will be held on the third Friday of each month. Why Friday? Because it's the day after Safety Thursday. People will be more aware of safety on a Friday, having seen their supervisors wear their Safety Shirts the previous day. Let no man here make any mistake about this. We WILL have a safe plant."

He paused, pointed in the general direction of the main factory floor. "People tend to forget about safety until there's an accident. That's what happened on the Case Line. An electrician forgot about safety. Now he's dead. These white Safety Shirts are to remind people that at Ford Motor Company, safety is job one. If your people fail to work safely, well, we have a solution for that too. It's called the form 4600.

"I want to emphasize that Safety Thursday is not required by OSHA. This is action taken over and above OSHA requirements. It shows OSHA that Ford is totally committed to a safe work environment. OSHA *does* require us to hold monthly safety meetings in each and every department on every shift, and we will certainly do that."

He looked around the room. Everyone remained silent, still struggling to stay awake, but trying to appear alert and interested.

Roger continued, "What will be involved in our monthly safety meetings? First and foremost is the record keeping."

Roger held up a piece of printed paper. "This is the safety meeting record sheet. Every foreman on every shift will be given one of these on the third Friday of each month. On the top left are the date, department, and shift. On the top right is a line for the foreman's name. Beneath that is a line for a description of the topic of the safety meeting. The lines in the body of the report are for the names and last four of each of your employees. The foreman will sign on the bottom, indicating that he talked to each and every man in his department about that safety topic on that date."

Even though nobody asked Roger any questions, he asked them for us. "What safety topics will be discussed? That is up to each individual foreman. Ford will provide a list of recommended topics, but a foreman can choose any safety topic. It can be safety at work, at home, on vacation, whatever. A man can be injured anywhere, not just at work. You can talk about safe driving habits, safety in the swimming pool, safety doing yard work. Any safety topic can be discussed."

The 252 foreman leaned over and whispered to Screaming Jim, "What the fuck, man? Are we supposed to flat shut down our department and talk about cutting your lawn and shit? What about our numbers? How are we supposed to make our numbers when everybody is standing around listening to us talk about swimming pools and shit?"

Screaming Jim shrugged his shoulders.

Roger continued, "No foreman will use safety meetings as an excuse for not making his numbers. The production requirements in each department will not change as a result of safety meetings. Safety is an integral part of each department, and not a separate item. No machines will be shut down and no production will be lost. Each foreman will go from machine to machine and talk to each employee about safety while he is running his machine."

When the meeting ended, everyone went to a table stacked with YOUR SAFETY IS MY BUSINESS shirts and picked out his size. On the way home I heard a news report that the government had proven a link between smoking and lung cancer. I had my first safety meeting topic.

The following Thursday there was a lot of eyeballing of the foremen. Red jackets had been replaced by Safety Thursday shirts.

We quickly grew tired of being asked, "If my safety is your business, then how come______."

A foreman would remove an ear plug, listen to the question/complaint, and say, "Go to hell."

The next day was Safety Meeting Friday. I retrieved my safety report and started at the front end of 258. Assembler one pulled out an ear plug and looked at me as I said, "You should not smoke. The government has proven that smoking causes lung cancer."

Number one looked at me like I had lost my mind. Then he lit up a cigarette, said, "Fuck you" and went back to work. I wrote his name and last four on my report and headed for the welders. I was lucky, because both the north welder operator and the welder set up man were together. I would only have to do my thing one time.

I went to them, passing through a cloud of toxic vapors containing highly carcinogenic nitrous oxide from the vaporization spewing off of steel that has been liquefied from high temperatures in the welding process.

Both men removed an ear plug and looked at me. I fanned the vapors out of my face and said, "You shouldn't smoke. The government has proven that smoking causes lung cancer."

The welder operator looked at the set up man, who shrugged. Then he looked back at me and said, "Huh?'

I repeated the safety message and he said, "Is this a joke or what?"

I left the front end of the department and headed down the aisle. My hilo driver nearly slid into me as he skidded across the oil slick floor. I motioned for him to stop. He removed an ear plug and bent down so he could hear me.

I said, "You shouldn't smoke. The government has proven that smoking causes lung cancer."

He had a puzzled look on his face. Then he said, "What did you say?"

I repeated my safety message, and he starred at me for a full half minute, as though he did not comprehend what I was saying or why.

Then he said, "OOOKay," put his ear plug in and gave me a strange look as he drove off. Then he stopped, put the hilo in reverse, backed up to me, took his ear plug out and said, "Say, Bob, are you feeling okay?"

Safety Thursdays and Safety Meeting Fridays continued for a couple months. Then I learned from the clerk that nobody even looked at the reports. She was told to maintain the files, in case OSHA pulled an audit. The foremen in Zone 5 were simply changing the dates on previous safety meeting reports and resubmitting them. No one noticed. The foremen in that zone had stopped giving safety talks three weeks prior.

I talked to the other foremen in Zone 3, and we decided to see if we could get away with that. The clerk got us copies of our last report, we changed the date, and resubmitted it. Nothing happened. The next month we did the same thing. I began to wonder what would happen if we failed to wear our Safety Thursday shirt on Thursday.

On Safety Thursday I fearlessly walked into Zone 3 wearing my red jacket. I got a lot of stares from envious foremen. Nobody really wanted to wear those goofy white shirts. Screaming Jim looked at my red jacket and said nothing. He did not want to wear the shirt either. The next

Thursday there was not a white shirt to be seen in Zone 3. No one was reprimanded.

Shortly after the discontinuance of Safety Thursday the men in the Press Room permanently opened the gigantic lead lined doors around the 1600-ton presses and never closed them again. OSHA was nowhere to be seen. The safety program at Sharonville had died a quiet death.

CHAPTER 13:
FOREIGN DEVILS

By the beginning of the following year, virtually every American-made vehicle was hitting the bottom of the quality charts. I talked with friends who worked at both GM and Chrysler. For every outrageous story I could tell them about Zone 3, they could counter with an even more outrageous experience. Ford Motor Company was not the only social and economic atrocity in corporate America. It was the entire auto industry.

Consumer's Report magazine advised people to avoid purchasing several models of Chrysler vehicles because they were being dumped onto the used car market by thousands of frustrated customers. They were, quite possibly, the worst-quality cars ever built in this country.

Lemon laws were passed in 33 states to protect customers from the Big Three when they refused to make good on poorly built vehicles that constantly broke down. Under the Lemon laws, people would have a comeback, even if the warranty had expired.

Japanese and German cars were in such high demand that you had to put your name on a waiting list to buy one. Their salesmen didn't have to do much selling, but rather just took orders because everyone was aware of the superior quality of imports over American-built cars. But Ford dealers sat on bulging inventories that few people were buying, even though they offered big discounts, zero percent financing and rebates. Chrysler offered a $50 check to any serious car buyer who was willing to test drive one of their cars. It was an act of total desperation.

Then Honda dropped the equivalent of another Pearl Harbor on Detroit when it announced that it was going to build an auto plant in Marysville, Ohio. Hondas would no longer struggle under the label of "import." They would be designed and built in America.

Before long, both Toyota and Nissan announced that they, too, were searching for appropriate locations to build auto plants in America. The flag waving card was being taken from the arsenal of marketing weapons of Detroit. They would soon have to compete with superior cars built in America by American workers.

There was a sense of impending doom at Sharonville that had never been present in past downturns. In previous recessions there were mass layoffs. But everyone knew that when the economy picked up again sales would boom, everyone would be recalled to their jobs, and all the lost wages would be more than made up for by nearly unlimited overtime.

But there was deep fear that something had changed, and the whole apple cart had been upended. This downturn would be like no other. This time there might not be any boom following the bust. What if people bought Hondas and Toyotas instead of Fords? Who in the hell did the Japs think they were, selling good quality cars in our market? Something had to be done, and it had to be done fast.

For the first time in history, Ford Motor Company and the United Auto Workers found themselves on the same side of the bargaining table. Survival of the industry depended on them working together instead of fighting each other. They would use their combined clout to fight the foreign devils.

Everyone at Sharonville had their own ideas about how to fight the foreign enemy. Every idea involved the heavy hand of government stepping in to smite the invaders and protect the innocent auto companies and their workers. There was no lone voice in the wilderness crying, "We did this to ourselves." It was like the emperor that wore no clothes. Everyone was aware, but no one wanted to see.

Langley, my outspoken black balancer set up man saw the problem as white oppressors being replaced by yellow oppressors.

Yet his solution was identical to that of the white auto workers. "Make laws. Why let them bastards bring their cars to America? If they want to sell cars, let them sell cars to their own people. Put a 100% tax on imports. Then we will see how many Hitler and Tojo cars people buy."

I asked Screaming Jim if he thought foreign cars threatened our jobs. He went into a fifteen minute vulgarity-laced rant that could be heard in the next zone.

"Hell no they ain't gonna be no threat. You wanna know what is gonna happen? Some turncoat traitor son of a bitch is gonna pull up at a stop light in his Toyota. Four or five guys is gonna open his door and pull his ass out of that Jap piece of crap. Then they are going to beat the living shit out of him. That will make the news. People all over the country will see it on TV. Pretty soon other guys, all over the place, will pull them traitors out of their imports and beat the shit out of them. Then people will be afraid to buy imported cars. That is what is going to happen."

Screaming Jim got a crazy look in his eye, like he was ready to start a riot. "How stupid do you think we are? Do you think we are going to be attacked, fight a war, and then let them come over here and take our jobs? We got a lot of dumb people in Washington, but they ain't that dumb. Chrisake, I was shooting them bastards a few years back. They killed my brother. Did you know them slant eyes killed my brother on Tarawa?

"We ain't gonna let them build no plants here either. For one thing, what American is gonna work for a fucking Jap? Ain't no American gonna go work in a Jap factory. But it don't matter, because there ain't gonna be no Jap factories in America. They try to build a Jap factory over here, somebody is gonna blow it up, just like they blowed us up at Pearl Harbor."

Screaming Jim shook his head and said, "People worry too much. They ain't got nothing to worry about. Sure, things is slowing down. But look at how busy we was for the last four years. We go like hell for three or four years, then the bottom drops out. People go on layoff for awhile. So what? They need the rest. Then things pick up, everybody gets called back, and we are back to normal.

"Let me tell you something. You get a few weekends off, you better enjoy it. Because when all this shit about bad quality and Jap cars blows over, we will be back on a seven day work schedule. Ain't nothing going to happen to Ford Motor Company. We are one of the biggest companies in the world."

The UAW held a press conference and demanded that we slap a 100 percent tariff on every imported car immediately. Ford, Chrysler, and General Motors appealed to the government to set strict import limits. Then the bumper sticker war started.

The first bumper sticker I saw read: *Are your kids hungry? Let them eat your import.* The next one I saw had a swastika: *Every time they sell a VW, Hitler's ghost smiles.* Another one stated: *The people that brought you Pearl Harbor now sell you Toyotas.*

If you were an auto worker and did not have a bumper sticker, your loyalty was suspect. Steel workers displayed bumper stickers in sympathy for their union brethren.

In Detroit, import hating grew to an art form. Foreign cars were shot at in the city, windows were smashed in parking lots, and travelers who owned imports were strongly advised to avoid driving in or near Detroit.

The United Auto Workers sponsored "import bashings" for the press. Imported cars were smashed with sledge hammers in front of TV cameras. Children of auto workers were aided in swinging sledge hammers by their fathers. Bystanders were invited to take a swing at an import. American Flags fluttered in the breeze, and a blown up picture of burning ships on Battleship Row on December 7, 1941 was displayed.

Articles about the economic consequences of losing our auto industry began to show up in newspaper editorials and in magazines. Dire consequences were predicted. The entire Midwest would become an economic wasteland where gangs of looters and anarchists roamed freely. There would be mass unemployment in the steel, glass, and plastic industries. Families would crumble, as men were unable to earn living wages. The entire middle class would be destroyed, and America would end up in the economic ash bin of history.

Yet with all the hand wringing and public whining, I saw no evidence whatsoever that anything had changed at Ford Motor Company to combat the foreign devils. It was business as usual at the Sharonville Transmission Plant. I was astounded that Ford did not seem to be taking a hard look at how it managed the company, so it could formulate a real plan about how to deal with the new foreign competitors.

That was when the letter arrived at my home.

It was a registered letter from Ford World Headquarters in Dearborn. It described a new initiative that Ford would be undertaking to revitalize the company by tapping the potential of all employees, both salaried and hourly. The new program was called the "*Let's Talk*" program.

Let's Talk would open up a communication channel between hourly employees and management. Every hourly employee would have an opportunity to communicate ideas directly to management via a paid suggestion program. No one was more qualified to analyze jobs and methods than the people who did those jobs every day. Ford wanted to hear from the employees themselves how things could be improved, and handsome rewards would be given.

Every single suggestion submitted would be given consideration. It could be an idea about improving quality, improving productivity, or making the work environment more conducive to producing good quality vehicles. If an employee's suggestion was accepted, and resulted in a cost savings, that employee would be paid, in cash, the full amount of the first year's savings.

Every Ford employee received a letter at home, sent from World Headquarters, detailing the *Let's Talk* program. The letter explained how important it was, in the face of the emerging foreign competition, for each of us to put forth any ideas we had that could help us better compete, and thus retain our jobs. This was the most important program in many years at Ford, and every employee was asked to put aside past differences with the company, in the common interests of everyone who looked to Ford to provide a living for his or her family.

Employees who made the best suggestions would be flown to Detroit, put up in a fancy hotel, and be treated to an appreciation dinner with top management and union officials. The Ford/UAW team would deal a fatal blow to the impudent foreign devils with the help of the *Let's Talk* initiative.

By the end of the week, suggestion forms and the ballot boxes for submission were placed throughout the plant. People were tearing off suggestion forms and there were animated discussions in every department about the program.

I had never seen anything like this at Ford. I began to question my harsh judgment of management. Maybe they were not hired thugs wearing neckties after all. Maybe they could actually turn this thing around and go head-to-head with the Japanese and German cars. Maybe Ford would not go belly up after all.

Roger scheduled a Zone 3 management meeting about the new program. We filed in after the midnight shift, bleary eyed, and sat down. Roger praised the new program and talked about the piles of good suggestions they were receiving about how to improve.

Then he clarified with, "Okay, *all* of them are not good, like the one that suggested all managers be fired and new managers 'who actually have brains' be hired. But most of them are good suggestions."

Then Roger got to the meat of what he wanted to say, but was too cautious to say in plain English.

"We will be having visitors in a few days. People from Up North will be visiting to talk up the new initiative. They will be walking around, talking to people. They will be encouraging them to come up with good ideas about how we can fight the Japs and Germans."

Larry had a way of cocking his head so he could see clearly with his one good eye and he said, "Are you saying the Men From Up North are gonna be walking around talking to the hourly?"

Roger nodded grimly and said, "Yes, Larry, the Detroit Mafia are not coming to talk to us. They are coming to talk to the hourly."

Larry shook his head in disbelief.

Ed scowled and muttered, "Holy Christ."

Screaming Jim said, "They can't do that. They're supposed to talk to us. We run this place. They tell us what they want and we get it from the hourly. What in the hell is going on? First they say we don't make good cars. Then they let the slant eyes and krauts in. Now them People From Up North want to go around us and talk to our people behind our backs?"

Roger did not respond to Screaming Jim, even though he knew that what he was saying was on the minds of everyone in the room, except for me. I thought the whole thing was funny and I could barely keep from laughing out loud. They were like kids who were caught with their hands in the cookie jar and now somebody was going to tell.

Roger said, "This *Let's Talk* thing is all about having everybody think about how we can improve operations. Ford is starring at a double barrel shotgun. The Japs are one barrel and the Germans are the other. The boys at the top think some of those sorry pieces of meat might have some ideas that we can use.

"Here is what we can do. I want you foremen to talk to your hourly. Tell them that these People From Up North are not here to listen to bitching and moaning. They are here to encourage them to think how we can do things better. Unless you have a good idea, don't talk to these people. Make them realize that what they tell them could make a difference on whether any of us has a job. Don't say this flat out, but let them know that the whole auto industry, including Ford, is talking about shutting down plants and consolidating production. Put the fear of God in them, but don't beat them over the head with it."

Larry said, "Yeah, let your people know that they ain't supposed to be talking about things that people up in Detroit don't need to know."

Roger nodded and looked around the room. He wanted to be sure that everyone understood that the communication between the hourly and the People From Up North be controlled.

Then he said, "I want everybody in this room to know what your people are saying to the Detroit Mafia. I want a full report. I want the names of the hourly that did the talking, and I want to know what they said."

More than a week passed and no one from Up North showed up at Sharonville. But suggestions were pouring in by the hundreds. They were routed first to the General Foremen in charge of the area where the improvement was suggested. If he rejected the idea, that was the end of it, and Ford sent a thank you for participating letter to the home of the person who turned in the suggestion. If the GF approved the suggestion, it was forwarded to engineering for further evaluation.

Screaming Jim had a stack of suggestions on his desk. He also had an "approved" rubber stamp and a "rejected" stamp. I watched him glance over a suggestion, stamp it rejected, throw it on top of a big pile of other rejections, and look at the next suggestion. Then he repeated the process. I asked Jim how the *Let's Talk* thing was going.

He shot me a disgusted look and said, "Look at all this shit. Every night I come in and Ed and Larry leave a pile of this shit on my desk.

They claim they don't have time to fuck with it, and I do because it can help to keep me awake. Rotten bastards."

I said, "But are you getting some good suggestions?"

"Hell no. These people ain't smart enough to have any ideas. Chrisake, half of this shit I can't even read because them people don't have good handwriting. If they was smart enough to have good ideas, why would they work at Ford? Here, look at this one. Have you ever seen such bullshit in all your life?"

I read the suggestion. A press operator observed that on both 1600-ton presses oil is used to absorb the tremendous heat of friction when the dies slam down onto cold rolled steel to stamp out parts. When the parts come out of the press they are dripping with oil. Then they go into a high temperature detergent bath that washes off all the oil. When they come out of the bath, two men stand at the end of the line, manually grab the parts, and dip them into oil to prevent flash rust while they are in storage.

The operator suggested that Ford could save a lot of money by eliminating the bath and the two men hand dipping parts. The parts are already covered in oil when they come out of the press.

Actually, I had personally wondered about that very same operation every time I worked overtime in the Press Room. It seemed wasteful and redundant. I asked Jim why he thought that this suggestion had no merit.

Screaming Jim scowled at me, rolled his eyes, and said, "Ain't you learned nothing at Ford? Do you know what kind of hell you get put through if you try to eliminate jobs? There are a lot of jobs that they could combine and eliminate around here, but nobody wants to do it. Do you remember the Coffee Pot War? You ain't seen nothing until you try to eliminate jobs. These people will cut our balls off and hand them back to us. I'm too old to fight anymore fucking wars. I got four years left until I get my pension. I ain't gonna fight no more shit than I have to until then."

I said, "But any suggestion at all will require us to change the way we do things. Why bother with a *Let's Talk* program if we're not going to try and change to remain competitive?"

Jim laughed cynically, shook his head, and said, "You think this *Let's Talk* thing is real, don't you? Well, it ain't real. It got nothing to do with making improvements. They are trying to get me fired before I get my pension. They ain't shitting me. I know how Ford operates. They squeeze out everything you got to give. Then they get rid of you before you can draw your pension."

I was thoroughly puzzled by his response and said, "The *Lets Talk* program is about getting you fired? I don't know what you mean."

Jim stamped another suggestion, threw it on the rejected pile, and said, "Okay, I'll spell it out for you. Let's say I come across a good suggestion that will save us a lot of money. I approve it, it goes to engineering, they approve it, and they put it in. The guy that wrote the suggestion gets a lot of money. Do you know what happens next?"

I shook my head and said, "No. What happens next?"

"I get called into Roger's office. He says you run the show out there. You should have seen this better way of doing things a long time ago. But you didn't. Some dumb-ass hourly man had to tell us how to do it. Now we gotta pay the sorry bastard a lot of money when it was your job to see a better way of doing things. You're fired, you dumb son of a bitch."

I looked at Jim in astonishment and knew at that moment that the *Let's Talk* program would fail. There was a Screaming Jim in every department on every shift in every plant that Ford owned. Any meaningful suggestion would die on the top of a pile of rejections on all the desks of all the Screaming Jims in the company. Ford Motor Company had no chance whatsoever of tapping the knowledge, experience, and ideas of anyone.

A few days later the Detroit Mafia showed up at Sharonville to talk up the program. They walked around in new coveralls on top of white shirts and neckties, with phony smiles, glad handing the hourly. Most paid them no mind. A few actually talked to them. On midnights and afternoons we felt lucky because it was highly doubtful the Men From Up North would show up on our shifts.

When the Detroit Mafia came to town, they were received like visiting royalty, put up in the most expensive hotels and wined and dined by local management who did not want them to look too closely at how things were done in the plants. They never showed up until nine or ten in the morning, after a leisurely, expensive breakfast, and they were gone by five. By eight they were at local watering holes on Ford's dime.

Unfortunately for midnights, one of the Detroit Mafia did not follow that script. I did not know he was at the back end of 258 talking to Langley, my embittered black balancer set up man. When I looked back and saw him, I dropped my clipboard and did a double take. What the hell was he doing in 258 at two in the morning? Why wasn't he out at some bar putting the make on a local floozy? I picked up my clipboard and headed for the south automatic balancer.

When I got to them they both looked at me, the Man From Up North noted my red jacket, nodded at me, and Langley continued his conversation. "So the converters are locked up, right? We take and put them on this machine and – "

The man interrupted Langley and said, "What does locked up mean? Are they supposed to be locked up?"

Langley said, "No, they ain't supposed to be locked up. Locked up means it won't turn inside. None of the parts will rotate. If the parts don't rotate when you put your car in gear, it ain't gonna go no place. The transmission won't work."

"But if it is supposed to rotate, why doesn't it rotate?"

Langley shrugged his shoulders and said, "Ain't no way to tell. The torque converter is welded together and filled with oil. The only way you could tell why it don't rotate would be to saw it in half and look inside. A converter can be locked up for a lot of reasons. The stator could be upside down. The assembler could have put two washers in instead of one. The cover plate could be mashed down too tight on the impellor when it got welded. You could have an egg-shaped impellor and a round cover plate, which might not give the parts room to turn on one side. It could be a lot of things."

The Detroit man said, "Did you say egg shaped? If the torque converter is round, why would the parts used to build it be egg shaped?"

I broke into the conversation and said, "I'm the foreman of 258. Is there anything I can do for you?"

He looked at me and said, "No, thank you. This man is explaining some of the problems he faces in making torque converters." Then he looked back at Langley, who continued.

"Sometimes they don't give the die setters time to shim the dies right so we get round parts. Sometimes we get egg-shaped parts. When that happens the assemblers have to beat the two parts together with lead hammers. Sometimes that makes the converter lock up because an egg-shaped part don't fit right into a round part."

The Detroit man was profusely jotting down notes. He asked Langley for his name and last four.

Then he said, "This is Department 258, is it not?" but before Langley could answer he said, "So torque converters come down this line and are locked up for a variety of reasons. How many are locked up?"

Langley twisted his head inquisitively and said, "It all depends. Sometimes we only get five or six in a shift. Other times we get a couple hundred. It got worse ever since Ford started to let shit get through from vendors without no inspection."

"What do you mean by 'let shit get through'?"

Langley said, "They used to inspect all the components that we bought from vendors. But Ford wanted to save money and they arm twisted the vendors to cut their costs. One way to cut their costs was to cut way back on inspection. There was a time when every part that came into Sharonville was inspected. But now every one hundredth part that comes in gets inspected. We get bolts with no threads on them. We get plastic stators that are chipped and cracked. We get all kinds of shit that we never got when everything was inspected."

The man jotted down more notes. Then asked, "What do you do with locked up converters?"

Langley said, "We put them on this here expander. It pumps in pressure to force the sides out on the converter. That gives the parts more room to rotate. Once everything is loose inside, the converter will rotate internally."

"But does that solve the problem? If the insides are pushed out, won't the parts get knocked out of place or something? I am far from an expert on quality. But it seems to me that by blowing these converters out you run risks that other things are going to go wrong with them."

Langley said, "Well, to be honest, I wouldn't want an expanded converter in my car. But they seem to do all right, at least until the warranty is up. We don't get many expanded converters that fail in 12,000 miles. Nobody knows what happens after 12,000 miles because then it's not Ford's problem."

I headed for the zone office. I thought Screaming Jim's head might explode when I told him about the Man From Up North talking to

Langley. He had no idea that the Detroit Mafia would be in the plant on the midnight shift. He instructed me to write down everything that I could remember that Langley talked about.

After Screaming Jim gave his end of shift ass-chewing to every foreman, he and I and the Press Room foreman went to Roger's office. Jim had already given him notes on what the man had heard from Langley and from Carter in the Press Room. Jim and the other foreman were on edge, but I thought this entire episode was hilarious. Ever since my trip to Rollman's, I refused to let Ford Motor Company get me down.

Larry was already in Roger's office when we arrived. Roger said, "I don't think I have to tell you how much damage was done by your people talking to the Guy From Up North. The Detroit Mafia is looking for scapegoats. Someone has to pay a price for all this bad publicity about quality. After he left 258 he went to the Press Room and Carter, the 1600-ton operator that works with that hick who sells coffee, gave him an ear full about the Press Room. Langley and Carter gave the Detroit Mafia enough rope to hang us all."

Jim and the Press Room foreman looked at the floor like scolded children. Larry was shaking his head like a mourner at a funeral, but I had a hard time keeping myself from laughing. I no longer cared who swung from the gallows. I had no debt, was saving my money to break free, and ready to watch Ford go the way of all badly managed corporations.

Roger said, "I don't know what's going to happen. What I do know is this: I want Langley and Carter! What we are about to go through is all their fault. I want 4600s on those sorry pieces of shit. If it is my last act at Ford Motor Company, I will sign their termination papers. I don't care what you have to do to get 4600s. Follow them around, watch them like hawks, whatever it takes. Lie if you have to. But bring me 4600s."

As I was leaving the plant I remembered that Langley was staying over four hours to cover an absence on the day shift. I swung by the south balancer. Langley had his head stuck in the balancer, making adjustments.

I said, "Roger is pissed. I mean really pissed. He wants your head on a platter. Be careful."

Langley pulled his head out and said, "Thanks for the warning. But that half pint honky son of a bitch ain't smart enough to nail my black ass."

CHAPTER 14:
THE END OF THE SHARONVILLE COMEDY

The closer Ford seemed to get to the end of their rope, the more amusing every incident became to me. I felt that Ford and the UAW had dug their own grave, were standing and looking down into it, and did not recognize it.

The seven day production schedule continued, even as finished transmissions overstocked the warehouse. The nightly news hammered on about how unsold American-made cars were clogging dealer's lots, while Volkswagens and Toyotas could not be imported fast enough to meet demand.

Tension hung thickly in the air at Sharonville, and a bunker mentality prevailed in both management and the union. Just as Hitler and his henchmen pretended that victory was just around the corner even as Russian artillery shells exploded nearby, the Sharonville plant continued business as usual. But each incident of conflict caused tempers to explode like never before.

It was on a holiday that the UAW tried to get me fired. Every holiday was a triple time day. I always tried my best to get maximum production when Ford was paying us all three times our normal pay. I let nothing stand in the way of making my full quota of torque converters. That is why I became concerned when the south Inteco jammed, and converters were backing up all the way to the two south welders.

I knew the machine had simply jumped out of cycle, and that the simple solution was to push the reset button to restart the machine. I waited for Langley to do it. But the converters continued to back up, and Langley was no where in sight.

I climbed the step-over ladder that straddled the conveyor and went back to the south balancer. No one had seen Langley for awhile. I asked the burr hand to push the reset button and restart the machine. But he said, "Are you crazy? You want me to do set up work on overtime? I will do it if you order me to, but I want to see a committeeman. Pushing that button is the set up man's job."

I turned around and pushed the reset button myself. The Inteco groaned, hissed, clanked, and started back up. I watched approvingly as the line of converters on the conveyor started moving. Then I turned around to go back to my desk and almost ran over top of Langley.

He was so angry that his lips were trembling. He tried to speak, but the words fell out of his mouth like a backfiring motorcycle.

"You pushed the reset button. This is an overtime day. You are management and you did setup work. Get me a committeeman, and I mean right now, Jack."

I was in Roger's office. Screaming Jim and Larry sat in chairs on either side of me, as if to protect me from the storm that I was about to face. They each glanced at me as you might look at a corpse laid out at a wake. Roger tapped his pen on his desk and looked at his watch.

The door opened. The Salaried Personnel Manager came in, nodded to Roger, who nodded back, and took the seat at the end of the table. This was going to be Judgment at Nuremburg and I did not give a hairy rat's ass.

The door opened again. Committeemen started filing in like people at a restroom during intermission. The Chairman of UAW local 863 came in first. He was followed by every committeeman that I had worked with for the past six years at Ford Motor Company. They sat at the opposite side of the table from Screaming Jim, myself, Larry, and Roger and took up the entire table and then some. They had blood in their eyes. They had a foreman dead to rights, and intended to nail me to a cross.

I, the accused, was to sit at the end of the table opposite the Salaried Personnel Manager. I got up and moved to that position. My defenders, Larry, Screaming Jim, and Roger sat to my left. My accusers, the gang of committeemen, sat to my right. The judge of all things contractual, the Salaried Personnel Manager, faced the accused, which was me. Chairs squeaked, throats cleared, and the hearing began.

The Salaried Personnel Manager said, "Foreman Dewar, you are charged with violating the labor contract by performing hourly work. I will now hear the specifics of that very serious charge."

All eyes turned to the Chairman of UAW local 863. He cleared his throat, addressed the Salaried Personnel Manager in a clear and loud voice.

"This here foreman went and pushed a reset button on a machine in Department 258. It was on overtime, fer Chrisake. It wasn't bad enough that he done hourly work. He went and done it on overtime, which makes it twice as bad. If management ain't got enough hourly men to run the department, then by Gawd they ought to bring more men in on overtime instead of having management do hourly work. I want this foreman fired."

All eyes turned to me. The entire situation was ridiculous to me, and I must have been smirking.

The Chairman was clearly upset, and raised his voice, "Do you think this is funny? You wrote up men for minor offenses and never batted an eye. Now we caught you violating the contract and you got the nerve to sit there and laugh?"

The Salaried Personnel Manager said, "Foreman Dewar, you will change your attitude immediately. This is a formal management disciplinary hearing. There is nothing funny here, and I will not tolerate your blatant display of disrespect for these proceedings."

I tried to make a straight face, but it was difficult. I was getting very sleepy. I had been at Sharonville for more than fifteen hours, making triple-time pay – more money than most people make in two weeks. I was still on overtime as I sat there being charged with the crime of pushing a button. My head started to droop, and Screaming Jim kicked my leg under the table.

Larry said, "How do we know that Foreman Dewar pushed that button? Do we have any management witnesses that saw him, or are we merely taking the word of an hourly man? I protest having one of my best foreman harassed on the basis of hearsay, and I respectfully request that this hearing be terminated without prejudice."

The Chairman said, "You want witnesses? We got plenty of witnesses. We got the set up man. We got the burr hand. We got the whole damn department that knowed that line was backed up, seen Dewar climb over the conveyor, then seen the line start back up again. Was no possible way nobody else could have pushed that reset button but Dewar."

Screaming Jim said, "I want credible witnesses. I want management witnesses. Hourly men will say any damn thing you tell them to say. I do not accept the word of hourly men who claim to have seen management violating the contract."

I caught myself before my head drooped completely down and said, "I pushed the reset button. The line was backed up. We were losing production. The set up man was no where to be seen. My entire department was being paid triple time on the holiday. My job is to produce torque converters. That is why Ford gives me a pay check. I pushed that button and got that line moving. Throw me down in the coliseum and let the lions rip me apart. I pushed the damn reset button."

There was a total, shocked silence in the room. Every face but mine had a blank, uncomprehending gaze. I had just admitted, in a formal hearing, in front of management and the union, to willfully violating the labor contract. This was, quite possibly, the first time in the history of Ford Motor Company that a member of management had been open and honest.

The Salaried Personnel Manager slowly shook his head and said, "Foreman Dewar, you leave me no choice. A severe letter of reprimand will be placed in your file. This letter will remain in your file for as long as you are employed by Ford Motor Company. It will document your blatant violation of the labor contract, as well as your disrespectful attitude. This letter will be a factor in all future considerations, including merit raises and promotions. Do you have any questions, Foreman Dewar?"

I said, "Yes, I do. Can I go home now? If I can't, I am going to lay my head on this table and go to sleep. You might want to add that to your letter."

The *Let's Talk* initiative died a relatively fast, but dirty death at Sharonville. It did not take long for enthusiasm for writing suggestions to die when people realized that Ford was never going to change, and that any suggestion to improve operations would inevitably involve chipping away at some group's power base and eliminating jobs.

Suggestions stopped coming in, and the suggestion boxes quickly became coated with a heavy layer of filth from the air. The box by the time clock became the target for spitting contests when men were lined up to clock out. A few token suggestions that did not compromise any group's power base were accepted, and a $50 prize was awarded in ceremonies that were laughable. All the suggestion boxes were removed when someone stuffed a zip lock bag full of human excrement in one of the slots. The *Let's Talk* program was over.

The Friday after the hearing that disciplined the management criminal Foreman Dewar, all weekend overtime was eliminated. Once again, the warehouse was chock full of finished transmissions that could not be shipped to assembly plants that were partially shut down. Once again, power shifted from production management to Quality Control Management, and the graveyard of rejected parts grew like a cancer. I had seen this movie before, and it was getting boring.

Although I was no longer working weekends, and was able to reconnect with my wife and children, I was still working plenty of overtime. Five days a week I was either called in four hours early, or held over four hours at the end of my shift, or both. Foremen all over the plant were jumping ship like rats off the Titanic.

There was a general feeling throughout the corporation that this would be no ordinary downturn. There would not be the inevitable recovery, and the inevitable recalling of laid off workers. This time Ford faced real competition, and the way it managed its business, and the shoddy products it produced would not stand up to that competition. No one believed that Washington could continue, without end, to protect an uncompetitive business.

People at all levels of the company that had any real skills or education, and were not close to retirement, had their resumes circulating. When a foreman received a job offer at another company, he was gone. I found myself working overtime in departments outside of Zone 3 that

I had no clue how to manage. It did not matter. Ford had a red jacket to stand at the desk, and that was all that mattered.

I was continuing to document the unraveling of Ford, but unfortunately my "insider" clerk jumped ship. She left a handwritten note in my mail slot stating she was moving to Houston where her fiancé, who worked at NASA, was able to line her up with a good job. She wished me well.

I was called in early to cover the back half of the afternoon shift in 258 and Langley was also called in early. Langley and I avoided each other as much as possible. He tried to get me fired as well as other white foremen, but failed. As long as he did his job I let him alone.

It was a little after nine, and Screaming Jim had also come in early. He was heading toward my desk which seemed peculiar as he normally stayed in the office and worked crossword puzzles, even on overtime. He said there was a phone call in the office. Some woman, it sounded like, was screaming and crying. As best he could make out, she wanted to talk to somebody in 258. I hurried to the office.

I did not recognize the voice and she was in a panic. There was some kind of fire. A huge fire and someone was trapped. I tried to get her to calm down. I was finally able to understand that she was Langley's wife. I ran to 258 to get Langley to the phone.

Langley took the phone and blood drained from his face. He pulled off his safety glasses. Tears welled up in his eyes.

He said, "Oh, my God. How do they know she didn't get out?"

Then he slammed the phone down, threw his safety glasses up against the wall, groaned a strange, throaty noise, ran from the office, and sprinted down the aisle like an Olympic runner. I looked at Screaming Jim. He had a devious grin on his face.

Jim said, "If that nigger just left the plant, and I would bet my last dollar that he did, you flat got him by the balls. I count five violations. Number one is using the management phone. Number two is destruction of company property – safety glasses. Number three is going out on the floor without no safety glasses on. Number four is running in the plant. Number five is leaving his job without permission.

"That coon tried to get you fired over pushing a button. You never did nail him a while back when he ran at the mouth about expanded converters to the Detroit Mafia. Roger's balls is still frosted over than one. You wanna get back in the good graces of Roger you will nail that son of a bitch to the cross. If you don't, you ain't got a hair on your ass."

I said, "Jim, don't you think that we ought to find out what that phone call was all about before we plot to crucify Langley?"

"I give less than a damn about that phone call. What I care about is nailing that son of a bitch when we have a chance. He is smart enough that he don't give us a chance to nail him. Now we got one big ass chance. Don't blow it."

When I got home my wife asked if I had heard about the big fire at the Beverly Hills Supper Club in Northern Kentucky. It burned to the ground. Exit doors were locked. People tried to get out and burned bodies were stacked like cord wood in front of exit doors that would not open. The morning news was calling it one of the deadliest fires in American history. I told her about Langley and the phone call. I knew that his mother was a waitress at the Beverly Hills.

The contract gave Langley three days of paid bereavement leave. On the second day I found myself sitting in Roger's office, along with Screaming Jim and Larry.

Roger said, "I don't expect that you will waste any time when Langley gets back. Schedule a hearing with Labor Relations and the committeeman now. We will not let him return to his job. We will schedule the hearing at the beginning of the shift when he gets back."

I was absolutely revolted and sickened by Ford. I looked at Roger incredulously and said, "Roger, a man just lost his mother. She was burned to death. Are you saying that you want me to write this man up?"

"I want the full five step penalty sequence carried out in one step. We can jump penalty and terminate Langley. An employee's personal life is of no concern to Ford Motor Company. We all have our problems. We all have to deal with our problems, and come in to work, follow the rules, and give a fair day's work for a fair day's pay. This is a very clear cut case. The union will grieve the termination, but will have no leg to stand on. The series of violations were witnessed by two members of management."

There was a moment of silence, and all eyes were on me. I alone could hold the hearing, since I was Langley's supervisor. I looked into the eyes of Screaming Jim and saw a thirst for vengeance. I looked into the hard, cold, black eyes of Roger and saw no hint of emotion, just the monotonous stare of a functionary insisting on striking a blow when the opportunity arose.

I shook my head with conviction and said, "I cannot and will not take action against a man who just lost his mother under these horrible circumstances. There has to be some humanity in our actions. We cannot simply go by hard and fast rules. While I'm pissed at Langley, he is still a human being, and I will not stoop to kicking him in the teeth when he is down."

Roger was so mad the paper he was holding was shaking in his hands. He said, "You will take action against Mr. Langley, or I will take action against you. This is clear evidence to me that you cannot control the men in your department."

I said, "Well, Roger, you do what you have to do. My name is not Himmler or Eichman. You hired me to be a manager. You did not hire me as a hit man. I am tired, and I am going home."

As I got up to leave, Screaming Jim said, "You better think about this."

I left Roger's office, went home, and pulled out all my financial information. I looked at the *Paid in Full* stamp on my mortgage. I did some mental math. There was enough money for us to live for two full years. I put the records away, went to bed, and slept like a baby.

When I got to 258 the next night, Screaming Jim met me at the time clock. He said not to bother checking for absences; I would not be running Department 258 anymore. I was to go to the zone office and wait for him.

Jim had a grim expression when he came to the office. He sat down, took his safety glasses off, rubbed his eyes, and said, "Did you hear about Larry?"

"Did I hear what about Larry?"

"Larry had a heart attack. Right out on the floor in front of 251. He was chewing ass on that new foreman that ain't worth a pint of piss. The new college punk they hired. You know the one that I mean."

I nodded my head. Everyone in Zone 3 knew him. He was an arrogant air head that strutted around bragging about his degree in business administration. No one liked him, and he could not run 251.

Jim continued, "Larry turned white, started twitching, gasped for breath, grabbed his chest, and went down. That punk son of a bitch stood and looked down at him. Then he took his safety glasses off, pitched them up the aisle, and walked out of the plant. Ain't nobody seen him since. I don't imagine he will be back. A hilo driver saw Larry on the floor and called security. Right now he is in intensive care. It looks like he is going to be okay, but nobody can say for sure. That is why you ain't gonna run 258 no more."

I said, "So I am going to run 251 on days? Who is going to run 258 on midnights?"

Screaming Jim said, "No, you ain't going no place. You are staying right here. You have been promoted to my job. I am going to days to replace Ed, who will replace Larry. They hired a new foreman to run 258. He should be here any time now. Your next pay check will see a 12% bump. You are now a general foreman."

I fell silent and starred at Jim in amazement. I had fully expected to be fired. Instead, I was promoted. Was there no end to the mysteries and intrigues of Ford Motor Company?

I said, "Let me get this straight. You are the new Ed. Ed is the new Larry. I am the new Jim."

"Yeah, you got it right. We oughtta have a new foreman show up any minute now."

As I struggled to digest this information, I saw a young man in a suit and tie hesitantly come into the office. He still had a hint of acne, and I had no doubt that this was his first job out of college.

He said, "Excuse me, sir. I am supposed to report to a Mr. Dewar."

"I'm Bob Dewar."

"Mister Dewar, I'm Frank Carpenter. They said that I was to report to you and you would assign me to Department 258."

I studied Frank Carpenter and tried to look like a general foreman. Then I said, "Frank, Department 258 is a bitch and a half. You have got to let those men know who is boss. If you don't they will cut your balls off. If you want them to work, they have to be afraid of you. Do you think you can handle that?"

Frank said, "Oh, yes sir. I managed four guys at a pizza shop in Columbus. I can handle anything."

I nodded and said, "Okay Frank, I will give you a shot. But don't call me sir. I work for a living. Let me tell you this, I expect you to get me

2,400 converters out of 258, or a stack of 4600s, and I don't care which it is. Do you know what a 4600 is Frank?"

"No, sir, I don't"

"Don't call me sir. I put my pants on the same way you do. A 4600 is a formal disciplinary form. A man does his job or you rack his ass with a 4600. Do you understand that, Frank?"

Frank swallowed hard and said, "Yes, I do."

"Good. Then we understand each other. Now get on out to 258. I will be out in a few minutes to get you broke in."

Frank had a semi terrified look on his face as he went out the door. After he left Screaming Jim said, "You son of a bitch. You are a lousy, hypocritical son of a bitch."

I burst out laughing and said, "I have wanted to do that since the first day I started at Ford. You see, Jim, I am a secret admirer of general foreman. When I grow up, I want to be just like you."

"Go to hell, Dewar."

The Langley issue was swallowed up by the heavy negativism that blanketed the plant. It seemed like every day the mood became more depressed as people waited for the end. There were no consequences for my refusal to take action against Langley. All joking disappeared from Sharonville. I had few problems adapting to my new role as GF. Everyone did their jobs because they worried about the future. There was no room for the typical nonsense. Everyone knew that all of our jobs hung in the balance. There is no more powerful motivator than fear.

That October a delegation of the Detroit Mafia came to Sharonville. Everyone knew that they were not coming to deliver cheerful news. They were grim faced. This time no one jumped up on a table. Instead, big speakers had been installed all around the salaried cafeteria and the Man From Up North talked into a microphone.

"Gentlemen, I do not have to tell you that our entire industry faces some daunting challenges. Sales have essentially collapsed. Our government has chosen to abandon us and let foreign manufacturers come in and rape us and steal our markets. I would appeal to every person in this room to sit down and write letters to your congressmen and senators about this despicable economic betrayal.

"I will get right to the point of this meeting. Ford Motor Company is forced to make massive production cutbacks. Some plants will be closed. Others will have vastly reduced production schedules. In the case of Sharonville, the plant will remain open, but there certainly will be major changes."

Everyone in the room sat quietly, solemnly listening. I had to imagine nobody was entirely surprised by the news.

The man continued, "Before I get to the specifics of those changes, let me say this: The Sharonville Transmission Plant has the lowest quality rating of any plant in the entire transmission and chassis division. Both Sharonville and Livonia manufacture the C-4, but Livonia has better quality and better efficiency. Obviously, if a transmission plant has to be shut down, it will most likely be Sharonville. You should all endeavor to improve quality and productivity in the interests of keeping this plant open. I do not want to dwell on this point, but I do want to make sure that every man in this room understands it.

"Okay, here is what is going to happen right now. The Fairfax Plant will be closed permanently. The entire management group from that plant will be transferred to Sharonville. The hourly workers at Sharonville will be reduced from just under 5,000 to just over 2,500. The cutoff point, I believe, is twenty years. If an hourly employee has less than 20 years at Ford, he or she will be laid off."

People in the room were getting visibly antsy, one foreman started sweating and wiping his brow, but nobody said anything, and the grim news continued.

"What does this mean to the people in this room? It means that by cutting our work force in half we will end up with far more foremen, general foremen and superintendents than we can utilize. But there is more. When the entire management group from Fairfax arrives, which will occur in dribbles over the next several weeks, we will have approximately three management people for every management job. I do not believe that I need to explain why we cannot keep on the payroll three people for every one job.

"Gentlemen, I have the very unpleasant task of announcing to you that for the first time since the Great Depression, Ford Motor Company is forced to lay off management people. I think everyone in this room knows that we have no real choice in this matter, regardless of our past policy of always retaining our knowledge and skill base. In past downturns, we could project ahead the need for these people when the economy turned around. Unfortunately, as we project ahead today, we can see no upturn that would justify retaining management people that we cannot use presently. Indeed, there are some in upper management who project that Ford Motor Company has already seen its peak employment numbers."

I was thinking about my bank account, and relieved about my financial status, but looking around the room, I noted panic in the eyes of several foremen who would be hard-pressed to get work elsewhere. Some were shaking their heads, looking at the ground in disbelief.

"How will we choose who stays and who leaves? We will follow the same basic pattern as we do with the hourly. That is, seniority will rule. The only exception would be in cases where a man has several unsatisfactory performance reviews and/or letters of reprimand. Those cases will be thoroughly investigated, and there may be cases where a higher seniority manager is let go in favor of a better performing lower seniority man. When this meeting is over, each zone office will have the layoff schedule posted.

"Let me end this meeting on a positive note. It is a very positive note, indeed. Ford has broken ground on a new transmission plant right here in Ohio. It will be located at Batavia, twenty five miles east of Cincinnati. When this plant is completed in two years, those of you who get laid off may well find employment at our new Batavia Transmission Plant.

"The Batavia Plant will have the most sophisticated, high technology equipment of any plant in the world. It will produce the best quality, most gas efficient front wheel drive transmission in the world. In fact, Ford fully expects to supply some of our foreign competitors with transmissions from Batavia because they will be far superior to anything that Toyota, Nissan, VW, or any of the rest of the imports can produce. This means that the imports that are giving us problems now will provide jobs for us later."

The layoff schedule was posted in the zone office. Every foreman with less than 20 years seniority was on the list. The list was staggered, with a few foremen being let go each week over a two month period. My name was listed, and I was the only GF to be laid off. All the others had been at Ford for over two decades. Every foreman and general foreman in the plant who was a college graduate was being let go, while the likes of

Screaming Jim, Ed, and Larry were being retained. It was the equivalent of throwing out the baby with the bath water.

My last act as general foreman was to lay off Frank Carpenter. Then I was reduced back to foreman of 258, midnight shift. Larry came back to work, and was infuriated that he would not have a chance to fire the foreman who walked away and left him lying on the floor. The midnight shift was eliminated, and we all went to the day shift.

There were so many foremen and general foremen milling around that they kept bumping into each other. Everyone tried to keep busy in order to not think about the future.

When my turn came I turned in my red jacket, safety glasses, and Ford I.D. card. I thanked every man who had worked for me for helping to make 258 a successful department, and wished them well.

Even though I felt a tremendous sense of liberation as I left Sharonville for the last time, I also felt sadness. I knew that many of those people would never again find work that paid the kind of money that they had made at Ford Motor Company, and that their lives would be turned topsy-turvy because of it. In fact, over the next two years I learned of five divorces and one suicide of men who had worked for me in Department 258.

EPILOGUE

Escape from economic bondage was actually frightening. We had no debt, and saved enough money to live for two years without income. But we had two kids with a third due shortly, and no future income stream. Ford classified me as laid off and continued to carry my medical insurance, but I did not know how long that would last. I wanted to work for myself as I had lost all trust in corporate America. My trust was in hard work, dedication, and purpose in life and none of these things were rewarded in the corporate world. I had worked hard and played by all the rules in life, but somehow had ended up with the bad guys.

Some of my friends advised that I should go to a smaller company. P&G and Ford Motor Company were richer than some small countries, and more corrupt than South American dictatorships, but there are a lot of smaller companies out there that operate much differently than corporate behemoths. As I contemplated my next step in life, surprises started arriving in my mail box.

First, there was a check for $6,000, tax free, from the U.S. government. They ruled that the massive layoffs in the auto industry resulted from "unfair foreign competition." Under something called the "Trade Readjustment Act" we were all entitled to tax-free compensation from the government.

Then I received a letter from Ford corporate headquarters advising that I was eligible to receive 95 percent of my base salary for a period of six months, and all of my benefits would be in effect for that time period. In addition, I was eligible for full unemployment compensation from the State of Ohio. All together I would have an income equal to my Ford pay, including overtime, for six months, even though I had no job.

I spent that time investigating business opportunities. But all I saw were franchises that were nothing more than extensions of some gigantic corporation. I was expected to put up my money, and they would tell me precisely what to do. I would take all the risks and put in all the work. If I was successful, they would skim off a major part of my profits without having any money at risk. If I failed, they would lose nothing, and I would lose everything.

The franchise option seemed like nothing more than a variation on the corporate oppression that I had seen at P&G and Ford. I would not be working for myself and my family; I would be working to enrich some corporation. I started investigating the option of working for a smaller company.

I interviewed with Signode Industries, and they offered me employment as a Plant Superintendent. I would be in charge of everything. Signode was a small company that operated like a big family. There was no hostility, distrust, or labor union. Management and hourly workers had golf leagues, bowling leagues and often socialized. Signode was truly a world apart from the cartoon life of a Proctoid or the prison-like Sharonville Transmission Plant. I began to wonder if I had been wrong in using the same brush stroke to paint all corporations. Maybe only the big ones were bad guys.

From the perspective of hindsight, I feel that Ford Motor Company operated similarly as organized crime syndicates. Yet it was a respected member of the corporate community, and nothing that it did was considered a criminal act. In fact, Henry Ford has been packaged as an American hero and sold to the American people as a national icon. I could think of nothing more ironic.

Over the years, I've continued to read everything published about the U.S. auto industry. Just as I expected, there is continued deterioration. The Big Three struggle to compete with better managed foreign companies who build better cars.

Chrysler slipped into bankruptcy, and Lee Iacocca went to Washington to beg the government to save the company. I found it incredible that he walked away with more than one billion dollars of taxpayer money, and we all paid to subsidize bad management. What about free markets? What happened to "may the best man win"?

Numerous articles and books about the auto industry kept Detroit's mismanagement in the public eye. Newspapers, magazines, and TV news reported on the 160 fires in Ford Escorts and Mercury Lynxes that were being probed by Federal Safety officials. Harper's magazine published an article entitled, The Wreck of the Auto Industry. GM was forced to recall 77,000 defective vehicles. A book entitled, The Decline and Fall of the American Auto Industry was featured in the Fortune Magazine Book Club. Yet none of these fine pieces of writing delved into the root of Detroit's problems – what is happening inside the auto plants and how the auto companies treated employees and customers.

While these articles zeroed in on the big picture of Detroit's problems, a breaking news story had a direct link to the Sharonville Transmission Plant. The National Highway Traffic Safety Administration issued the largest recall in auto history. Sixteen million Ford, Lincoln, and Mercury vehicles were ordered recalled for defective automatic transmissions. Every transmission that Ford manufactured during my six-year tenure was ruled defective.

The most dangerous, but certainly not the only defect was transmissions jumping out of park and into reverse. More than one hundred people were run over and killed when they put their car in park, and were retrieving items from their trunks. More than a thousand more were injured. Transmissions that leaked oil, or failed shortly after warranty expiration, or had torque converter wipeouts paled in comparison to the deaths and injuries from jumping from park into reverse.

Ford made an urgent plea to the White House to void this recall. If Ford was forced to recall and repair sixteen million vehicles, it would be forced into bankruptcy. This would push hundreds of thousands of people onto the unemployment roles, and probably cause a severe recession just as the U.S. was pulling out of a recession. If the government could save Chrysler, why could it not save Ford?

I felt that the moment had arrived for Ford Motor Company to be judged in the court of public opinion for the economic crimes it had committed at Sharonville. Surely more than one hundred deaths and over one thousand injuries would spark interest into how Ford Motor Company built transmissions. But I could not have been more wrong.

The Wall Street Journal reported on lawsuits that were being filed against Ford for deaths and injuries from defective transmissions. A Ford engineer came forward and reported that he had sent a memo to upper management warning of a design defect in C-4 transmissions that could cause injury or death.

That engineer died at a young age, and his wife sued Ford on the grounds that the company brought about the man's death through unbearable stress and harassment to keep his mouth shut. Ford Motor Company became the only corporation in American history to be charged with reckless homicide because of transmissions that were built at Sharonville.

Incredibly, the Reagan Administration complied with Ford's urgent request. With the stroke of a pen, President Reagan removed the authority of the National Highway Traffic Safety Administration to issue auto recalls. They could issue safety advisories, but they could not order auto recalls. Ford was instructed to mail out sixteen million stickers advising Ford, Lincoln, and Mercury owners that the transmissions in their cars could cause injury or death.

It was incomprehensible to me that the United States government would put the financial interests of a gigantic corporation above the safety of American citizens. I began to wonder if writing this book would be dangerous to publish. I had no doubt whatsoever that Ford would not hesitate to harm me or my family if laid bare economic crimes and social deviance in their car plants.

If Ford did take action against me, my wife, or my children, I felt that I could count on no protection from the government. If they looked the other way while more than a hundred people were killed, why would they protect my family? If Ford harassed one of their own engineers, causing his early death, because he spilled the beans, what would stop them from coming after me and my family? In my mind, Ford Motor Company was on the same moral level as organized crime, and I had a wife and three small children to protect.

I purchased file boxes and carefully inserted my partially written book, my documentation, and notes that I had made while running 258 and stored them in my attic. They laid there for twenty five years. I vowed that I would write my book one day, when I no longer feared retributions from Ford. I felt that sooner or later Ford would be given enough rope to hang itself and the American taxpayer would tire of bailing out a badly mismanaged industry. When that day arrives I would retrieve my file boxes and finish A Savage Factory.

I kept my eye on Ford and events in the auto industry. The new, high technology transmission plant was opened at Batavia. Ford invited the news media to record the historic event of a state-of-the-art Ford plant that would blow away all competition. Meanwhile, people were being burned to death from rear end collisions in Pintos, and Ford SUVs were rolling over on sharp turns. Yet Ford was again profitable, and had recalled many of the laid off workers, including me. I refused, and terminated my relationship with Ford.

I was happy as a Plant Superintendent at Signode Industries. It was a close knit, well managed company that produced very high quality hand tools and steel strapping. I was able to work a leisurely 50-hour work week and spend every weekend and holiday with my family. Then it all came to an end.

A giant corporation swallowed up Signode Industries like a great white shark snatching a baby seal. More than 90 percent of the employees were laid off, and once again, I lost my job. Signode became a minor division of Illinois Tool Works.

But I had never lost my dream of breaking free from corporate bondage and having my own business. While I was happy at Signode, I had seen enough to never fully trust a corporation, and continued to tuck money aside for the day that I would strike out on my own.

My wife and I hunkered down and squeezed every unnecessary dime from our budget. I installed a wood burning stove, bought a chain saw, and we cut our heating costs in half. We planted an immense vegetable garden, grew nearly all of our own food, and reduced our food costs by a colossal amount. My wife became the family barber and tailor. We got ready to tough out the rough early years of a new business.

Our new business would not only provide us with a sane, reasonable living, it would be a training ground for our three children. They worked with us in our new business, and learned the difference between what they wanted and what they needed. If they wanted things that were over and above their needs, they could work for us to earn the money to buy those things. They quickly learned the value of money, and that they did not need most of the things that advertising was trying to cram down their throats.

We started a packaging business, packing and shipping for retail and commercial customers. Later we expanded and began selling packaging supplies to small businesses. Our business was a success, and is now in its twenty third year of operation. We have a retail store, a warehouse, two delivery trucks, and three employees. Our small business enabled us to help our three children achieve college degrees. All three are now successful professionals. We were also able to accumulate substantial retirement investments. We have broken free of economic bondage and corporate tyranny.

I have had three heart attacks, and am now sixty-five years old. For a quarter of a century I have never taken my eye off Ford Motor Company. I have waited patiently for the time to come for that company to be judged in the court of public opinion.

For the past fifteen years the entire U.S. auto industry has been in a tailspin. General Motors closed its assembly plant at Norwood, Ohio, which is a Cincinnati suburb, as well as its body plant in Fairfield. Chrysler closed its radiator plant in Dayton. The highly publicized Batavia Transmission Plant now sits empty. Ford was never able to produce quality transmissions, and after twenty seven years simply closed the plant down and put it up for sale. Rollman's Psychiatric Hospital closed its doors when the auto plants shut down. The need for psychiatric help declined in direct proportion to the decline in the number of auto workers.

Yet foreign auto plants now employ thousands in the Cincinnati area. Toyota has located its North American headquarters twenty miles south, in Hebron, Kentucky. Many of the workers from the U.S. auto industry are employed by Toyota and Honda. There is no union, and none of the rancor and discord that was at Sharonville is present in the foreign-owned plants. There could be no greater indictment of the incompetent, even criminal management in the U.S. auto industry than closed Ford, GM, and Chrysler plants and thriving, profitable, nonunion Japanese auto plants.

I do not know if Ford Motor Company will ever be held accountable for its economic and social crimes. I do know that the company is losing billions of dollars, has borrowed against every asset it has to raise cash, and has offered buyouts to virtually all of its hourly employees with plans to replace them with low wage, inexperienced workers. I feel that Ford Motor Company will soon have to lie in the bed that it has made. That is why I retrieved my file boxes from my attic and finished this book.

NOTES

1979

Chicago Tribune: "Preventing Deaths Not Worth $11 a Car, Ford Study Said." Saving 180 people from burning to death and another 180 from suffering serious burns in car fires each year would not be worth the cost of adding $11 per car for safety improvements, Ford Motor Company concluded, in a financial study....

1980

Cincinnati Enquirer, June 12, 1980: "Faulty Transmission Could Spur Record Recall." The Transportation Department announced Wednesday that investigation indicates there are transmission defects in 16,000,000 Ford Motor Company cars and light trucks, raising the possibility of the biggest auto recall in American History.

Cincinnati Enquirer, September 17, 1980: "Batavia-Made Transmissions Encounter Early Problems." Chuck Gemushian, a Ford spokesman said Ford is having noise and vibration problems in transmissions produced at its new, state of the art $500,000,000 transmission plant near Cincinnati....

Tucker, William. (1980, November). The Wreck of the Auto Industry. *Harper's Magazine.*

1981

Cincinnati Enquirer, January 11, 1981: The report of Oct 5 showed scrap costs last week were $122,313.03, the highest since the new, high technology plant opened....

Cincinnati Enquirer, March 24, 1981: "Ford to Keep Job Level at 25% Below 1978 Peak." Ford had 500,000 employees at its all time peak in 1978, but will never again reach that level of employment, according to Ford President Donald E. Petersen.

Business Week, November 9, 1981: "Why Detroit Still Can't Get Going."

1982

Cincinnati Enquirer, January 7, 1982: "Fairfax Hopes to Find Tenant for Closed Fairfax Transmission Plant."

From a letter sent by CAMPAIGN FORD RECALL on February 3, 1982: Dear Ford Owner, This letter brings you up to date on our efforts to obtain a recall of the Ford vehicles with automatic transmissions that jump from Park into Reverse. Since the Department of Transportation (DOT) agreed to let Ford mail warning labels to 23 million Ford owners rather than repair the vehicles, 15 more people have been killed when Fords failed to hold or engage in Park, bringing the known death toll to 154. The fact that 8 of these fatalities occurred since the completion of Ford's warning label campaign tragically illustrates the ineffectiveness of the warning labels....

1983

Bonner, Raymond. *New York Times,* February 15, 1983: "Ford Quietly Settles Transmission Lawsuits." Ford Motor Company is paying about $20,000,000 as a result of lawsuits charging that defective automobile and truck transmissions caused scores of deaths and injuries, according to private lawyers and a non-profit safety group. The lawyers say documents obtained from Ford in the litigation show that as long ago as the early 1970s the company was well aware of a defect in the transmissions of millions of cars and light trucks and could have corrected it for three cents a vehicle....

Cincinnati Enquirer, March 2, 1983: "Transmission Flaw Forces '83 Ford Recall." Ford Motor Company said Tuesday it is recalling 140,000 1983 model vehicles because faulty parts in transmission systems might cause the vehicles to remain in neutral when parked or fail to shift into appropriate gears.

Cincinnati Enquirer, March 17, 1983: "Ford Recalling 99,863 Cars." Ford Motor Company said Monday it is recalling 99,863 cars because they may have metal fan blades that could break and fly off. Ford already has recalled more than 2 million cars and trucks for the same problem....

Sease, Douglas R.*Wall Street Journal,* April 4, 1983: "GM, Hoping to Avoid Big Recall, Tells U.S. Government Loss of Rear Wheel, Axle Isn't Dangerous."

Cincinnati Enquirer, April 6, 1983: "Federal Safety Officials Probing Fires in Ford's Escorts, Lynxes."

<u>1984</u>

Philadelphia Enquirer, December 31, 1984: "Nader Group Cites Ford Death Toll After '80 Accord on Transmissions." The Center for Auto Safety, a group founded by consumer advocate Ralph Nader, said there had been more than 3,500 accidents involving Ford transmissions that slipped into reverse....It charged that the government's highway safety agency, the National Highway Traffic Safety Administration "has concealed the alarming increase in deaths.....by manipulating fatality statistics and by refusing to investigate - and thus count - dozens of reported deaths."

Wall Street Journal, date unknown: "White House Accused of Hampering Recall." Consumer advocate Ralph Nader charged Friday that White House influence is one reason why the government has not ordered a massive recall of Ford Motor Company vehicles that can jump out of "park" and into reverse...Nader asserted ...there are so far 70 deaths attributed to the faulty transmissions...it would be the largest auto recall in history....

1985

Conte, Christopher. *Wall Street Journal,* July 15, 1985: "Bid to Reopen Ford Inquiry is Rejected by Safety Agency; Probe Ended in '81" The Center for Auto Safety contends that 1966-1979 model Ford vehicles tend to jump, without warning, from "park" into "reverse" and, by the agencies count, 199 people were killed in accidents involving runaway Fords.... As part of the settlement Ford agreed to send owners of 23,000,000 of the vehicles special warning stickers to be pasted to cars' dashboards.

Cincinnati Enquirer, August 8, 1985, pg 4: "138 Deaths Blamed on Unrecalled Fords."

The Kentucky Post, August 20, 1985: "Rolling Lemons Leave Car Buyers with Sour Taste."

Cincinnati Enquirer, October 9, 1985: "Government to Examine Fords." Federal officials announced Tuesday that they are starting an investigation of almost a half million 1975 through 1984 model Ford Motor Company light trucks whose rear wheels can fall off....

1986

Miller, Edward. *The Associated Press,* May 10, 1986: "Potential for Liability Causes Worry at Ford." Ford Motor Company has revealed to the federal government that the company has billions of dollars in potential product liabilities, including an estimated $1.2 billion in lawsuits over allegedly faulty automatic transmissions....

Cincinnati Enquirer, November 17, 1986: "Fairfield UAW Seeks Agreement." An older model Toyota was destroyed by sledgehammer blows at a Sunday afternoon rally, sponsored by members of United Auto Workers Union Local 863 "import bashing"....

1988

Wall Street Journal, April 14, 1988: "On and On Grinds Fight Over Old Fords That Slip into Reverse." Endless safety battle drains all who try to settle it, and still the cases come.... Defeat of a monster recall.... Ford settles many cases out of court, refuses to disclose financial terms to victims.

Emshwiller, John R. *Wall Street Journal,* April 14, 1988: "For Ford Engineer, Life Became Unbearable Ordeal of Inquisitions." As an engineer at Ford, Douglas R. Dixon lived the kind of pleasant, unremarkable life of countless auto industry professionals: a house in the suburbs, duties as a scoutmaster, fishing with his sons. Then it was all torn apart by two sheets of paper. Two brief memos Mr. Dixon wrote in 1971 revealing serious defects in its shift mechanisms eventually led to enormous emotional stress, according to papers produced in connection with two separate lawsuits arising from his premature death....

Emshwiller, John R. *The Wall Street Journal,* October 25, 1988: "Ex-Worker Riles Chrysler in Role as Expert Witness." Chrysler Corporation is trying to silence Rahn Huffstutler in a dispute that raises thorny questions about the rights of expert witnesses to testify against former employers....

Wall Street Journal, date unknown: "Ford to End 'Secret' Warranties." Ford Motor Company agreed Thursday to notify customers about potential problems they otherwise might not know about until their cars break down the Federal Trade Commission said Thursday....Under the agreement, at least 84 full-page ads will appear in such publications as *Time, Newsweek, U.S. News & World Report, Sports Illustrated, People and Reader's Digest* containing the information.

2007

Cincinnati Enquirer, October 5, 2007: "Ford Retraining Center to Open." The formal opening of a training center for 1822 workers who will loss their jobs when Ford closes the Batavia Transmission Plant, the third largest employer in Clermont County, will take place....

Cincinnati Enquirer, December 9, 2007: "Special Report: Japanese Car Plants Alter Employment Landscape in Southern Ohio."

2008

Cincinnati Enquirer, January 1, 2008: "Ford Offers Buyouts to 54,000."

Cincinnati Enquirer, March 29, 2008: "UAW Ranks Dip to WWII Level." Membership now less than 500,000, which was once the number of UAW workers employed by a single company, Ford....

AUTHOR CONTACT PAGE

The author of this book is Robert J. Dewar. You may contact him with comments, questions, or discussion by email at rdumore@aol.com or you may contact him at his home, which is 511 Beechtree Drive, Cincinnati, Ohio 45224. The author welcomes any feedback from readers, and will give a timely response to that feedback.

www.asavagefactory.com
www.thedewarchronicles.com